D1599205

The Petersburg Campaign
The Battle Of The Crater
"The Horrid Pit"
June 25 - August 6, 1864

The Virginia Civil War Battles and Leaders Series

VIRGINIA

SIC SEMPER TYRANNIS

2nd Edition

Michael A. Cavanaugh   William Marvel

Manufactured in the United States by
H. E. Howard, Inc., Lynchburg, Virginia

Printed by H. E. Howard, Inc.

ISBN-0-930919-77-7

Dedicated to any unknown soldiers
who remain buried in the Crater,
whatever their allegiance

THE HORRID PIT

"And now the scene within the horrid pit was such as might be fitly portrayed only by the pencil of Dante after he had trod 'nine-circled Hell.' From the great mortars to the right and left, huge missiles, describing graceful curves, fell at regular intervals with dreadful accuracy and burst among the helpless masses huddled together, and every explosion was followed by piteous cries, and often-times the very air seemed darkened by flying human limbs. Haskell, too, had moved up his Eprouvette mortars among the men of the Sixteenth Virginia — so close, indeed, that his powder-charge was but one ounce and a half — and, without intermission, the storm of fire beat upon the hapless men imprisoned within."

Captain William Gordon McCabe

Southern Historical Society Papers,

"Defence of Petersburg"

TABLE OF CONTENTS

Table Of Maps

Acknowledgements

When one has studied a single Civil War battle for over twelve years it is almost impossible to give credit to all those who helped supply the bits and pieces to the great puzzle. Many have endured my constant ramblings about the battle of the Crater, but have always been most receptive to my requests for information and assistance.

Several who must receive personal recognition are Chris Calkins, historian at Petersburg National Battlefield. Chris has always made me aware of any new information on the battle and has always been a genial host on my countless visits to the park. Another who has always made my visits to the Petersburg area fruitful and enjoyable is Bill Henderson professor at Richard Bland College. His knowledge of the Petersburg area is second to none. Rick Sauers of the Pennsylvania Capitol Flag Preservation Committee deserves special thanks for his assistance in providing me with the rich sources of information in the *National Tribune* newspaper and the Pennsylvania State Archives.

My thanks for the fine maps in this work go to my good friend and partner Blake Magner. Thanks also go to Dr. Richard Sommers, Mike Winey and Randy Hackenburg at the U.S. Army Military History Institute. They alway made me feel welcome on my many visits to the institute to explore their fine manuscript and image holdings. For the fine selection of photographs and drawings in this book I would like to thank David W. Charles, Tom Lovell and the Greenwich Workshop Galleries, Herb Peck, Henry Kidd, Richard Couture, Michael Taylor, and Fred Bell.

Other institutions and individuals who are also deserving of special thanks are Russ Pritchard, Civil War Library and Museum in Philadelphia; Leo Ward, Historical Society of Schuylkill County, John E. White, Southern Historical Collection, University of North Carolina at Chapel Hill; Ervin L. Jordan, Jr., University of Virginia, who alerted me to the extremely important Hugh Thomas Douglas papers; Benn Trask, Norfolk Public Library; Gary Gallagher, Pennsylvania State University, a great asset with the papers of E. Porter Alexander; Marie and Bob Melchiori always ready to help at the National Archives and Library of Congress; Bob Krick, Fredericksburg, N.M.P.; Wendy Clark, Virginia State Library; Beverly S. Powers, Auburn University Archives; Paul R. Begley, South Carolina Department of Archives and History; Elfrida M. Raley, The South Carolina Historical Society; Brian Pohanka and Harris Andrews, Time Life Books; Martin L. Everse, Brierfield Ironworks Park Foundation (Ala.); B. F. Emanual, Lancaster County (S.C.) Historical Commission; Francis B. Beddall; Garold L. Cole; Thomas E. Corbin; the late Mrs. Henry Pleasants, Jr.; Edward Longacre; Maynard P. Creel, Jr.; Bill Smith, descendent of Sergeant William Crawford Smith, 12th Virginia Infantry; Dr. James I. Robertson; David Coles; Allan J. Zellnock; Tom LoPiano, Jr.; Bill Stoudt, a rich source of information on the 48th Pennsylvania Infantry; Allan Tischler on General Julius White; Roger L. Heiple; the late James Haas of Harrisburg, Pa., former newspaper reporter in Schuylkill County. Jim was always ready to share material on the county, the 48th, and the Crater. Last, but certainly not least, is Lee Wallace of Falls Church, Virginia, past historian at Petersburg Battlefield Park. His interest in and knowledge of Petersburg and the battle of the Crater has been a rich source from the very beginning of this adventure.

The staffs of the following institutions were also very helpful: Alabama Department of Archives and History; Bentley Historical Library and William L. Clements Library, University of Michigan; Georgia Department of Archives and History; Massachusetts Historical Society; Historical Society of Delaware; North Carolina Baptist Historical Collection, Wake Forest University; North Carolina Department of Archives and History; Pattee Library, Pennsylvania State University; Pottsville, Pennsylvania Public Library; Historical Society of Pennsylvania; The South Caroliniana Library, University of South Carolina; The University of Texas at Austin; Vermont Historical Society; Virginia Historical Society and the Virginia Military Institute.

Special thanks go to Bryce Suderow of Washington, D.C. His help with the chapter on Hancock and Sheridan at Deep Bottom and the Confederate casualties at Deep Bottom and the Crater have greatly enhanced this work. His research on Confederate casualties during this time period are, I believe, the most accurate to date.

One of my really brilliant ideas was to ask Bill Marvel to co-author this work. His research on the Crater and his skills as a writer have made this work so much better than if I did it alone, not to mention getting it finished on time for the 125th anniversary of the battle. Thanks to Harold Howard, publisher of the Virginia Civil War Battles and Leaders Series for his help and confidence.

My thanks to my wife, Marianne and my family and friends for putting up with this obsession over the past twelve years and to all those not mentioned by name, I thank you. This book has a little part of all of you in it.

Michael A. Cavanaugh
Cinnaminson, New Jersey
July 30, 1989

Acknowledgements

The Crater battle has haunted me since I was a boy, growing up in the same rural district that had been home to a teenaged color sergeant killed there. I did the preliminary research for a book on that subject, only to put it away when I discovered that someone else had a ten-year jump on me. Much to my surprise and pleasure, I received an invitation from that very person to collaborate on the work, and I would therefore like to thank my co-author — in his own book — for the opportunity.

My participation in the project began so late that I have but few debts to note. Most of my own material was gathered during research on the 9th New Hampshire and the career of Ambrose Burnside; the rest (four cartons of it) was supplied by Mike Cavanaugh. Neverthless, I need to thank a few people specifically. These include Steve Cox, Debbie Tapley, and Bill Copeley, of the New Hampshire Historical Society, who helped me over several years to review the manuscripts of three New Hampshire officers used herein; Chris Calkins, Park Historian at Petersburg National Battlefield, for his prompt and thorough response to questions about reburial of the Crater's dead; Ted Alexander, on the staff of Antietam National Battlefield, and Bill Christen, of Wyandotte, Michigan, for their help in identifying those Indian marksmen of the First Michigan Sharpshooters; and Blake Magner, our cartographer, whose fine maps inadvertently went without acknowledgement in my last book.

Finally, I cannot refrain from remarking on a young lady who, patient though she may be, is occasionally heard mumbling about the formation of what she calls the Association of Civil War Widows.

William Marvel
January 11, 1989

CHAPTER I

The Thing Should Be Done Soon

After six weeks of turning movements against the right flank of the Army of Northern Virginia, Ulysses S. Grant found himself confronted by the deceptively calm waters of the James River. In one of the rare instances in which anyone ever fooled Robert E. Lee, Grant feinted at Richmond and bridged the river, driving his army straight toward Petersburg.

The "Cockade City," as Petersburg was known, was one of the most strategically important points in the Confederacy. The city of 18,000 was only twenty-two miles south of the capitol: its factories, roads and numerous rail lines made it the last big depot in the supply system for Richmond and Lee's army. In 1862 a Confederate engineer, Captain Charles Dimmock, had built a string of 55 batteries in a ten-mile arc around the city, anchoring it on the Appomattox river and tying the little forts together with lofty earthen parapets. The works were made strong enough to enable even a small force to delay a major attack until help could arrive.

For some time, Lieutenant General Grant had been expecting Ben Butler to take Petersburg with his Army of the James. Butler was ensconced at Bermuda Hundred, a thick neck of land between Richmond and Petersburg where the James and Appomattox converge. The personification of the political general, the tubby Butler had poked faintly at the city from both the north and east, but had come away with his fingers nipped. With a few thousand Confederates, General Pierre G. T. Beauregard drew a line across the throat of Bermuda Hundred and effectively neutralized Butler's army. All this had happened while Grant was pounding at Richmond from the northeast; his lack of success there convinced him that he, rather than Butler, ought to move on Petersburg. Thus, he decided to cross the river.[1]

Grant took William Smith's XVIII Corps from Butler. "Baldy" Smith attacked the fortifications northeast of Petersburg on June 15, taking Battery No. 5 and a good deal more of that section of the Dimmock Line, but his undue caution allowed momentum to falter. Winfield Scott Hancock came up with his II Corps late in the afternoon, and the attack was resumed in the morning. The V, VI, and IX Corps, under Generals Gouverneur K. Warren, Horatio G. Wright, and Ambrose Burnside respectively, eventually reached the field, and throughout June 16, 17, and 18 the outnumbered Confederates inched stubbornly but steadily backward,

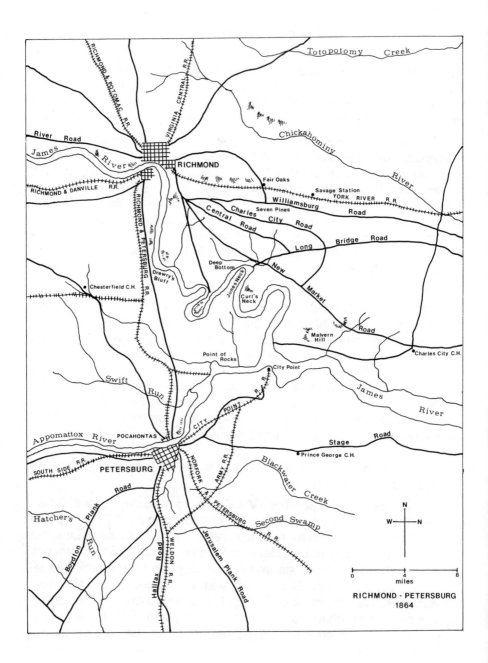

RICHMOND - PETERSBURG
1864

2

digging new trenches wherever they made a stand. These fieldworks proved so intimidating to the battle-weary Union troops — especially after Lee's army filed into them — that Grant gave up his costly frontal assaults and, on June 19, settled in for a siege. Soldiers on both sides began digging ever-deeper entrenchments and infantry obstacles, and the rolling farmland east and south of Petersburg was churned into a moonscape within a matter of days. The opposing lines stretched from White Oak Swamp, east of Richmond, across Bermuda Hundred, and south to the Jerusalem Plank Road below Petersburg. The tandem ramparts ran for twenty-six miles, crossed two major rivers, and bored through parts of four Virginia counties.[2]

Grant gave Butler and what was left of the Army of the James responsibility for defending the lines north of the Appomattox; George G. Meade's Army of the Potomac was charged with guarding the lines south of the river. Meade had the II, V, VI, and IX Corps, as well as the XVIII Corps, detached from Butler. Facing him was General Beauregard, who had his own troops from the Department of Southern Virginia and North Carolina buttressed by divisions from Richard H. Anderson's and A. P. Hill's corps of Lee's Army.[3]

Burnside's IX Corps turned in one of the more valiant Union performances during the first four days of fighting. His men marched twenty-two hot and dusty miles in fifteen hours — without a meal — to get into the fight on the 16th; on the 17th, with an hour or two of sleep, Robert Potter's second division made a spirited predawn attack at the Shand House. His and General Orlando B. Willcox's divisions lost heavily that day, as did James Ledlie's first division. But Ledlie was negligent at best, and drunk at worst, and by nightfall his division lost much of what it had gained. Some of Ledlie's staff shielded him from the corps commander, who never learned of his condition. Burnside attributed the failure of Ledlie's division to its large number of heavy artillerymen. Grant had activated several huge regiments of "heavies" and sent them to the field as infantry; the artillerymen were "worthless," said Burnside on June 18. "In the attack last night I couldn't find thirty of them."[4]

Ledlie's division was confined to the reserve on June 18, while the rest of Burnside's men made another good showing. They covered much ground abandoned by the Confederates until running headlong into new, heavily-defended works on the far side of the Norfolk and Petersburg Railroad. Much time was lost as Meade's staff tried futilely to coordinate a concerted attack by all corps, but late in the afternoon a frustrated Meade issued orders for every corps commander to make an assault without regard to neighboring troops. Incredibly, he meant for the attack to be pell-mell, every general for himself. It was an injudicious directive from a commander pushed to the edge of his patience, but Burnside's sec-

3

ond and third divisions dutifully braved devastating fire to cross an en-filaded cut in the railroad bed. Next they approached Taylor's Creek, which the Confederates fully commanded from their works. Potter's division even crossed the creek, battling to within a hundred yards of the deadly fortifications; no other Union soldiers came so close, and there the day's fighting closed. Despite a certain antagonism toward both Burnside and the IX Corps, General Meade issued a most complimentary order congratulating the corps for its gallantry.[5]

Early the next morning, General Potter peeked over the moist red clay of the freshly-banked trenches and noted just how close his lines were to the enemy's: a new Confederate redoubt loomed less than a hundred yards from his main trench. It occurred to the balding young general that it might be possible to tunnel under the fort and blow it up without the loss of a life, and he wrote a note to Burnside on the subject.[6] The corps commander made no reply, perhaps because he was too busy, and the IX Corps continued to dig in between Warren's V Corps, on its left, and the II Corps, temporarily under the command of David Birney, on the right.

Attrition in Burnside's divisions had left some brigades under the command of relatively junior field officers, among whom was Lieutenant Colonel Henry Pleasants of the 48th Pennsylvania Infantry. He had inherited Potter's first brigade, which was nearest to the Confederate redoubt. Pleasants was the son of a Philadelphian who had married a Spanish nobleman's daughter in Argentina. He had a thoroughly Latin look to him, as well as a touch of temper. After his father's death Pleasants had been sent back to Philadelphia to live with his uncle, and he subsequently achieved success in the Pennsylvania coal fields as a mining engineer. He had just buried his bride when the war began, and despair, more than patriotism, led him to join one of the early three-month militia units. After his discharge he had taken a commission in the 48th, which was raised in his own Schuylkill County. Most of the original men in that regiment were miners. After nearly three years of fighting, there were still about a hundred of those miners left among the survivors.[7]

The thirty-one-year-old Pleasants corroborated Potter's suspicion about the vulnerable fort. He told the division commander that, given some picks, shovels, handbarrows, and a couple of instruments, his men could tunnel twenty-five to fifty feet per day and be under the Confederate battery in two or three weeks. The miners in his regiment were, in fact, most anxious to give it a try. On June 24, Potter sent this information — in the form of a proposal — on to General Burnside.[8]

Potter was a model division commander, in whom Burnside had great confidence. Now that things had stabilized after the standup fighting of the week before, Burnside gave his proposal serious consideration. He called Potter and Pleasants to his tent that evening. In the flickering candlelight the former commander of the Army of the Potomac clenched a cigar beneath his famous wraparound whiskers. He scratched the gleaming dome of his head, asked a few questions about ventilation, and came to the conclusion that the plan would work. Burnside himself took the idea to army headquarters, where he revealed it to General Meade and Major James Duane, Meade's chief engineer.[9]

Meade and Burnside were not getting on well. Like many other officers in the Army of the Potomac, Meade had a low opinion of the IX Corps commander because of his infamous failure at Fredericksburg. Since the IX Corps had been assigned to his own army, the irritable Meade had been unjustifiably severe and sarcastic with Burnside. He told him now that he had no control over siege operations, and that he would have to pass the idea along to Grant.[10]

Duane, too, usually spoke ill of Burnside. It had been Captain Duane who, as General McClellan's chief engineer, led Burnside to the wrong ford at Antietam Creek, contributing greatly to a delay in the capture of Burnside's Bridge for which Burnside had been blamed. He also had an indirect hand in the tardy delivery of some pontoons that had been essential to Burnside's campaign at Fredericksburg. The mangnanimous Burnside had never criticized hirn, but the disparaging tone Duane always assumed in regard to that general seems suspiciously defensive. Major Duane flatly condemned the proposed mine as impossibly long. A comparable tunnel had never been dug; hence, none could be dug now. Burnside left headquarters with nothing more than Meade's reluctant promise not to make an immediate objection if the tunnel were started.[11]

In fact, the digging had already begun. The Union lines occupied the slope of a ravine carved by Taylor's Creek — often called Poor Creek by local residents. The Confederate fort was a hundred yards farther up that slope, though the pitch there was much gentler. Another ravine ran behind the enemy works. This was one of the many parallel ridgelines that had made Petersburg so defensible. At noon on June 25, Pleasants had opened his mine a hundred feet behind his own breastworks. The mouth was far enough below the Confederates' line of sight that his men could come and go safely.

In order to increase speed and conserve scarce timbering materials, the shaft was kept small. It entered the earth in the shape of a lopped-off pyramid, a little over four feet wide at the base and two feet wide at the top. The average height was four and one-half feet.[12]

From the start, Colonel Pleasants put one man in charge of the work on the mine. He chose Sergeant Henry Reese, a burly, redheaded Welshman from Minersville, Pennsylvania. Reese had been a miner all his adult life; for so many generations had his family burrowed in the ground for coal that, to him, it was an atavistic impulse. Though he was then just short of twenty-nine, his lungs were already coated with the dark dust that would end his career a quarter-century later. Reese spread his blankets at the mouth of the mine. No one entered it without his knowledge, and anyone who did belonged to him. By July 3, Reese had most of the enlisted men in the regiment working under him. Several shifts kept the dirt moving day and night.[13]

While still a captain, James Duane had written a manual for military engineers on the subject of mining operations. In it he had listed forty or so pieces of equipment — exclusive of surveying instruments — vital to such a project. Duane's department provided not one of these to Colonel Pleasants. The colonel was on his own, except for the help Potter and Burnside could give, but the resourceful Pleasants was able to improvise most of what he needed. No wheelbarrows were forthcoming, so he manufactured some handbarrows: he had his pioneers nail pairs of hickory poles across the bottoms of cracker boxes, and reinforced the boxes with hoop iron from discarded barrels. Crouching teams of soldiers were thus able to carry three or four cubic feet of earth as they would a man on a stretcher, dump it in a pile, and trot back into the shaft. The picks used in the mine were taken from the regular brigade supply, modified to mining specifications in the forges of artillery batteries. Pleasants cannibalized timbering material from a nearby bridge, but when that ran out he had to ask Burnside for a pass to send his men foraging. He discovered an abandoned sawmill, and put two of his companies to work as lumbermen.[14]

At first the excavated material went into sandbags for use along the parapets, but before long there was such a surplus that the mound of refuse became conspicous. Pleasants had to find areas behind the works that needed filling, and at the end of each day the regiment's axemen cut brush from the fast-receding vegetation, tossing it over the dark, damp clay to hide it from prying Confederate eyes: the few trees remaining on top of the ridge offered the enemy a clear view of the Union rear, and a glimpse of the fresh dirt might have given the secret away.[15]

The summer of 1864 was one of the hottest and driest in memory. The men in the tunnel worked hunched over, straining and sweating in the stale air with the added heat of the bull's-eye lanterns that lighted their way. Their only advantage was their protection from the blazing sun. Until near the finish of the digging, Pleasants — or perhaps Henry Reese — limited every man to less than three hours' tunnel duty each day; after that the clay-caked crews would stumble like so many troglodytes into the raw daylight and draw a gill of whiskey. The regiment was excused from picket duty because of the project, but the enemy did not excuse it from sharpshooters, or from the mortars that sent occasional shells looping over the trenches. At least one officer and a private in the 48th were killed, and two other enlisted men badly wounded, during the preparation of the mine.[16]

The suffocating weather was, if possible, even worse for those who did not enjoy the distraction of useful labor. Members of the 48th Pennsylvania were easily distinguishable by their muddy boots and the dried clots of clay on their pantlegs; but any other soldier fresh from the front was just as readily identified by the veneer of dust that coated his clothing, his body, and his equipment. As the random forest growth was leveled for breastworks and bombproofs, the landscape outside Petersburg became one immense broiler. The dust hung like fog in the streets of Petersburg, where all the grass had withered away. It grated in every bite the inhabitants could find to eat; its fine, yellow smell invaded every breath.[17]

The citizens of the city were, however, suffering from more than the drought, the dust, and the sudden shortage of food. The Yankees had come within range of Petersburg, and civilians going about their daily business were subjected to the same sporadic artillery fire as the men in the trenches. The postmaster, shelled out of the boarding house where he took his meals, moved across town. His post office was directly in the line of fire, and mail seldom made it into the city, but he continued to keep it open though eventually he moved to a safer location. Many residents refused to relocate, even under steady bombardment. Periodically someone, usually a woman or a slave, was killed by a stray projectile, but only the richest bothered to barricade their houses with cotton bales. Homes and hospitals were burned to the ground by shellfire. Yet the only particular anxiety surfaced just before the Fourth of July, when a rumor circulated that Grant intended to match his Independence Day capture of Vicksburg with an all-out assault against Petersburg, after which he planned to put the city to the torch. When July 4 had safely passed, life returned to what passed for normal under the siege.

Rumors about a July 4 holocaust may have had their source in the mine. It was virtually impossible for the operation to be kept secret, and word soon leaked across the picket lines with the usual degree of exaggeration and distortion. The Confederates may have heard quite early of a mine, but they had no idea how much truth there was to the information, and no notion at all where such a work might be progressing. What seemed at the time more pressing matters occupied their attention in the endless list of shortages. Southerners had long since become accustomed to short rations and insufficient clothing, but now an even more basic part of the soldier's equipment was growing scarce: the pig iron and lead needed for his ammunition. Now that the battle lines were static, and the men were growing bored with the tedium of the siege, Confederate authorities were able to relieve both the shortage of metals and the ennui by ordering a daily scavenger hunt. Soldiers ranged behind their lines, picking up all the ordnance the Yankees had thrown at them. An unofficial competition among the Confederates of Bushrod Johnson's division, opposite the IX Corps, appears to have been won by Private J. A. Reamy of the 34th Virginia, who collected 1,567 bullets and four artillery projectiles in a single day. Archibald Gracie's brigade accumulated almost four hundred pounds of lead and a thousand shot and shells in one day. All of this went up to Richmond to be recast or rearmed, after which it was shipped back to Petersburg and unceremoniously redelivered to the Army of the Potomac.[18]

Back across the trenches, the Pennsylvanians bored quickly through soft sand and sandy clay until they struck a stratum of solid clay that slowed them considerably. The shaft was driven fifty feet the first day, but only forty feet each of the next two days.[19] The farther the porters had to carry the waste down the tunnel, and the more distant the dumping places became, the less progress the miners made.

The only real trouble came when the horizontal path of the tunnel carried into a vein of marl. The soft, slippery deposit gave way under the concentrated weight of the timbers, and the roof of the mine sagged dangerously. Harry Reese brought in more lumber and planked over the floor to distribute the weight more evenly, but it was obvious the mine was going deeper into the marl and would soon be surrounded by it. Pleasants countered by putting an incline of something more than thirteen percent in the direction of the tunnel. Within another hundred feet he had cleared the marl, and was back into dense clay. Farther on the marl appeared again, but it was merely a hump in the vein and posed no real problem. The soldiers collected wet lumps of this clay when their shifts ended and shaped it into pipes, figurines, and IX Corps badges that dried quite hard when baked in the hot sun. Many pounds of the sacred soil of Virginia made its way to Pennsylvania via the U.S. mail, in the form of such souvenirs.[20]

Colonel Pleasants had to be very careful about changes in direction and elevation, lest the tunnel approach too near the surface and cave in. Neither would it do to drive it too far, and go beyond the enemy fort, or to fall short. Without the instruments with which to triangulate the distance exactly, he could not be certain to avoid such an error.

It was not as though Colonel Pleasants could ask the Confederates to hold their fire for a few minutes while he paced off the yardage. A number of officers had been shot while making observations from the Union works directly over the mine, among them a captain from his own regiment and a division staff officer with whom Pleasants had been standing.[21] Burnside requested a theodolite from Meade's engineer, so Pleasants could make the calculations quickly and with as little risk as possible, but it soon became evident that Major Duane's theodolite would be needed at army headquarters. Burnside was forced to rely on acquaintances in Washington, who sent down an older model of the same instrument.

With Confederate sharpshooters less than four hundred feet away, Colonel Pleasants peered from the outermost works at the four-gun fort he hoped to destroy. He sighted through his instrument, then dropped down to figure with his pencil. Not trusting either himself or his theodolite, he sighted again and again, ciphering betweentimes, until he was satisfied he had the correct distance.[22]

The greatest difficulty in such a long mine, aside from the need to conceal its location, was ventilation. Burnside had wondered about it from the start, but Pleasants suggested an ingenious solution. Although the plan had not impressed Major Duane, it worked very well in the end. Pleasants had his men build an eight-inch-square wooden duct, which they extended with each day's digging. Then, a hundred feet or so into the mine, they bored a shaft straight up, opening at a point just behind the Union trenches. This air shaft ended at the side of the tunnel; at its base was a little furnace in which the soldiers kept a fire constantly burning. To avoid drawing attention to this fire, others were lighted up and down Burnside's line. Between the firebox and the mouth of the mine Pleasants rigged a burlap partition, which forced the fire to draw oxygen from within the mine. This created a draft from the entrance of the tunnel through the duct to the end of the mine, back down the mine shaft, and up the air shaft. Fresh air was thus flowing continuously around the work area, and carbon dioxide was pulled down the tunnel and up the shaft. Pleasants drove his mine nearly twice as far as his superiors thought possible, and his workmen never suffered for want of air.[23]

The geology of this part of Dinwiddie County is what laborers have always called "good digging," with much soft clay and very little in the way of rocks. In fact, the only foreign object anyone recorded coming out of the tunnel was what some believed to be part of the thighbone of a mastadon. Still, the hours of toil in a confined space told on the miners. Back problems proliferated, probably from lifting heavy boxes of earth while stooping. The assistant surgeon of the 48th Pennsylvania also remembered treating myriad abrasions; he recalled, half a century later, that by the time the enterprise was finished the whole regiment was "used up."[24]

Not only were the tunnelers unusually strained, sprained, and scraped by their subterranean duty, they were also confronted in the midst of their labors with the news that a significant force of Confederates had migrated up the Shenandoah Valley and crossed the Potomac. Their anxiety was heightened by the inexact report that Jubal

Early's Southerners were raiding in both Maryland and Pennsylvania. The logical route out of the Shenandoah Valley would eventually lead those Confederates into Schuylkill County. At the time, Early's troops were actually all in Maryland, but in little more than a fortnight he would send some cavalry to burn Chambersburg, Pennsylvania — one hard day's ride from the Schuylkill County line. Colonel Pleasants tried to calm his men with what one soldier described as a "very friendly" speech, emphasizing his appreciation for their hard work. As he no doubt predicted, the newspapers soon carried word of Early's withdrawal back into Virginia. The enemy had, in fact, been retiring as Pleasants spoke, albeit only temporarily.[25]

General Burnside also complimented the men. He visited the tunnel on several occasions, once in the company of Senator Henry Sprague of Rhode Island and David Tod, ex-governor of Ohio. The general and his political friends were the only celebrities to brave the dank shaft, or even to sightsee at the maw, and they bantered with the miners, accusing them of laboring so hard just for a ration of whiskey.[26] Clearly, enthusiasm for their effort stopped along the chain of command at Burnside's tent. Few above him expected it to work, and one gets the retrospective impression that some even hoped it would fail. Given the animosity between the rest of the Army of the Potomac on the one hand and Burnside and his corps on the other, it is understandable if Burnside suspected such ill will from army headquarters.

The tunnel reached a depth of just over 510 feet early on July 17, putting it precisely where Pleasants had calculated the center of the Confederate fort would be. That same morning three deserters from the 49th North Carolina vaulted the picket line and were interrogated by Burnside's staff. Colonel Pleasants no sooner reported the completion of the main shaft than he was ordered to put away the picks and listen — the deserters revealed that the Confederates knew that their works were being undermined, though the location was still unknown. One of the Tarheels had, himself, been working on a countermining operation.[27]

At least one Confederate had suspected the mining project on Potter's front for more than two weeks. General E. P. Alexander, artillery chief of the Army of Northern Virginia's First Corps, had observed in late June that the Yankees in this sector maintained a constant fusillade that abated noticeably a hundred yards either side of Elliott's Salient. He guessed they were planning to reduce the four-gun battery by means of a covered approach, but when no such trench began wriggling toward the salient he deduced they were tunneling under it. He came to the conclusion as early as June 30, but that same day he was wounded by a sniper and sent home on convalescent furlough. Before commencing the roundabout rail journey to Georgia, Alexander dropped by General Lee's headquarters to report his theory about the mining operation. A visiting correspondent of the London *Times* scoffed when he heard him estimate that such a gallery would have to run about five hundred feet, and in the manner of James Duane remarked that the longest military mine to date covered only four hundred feet. The Englishman suggested nothing greater could be accomplished without suffocating the miners. With unbelievable premonition, Alexander responded that "in the Federal Army were many Pennsylvania coal miners who could be relied on to ventilate mines any distance that might be necessary."[28]

A little over a week before, a Virginia engineer captain had been ordered to Petersburg with his company of pontoniers. He immediately transformed them into sappers, and by July 10 they had been put to work on those salients of the Confederate line that were nearest the Union trenches. The captain, Hugh Douglas, at least had the assistance of his army's chief quartermaster, but he faced many of the same problems that troubled his Union counterpart. He had too few men; equipment was lacking despite the quartermaster's cooperation; his examinations of the ground had to be made at pointblank range; and he had to go to great lengths to conceal his excavated material if he expected to catch the Yankees by surprise. Like Pleasants, Douglas ordered the dirt carried out in cracker boxes; like the Pennsylvanians, his men had rations of whiskey doled out to them to maintain their vigor.

The listening shafts Douglas built were different from the tunnel he sought. Each of them was sunk a few feet into the ground, like a well, before galleries fully six feet high and three feet wide were run to the left and right. Once inside the galleries, Douglas himself would bore into the floor with a one-inch auger, looking for the soft spot that would reveal the enemy passageway. He dug a few of these shafts, one of them very near the actual Union mine, but his manpower was too limited for effective countermining. On July 15, he gained a detail of five dozen men from Henry Wise's Virginia brigade and Robert Ransom's North Carolinians — at least one of whom promptly deserted and told the Yankees his story. A few days later Douglas received another detail of a hundred more men from Bushrod Johnson's division. With these additional men, he was able to push his listening galleries nearly as far, laterally, as had Pleasants. The principal problem, it seems, was that Douglas did not go deep enough: his deepest tunnel was ten feet below grade, and the auger could not have penetrated much more than five feet beyond that. Judging from the most conservative estimate of the depth of the mine crater, the Pennsylvanians were at least twenty feet underground.[29]

Colonel Pleasants went into the mine with a couple of other officers on the afternoon of July 17. They lay there for some time. Above, there was the thump of something like hammers, but at last Pleasants decided it

11

was unrelated to a countermine, and he was allowed to resume work that evening. His men began a pair of lateral galleries, which were carefully run left and right beneath the doomed fort. Each gallery was nearly forty feet long and contained several large magazine rooms. The miners moved quietly now: timbers were cut and fitted together outside, dismantled, and finally assembled in place with nothing more resounding than the slap of a hand. Henry Reese frequently made his men drop their tools and feel for the tell-tale vibrations from above. At one point, as they were beginning the right gallery, the miners started at the sound of digging overhead. They called for Colonel Pleasants, who decided it was either an observation shaft coming down toward them or a gun platform under construction. In either case — since the shock of a recoiling fieldpiece might tumble the mine — he deemed it more prudent to curve the gallery around that point.[30]

The ground was unexpectedly damp in the chambers intended for magazines. A number of springs were uncovered and drained off, and the wide rooms required sturdy framing to prevent them from caving in. Pleasants notified Potter the shafts were complete on the evening of July 23, but for the next four days his men had to occupy themselves in maintaining a dry storage area while previously-uninterested army commanders decided when to explode the mine. It was not until July 27 that Pleasants was given permission to start carrying in the powder. His original request for six tons of powder had been reduced by army headquarters to four tons, and it was delivered in twenty-five-pound kegs. These 320 kegs went into empty sacks, which the men slung over their shoulders and carried to the mine through covered ways exposed to shellfire. Once the powder began going into the magazines, it was imperative that the rest of the operation be concluded quickly, lest the charge grow damp. While his entire regiment was busy hauling the cumbersome explosives, the colonel went to work on the fuse.[31]

By then, Pleasants was probably already aware that the fuse he had ordered was not what had been delivered. What he wanted was safety fuse, in lengths of a hundred feet or more. What he got was common blasting fuse, not impervious to moisture, and all in short lengths; some pieces were no longer than ten feet. Once again, Meade's staff seemed to be working against the project, for the fuse had come from Fort Monroe on the order of Meade's chief of artillery, Henry Hunt. General Hunt was hardly the sort to deliberately sabotage the operation, but it is a measure of how lightly he regarded it that he failed to specify the type and length of fuse he knew would be required. It was too late for Pleasants to ask for a new supply — Hunt had sent the original order to Fort Monroe on June 29.

As most engineers in his position would, Colonel Pleasants tried to overdesign. The fuse had to be spliced in so many places that he decided

12

to lay three of them, and to put them side-by-side in an open trough of powder.[32]

It was ten o'clock at night before the last of the powder had gone into the magazines and the fuse had been laid, but Pleasants began the job of tamping the charge immediately. For twenty consecutive hours the sweating Pennsylvanians hunched their way up and down the mine, stacking sandbags in the mouths of the magazines and at the deep end of the main shaft. When they were finished, there was nearly a thousand cubic feet of tamping to prevent the force of the blast from escaping down the tunnel. The only apertures were for the T-shaped trough of powder and the three knotted fuses.

Colonel Pleasants tied a fifty-foot tail of additional fuses, strung them on a dry section of the mine floor, and crawled out of the mine behind the last man. At six P.M., Thursday, July 28, a bleary-eyed Henry Pleasants notified General Potter that the mine was ready to explode, and that the thing should be done soon.[33]

CHAPTER II
The Order is Final

While the actual digging of the mine was accomplished virtually without an impediment, the above-ground planning associated with it was fraught with discouragement, misunderstanding, and interference. From the moment General Burnside mentioned it, both Meade and Grant frowned upon the notion. Meade regarded the site of the proposed mine as disadvantageous because the Confederate fort was really only a minor protrusion in the center of a long, shallow indentation in the enemy's line of works, which commanded the fort from either flank. General Grant viewed it similarly, but he and Meade allowed work to continue. For some time they thought of the tunnel as little more than an amusement for the men, to be stopped whenever it got out of hand. It was not as though Grant, at least, was inexperienced with mines. He had authorized such an operation at Vicksburg almost exactly a year before, but for lack of a sufficient charge or judicious use of lateral galleries — or both — that explosion had resulted in no great advantage.[1]

Just as Colonel Pleasants was dealing with the troublesome deposit of marl in the bottom of his shaft, an unfortunate correspondence transpired between Meade and Burnside that both illustrated the lack of interest in the project at general headquarters and aggravated communications between the two generals. At noon on July 3, in relation to an inquiry from Grant, Meade asked Burnside to evaluate the possibility of making a successful assault on his front. Nowhere did he mention the mine, nor did he seem to consider it in the request.[2] He, and apparently Grant as well, contemplated a costly frontal attack without waiting for the completion of the tunnel.

Whenever he was asked for his opinion, Ambrose Burnside tended to go into great detail. Especially when dealing with someone who seemed prone to find fault, such as Meade, he tried to render his judgement for each of several potential circumstances that might apply, and if there were any ambiguity in the question he would answer both possibilities. He so responded now. He told Meade that if he had meant to ask whether an attack ought to be made now rather than later, he thought it should be postponed, at which point he plugged the mining operation again. But if Meade wanted only to know whether an assault should be made on his front or elsewhere, Burnside felt there was a good chance of success on his line. On two previous occasions when he ought to have succeeded, Burnside had failed to achieve his objectives because of a lack of proper

support. Perhaps with Antietam and Fredericksburg in mind, he attempted to predicate his opinion on the presumption of appropriate support.
Not for the first time in his career, he phrased his thoughts badly. He
predicted a favorable result ". . . provided my corps can make the attack
and it is left to me to say when and how the other two corps shall come in
to my support."

By almost all accounts, George Meade was a testy individual. Even
his own staff found him profoundly irritable. When he read Burnside's
caveat he interpreted it as a haughty demand for the field command of
three corps, and he replied curtly that he, and not General Burnside,
would direct the army in any upcoming engagement.[3]

In justice to General Meade, it should be noted that he was in an extremely awkward situation. While he was commander of the Army of the
Potomac, and ought to have expected a certain amount of autonomy, the
commanding general of the armies of the United States had chosen to
ride shotgun with him. Grant tried hard to soothe Meade's feelings, even
risking a measure of inefficiency by continually pitching his headquarters
tent a mile or so from Meade's, but every movement of the Army of the
Potomac was subject to the approval of Grant. All the victories of the
spring — if they could be so called — had been attributed to "Grant's
army." Had any subordinate sought and gained control of three of the four
corps of his army, General Meade might as well have gone home.

What Meade failed to recognize, and surely ought to have known, is
that presumption and haughtiness were not part of Ambrose Burnside's
nature. Burnside had, in fact, been very kind to Meade when their roles
were reversed. He had promoted Meade to command of the V Corps after
Fredericksburg, replacing a popular political general despite significant
resistance from Joe Hooker. That new position had been critical to
Meade's elevation to command of the army the next summer. Then, when
Meade had been subjected to public criticism after the Mine Run campaign, Burnside had written him an encouraging note, expressing his
perfect willingness to serve under Meade in command of a corps. Such an
offer by a former army and department commander did not smack of over-
weaning ambition, and Burnside had often implied he thought Meade the
better general.[4] Still, Meade sizzled.

Abashed that he had so offended this very sensitive superior, Burnside made haste to correct his error. After he received Meade's stiff note,
he composed a letter disavowing any intention of infringing on his commander's authority, explaining that he would be happy to take orders from
Meade or, if necessary, from the other corps commanders. He reiterated
his good opinion of Meade as a military man and stressed his full support
for him. The letter was typical Burnside — self-effacing, sincere, and
generous; Meade was moved to thank him both for his compliments and

for the explanation, by which he hoped "all misapprehensions will be removed."[5]

Such misapprehensions, unfortunately, were not removed. Burnside's letter did not unequivocally demonstrate the reasoning behind the condition to his opinion, so Meade was probably left with an inflated impression of his subordinate's hankering for independence. For Burnside, the exchange did little but remind him how little it took to set Meade off. Their relations seem to have been no better, and were perhaps more fragile than ever, after the apology had been made and accepted.

Despite the inquiry, it began to look as though no assault would be made before the mine was completed, so Burnside began formulating a plan for his portion of any attack that might accompany the detonation of the magazines. He recognized, as had Meade and Grant, the danger of moving against the fort in that concave sector of the enemy line. The Confederates to the left and right would be able to pour a concentrated fire into the flanks of the attacking column and, eventually, into its rear. That disadvantage could be eliminated, he believed, by an assault on either side of the main objective, perpendicular to the Confederate works. The advantage of concentrated firepower would then revert to the Union troops, while the enfiladed enemy would have to abandon his fortifications to present a battle front. In all likelihood, the stunned and confused Confederates would spill from the far ends of the fortifications like loose birdshot pouring out a funnel.

In simple terms, Burnside planned to have most of the attacking column drive straight for the hill behind the presumably-destroyed fort, skirting the actual site of the explosion, while a portion of it peeled off from each side, wheeled into line perpendicular to the main attack, and swept the defenders from their trenches.[6] The battlefield commands necessary to accomplish this were a bit more complicated, and the required maneuvers were even more confusing. They would have been difficult to perform under heavy fire, even for troops who knew what each command entailed. With great good sense, therefore, General Burnside determined that the assault force ought to spend a good deal of time rehearsing its deadly choreography.

His choice to spearhead the assault was Edward Ferrero's fourth division, composed entirely of colored regiments. Ferrero, an Italian immigrant with a wispy imperial plastered on his pudgy face, had been a soldier less than three years. He had been a dancing instructor before the war, and except for some militia activity his principal military qualification seems to have been that he taught West Point cadets how to waltz. But he had led the 51st New York through the North Carolina campaign, under Burnside, and it had been Ferrero's brigade that finally carried the bridge at Antietam. Ferrero also had commanded a small division during the East Tennessee campaign, and Burnside appears to have been fairly satisfied with him.[7]

It was not because of Ferrero, however, that Burnside chose the Negro troops; it was, paradoxically, because they were relatively inexperienced in battle. Of the nine regiments, none had been in uniform before Thanksgiving, and most of them had been organized in the spring. They had first gathered as a division at Annapolis in April, and had marched into Virginia as part of the IX Corps, but Grant had taken them from Burnside as his corps crossed the Rapidan and set them to guarding the ammunition train. Not until the day after the siege began at Petersburg had the division been returned to Burnside, and since then it had been levied heavily for fatigue details by the generals of other corps. There was a feeling in the upper ranks that the black troops were valuable as laborers but not as soldiers. General Warren suggested they be permanently converted to engineer troops. Even one of Meade's best-educated staff officers regarded them merely as "hewers of wood and drawers of water," and shuddered to think of them going up against Lee's soldiers. "God help them," he had written early in May, "if the grey-backed infantry attack them."[8]

Burnside believed in his colored division. If the Negroes had not the practical experience of the white troops, neither were they battle-weary and shellshocked. Since the sixth of May, the first three divisions of the IX Corps had been almost constantly in touch with the enemy, either in open battle or in the equally lethal opposing trenches. Since June 16 there had been no respite. The corps had fought gallantly in the opening battles at Petersburg, but siege tactics had been employed when it was discovered that the soldiers could no longer be made to go forward in the face of an entrenched enemy. Burnside's white divisions had been especially decimated in their pointblank approach to the enemy lines. Even the staff member who so criticized the use of Negro troops noted that the best men, by virtue of their greater courage, were killed first in the spring bloodbath, while even the bravest of the survivors could only be driven to attack the enemy by the most fervent appeal. It was this that Burnside feared from his battered white divisions. More than in the other corps, which were positioned farther from the enemy's sharpshooters, Burnside's men had become enormously fond of the musty floors of their trenches. Few Southern marksmen could miss at a range of a hundred yards, and they lay for hours waiting for a target. Consequently the IX Corps was particularly demoralized. Burnside was somewhat ahead of his time in identifying the problem of battle fatigue, which only a few surgeons were then beginning to call "nostalgia;" he was certain that the Negroes, anxious to prove themselves as soldiers and undiscouraged by months of sustained combat, were the better gamble.[9]

When Burnside gave Ferrero his assignment, the dancemaster complained of the heavy work details made from his division for General Warren and others. Burnside had his inspector general file a report on the subject, and asked headquarters, in essence, to whose corps Ferrero's division belonged. Before the day was out, Ferrero's troops were exempted from fatigue duty outside the IX Corps.[10]

There were two brigades in the fourth division: four regiments under Colonel Joshua Sigfried, (the nominal commander of the 48th Pennsylvania), and five more regiments commanded by a young Mainer, Colonel Henry G. Thomas. The two brigadiers followed Burnside's advice to supplement their rough maps of the terrain by a personal reconnaissance. Like Colonel Pleasants, they found such observations hazardous, because every movement drew alarmingly accurate enemy fire. But, as others had discovered before them, a man could get a quick glimpse of the lay of the land by a primitive ruse. A hat propped on a stick or a ramrod would usually convince most of the sharpshooters to fire, after which it was relatively safe to put one's nose over the parapet until the Confederates reloaded. By this rather uncertain means, Sigfried and Thomas learned as much as it was possible for a Union soldier to know about the ground they would have to cover.

Meanwhile, the colored regiments gathered in their camps well behind the IX Corps front and began to practice the maneuvers they would have to perform after the mine was exploded.[11] For most of their time in the service these brigades had been broken up into company- and platoon-sized details, so they probably had forgotten much of what they once knew of battalion drill. A certain amount of basic marching instruction had to be reviewed, after which the better regiments could be chosen for the difficult flank positions. At first it was sheer chaos; it takes several days for even seasoned soldiers to perfect a large-scale wheeling movement. Within a week, though, the chosen troops knew exactly what was expected when the officers chorused "Right companies on the right, into line, wheel!" or "Left companies on the left, into line, wheel!" Even those who could not hear the commands could soon recognize the beginning of the movement when the marching column started to break apart, and since they knew it was coming they could simply follow along. It did not have to be pretty — there would be no reviewing stand. It merely had to be done with reasonable speed. There might be a little resistance, or there might be none; the important thing was to get the right number of rifles pointed in the right directions in time to assure that no more resistance could accumulate.

The blacks took great pride in their assignment. After months of guarding muddy wagons and spading up the dusty Virginia landscape, they felt like soldiers at last. Unlike the men in the immediate front, they could kindle fires at night, and in the evenings they would gather around those fires and sing a song one of them had made up, a single bar they repeated over and over.

> *We looks like men a marchin' on,*
> *We looks like men er war.*

First one man would begin it, then a few in his immediate group took it up, until the entire regiment or even the whole division could be heard droning the slow, steady rhythm. The sound, if not the words, must have drifted into the neighboring camps, reverberating for all the world like an eerie Gregorian chant leavened by the mournful African baritone. Even the Confederates must have heard it, and wondered what it meant.[12] It might have meant — it ought to have meant — the end of the battle for Petersburg and Richmond. But that was not to be.

On July 26, when the galleries were finished but not yet charged with powder, Burnside found his headquarters besieged by a small squadron of couriers and aides from both Grant and Meade. Their messages all arrived within a few hours, but the import of the last ones was directly contrary to that of the first few.

Initially, General Grant was concerned about countermining by the enemy. Burnside advised him there was no immediate need to worry, since nothing had been heard above the mine for two days. A rainstorm on the night of July 24, he presumed, had flooded the Confederate listening galleries. In his next note, Grant wanted to know if Burnside could maintain the mine for a few days, in case its explosion could be coordinated with advantageous circumstances above ground. At present, wrote Grant's chief of staff, the commanding general had no plans to assault the enemy's line in conjunction with the blast.

Within minutes, though, Meade sent a man to Burnside with a dispatch indicating that Grant had changed his mind — he now wanted to blow the mine as part of a larger operation, and Grant's earlier messages were obsolete. Fifteen minutes later, another aide arrived from Meade with directions to submit a plan for the detonation.

Burnside may have been too specific when he drew up this proposal. Meade's language, strictly interpreted, directed him only to explain the manner in which he would explode the mine; it implied, however, that he wanted to know Burnside's plan of attack, and Burnside sat down to provide that in detail. He diagrammed the galleries, gave his own estimates of the powder needed for each magazine, and revealed the system Colonel Pleasants had devised for setting them off. He proposed to explode the charge either just before dawn or in the early evening, and then detailed the manner in which "the two brigades of the colored division" would make the attack. All might have been well had he simply said "one division." He added that, if the heights beyond the Confederate position were gained, Ferrero's division ought to be thrown "right into the town." He hardly dared mention the issue of support, but finally referred to the need for "cooperation, at least in the way of artillery," from neighboring corps. He even modified this reasonable expectation by the redundant observation that Meade would have to judge the measure of cooperation necessary.[13]

Only then was the inadequate fuse delivered and the powder freighted to IX Corps headquarters — at least, two-thirds of the amount Burnside had specified. The next afternoon Colonel Pleasants began charging the mine.[14] On July 28, when Pleasants apprised him of the completion of the mine, General Burnside rode back to Meade's command post to make the final preparations. Not until that moment did he learn the news that would cut the legs from under him: the colored division, Meade said, could not lead the attack.

Burnside quickly explained that these troops had been trained especially for the difficult movements necessary to the battle plan. That, Meade went on, was of no consequence since he did not want Burnside to use that formation anyway. The leading division would simply push straight for the hill with the cemetery on it, beyond the fort. There was no need for any particular training or fancy footwork.

Then Burnside revealed his reasons for choosing the black troops: the white divisions were used to having the cover of their fortifications; they were excessively warworn and gunshy, as was much of the rest of the Army of the Potomac. Only the fourth division was fresh enough for open-field fighting after so many weeks of siege. Meade countered that it was precisely because they were untested troops that he could not allow it.

They argued about it for some time. Finally, Meade remarked that he was going to general headquarters that afternoon, and since Burnside was so earnest in his belief, he would put the issue before Grant. Perhaps satisfied that Meade would pose the question in a fair and objective manner, Burnside thanked him and went back to his own headquarters.

The afternoon of July 28 turned to dusk with no word from Meade, nor did the morning of the twenty-ninth bring the message Burnside was dreading. Later that day Burnside began to relax, deciding that Grant must have sustained him; otherwise, Meade would have communicated the news by now. The attack, after all, was scheduled for 3:30 on the morning of July 30.[15]

During the night, a deserter from Field's division of the Army of Northern Virginia had come into Burnside's trenches carrying the information that his division was marching for Drewry's Bluff, north of the Appomattox. This was just what Burnside had been hoping for. Hancock, back in command of the II Corps, was going to make a demonstration north of the James opposite Drewry's Bluff, so Lee would weaken his lines south of the Appomattox. News of Hancock's movement must have been leaked across the lines, prompting the Confederates to shift weight that way.[16] Burnside began to shed some of the gloom Meade's interference had left upon him.

Just before noon, Burnside called Generals Ledlie, Potter and Willcox to his tent. The commander of the fourth division knew precisely what was expected of him; those in charge of the white divisions needed coaching. With only fifteen or sixteen hours remaining before the mine was sprung, a conference could wait no longer. Ledlie arrived after Burnside began his instructions.[17]

Robert Potter had been with Burnside a long time. As the original major of Ferrero's 51st New York, he had served in the North Carolina campaign, where he was badly wounded, and had been in the IX Corps ever since, commanding it for some months in East Tennessee. He was a slight man with fast-thinning hair, but for all of his delicate appearance he was absolutely fearless.

Orlando Bolivar Willcox had been Burnside's classmate at West Point, and had graduated ten places ahead of him in 1847. Assigned to the IX Corps at the start of the Maryland campaign, he had commanded the corps briefly while Burnside led the Army of the Potomac. If Willcox had a failing, it was a reluctance to attack until supporting artillery was in place, a tendency learned at First Bull Run and demonstrated at both Antietam and Spotsylvania.

Burnside recited his last conversation with Meade for these two (and for Ledlie, when he finally arrived), describing the great anxiety it had caused him. He expressed a guarded hope that his plan had survived Grant's scrutiny intact. No sooner did he utter that sentence than Meade himself knocked on the tentpole. Burnside invited him in, and he entered with several other officers. Meade said that Grant had agreed the black troops should not lead the charge, not only because they were untried but also because a failure that resulted in their slaughter would have disastrous political ramifications. Meade did not, however, tell Burnside that this second argument was something he himself had thrown against the plan when he presented it to General Grant. In fact, Meade appears never to have shown Grant Burnside's plan at all, but only the orders Meade had drawn up for his own modification of that plan.[18]

Burnside asked, one last time, if Meade would reconsider.

"No, general," Meade replied, "the order is final."

With a sigh rising from despair, Burnside said he would do his best.

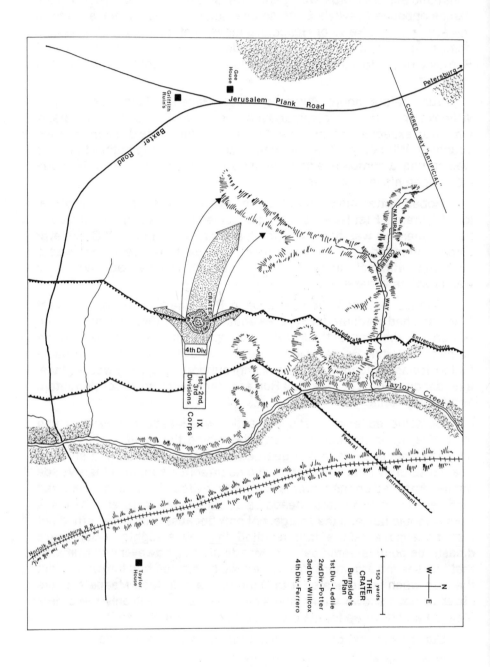

THE
CRATER
Burnside's
Plan

1st Div.—Ledlie
2nd Div.—Potter
3rd Div.—Willcox
4th Div.—Ferrero

150 yards

N
W   E
S

Gee
House

Griffith
Ruins

Jerusalem Plank Road

Petersburg

COVERED WAY "ARTIFICIAL"

Baxter Road

NATURAL COVERED WAY

CRATER

4th Div

1st & 2nd,
3rd
Divisions
IX Corps

Confederate

Entrenchments

Taylor's Creek

Federal

Entrenchments

Norfolk & Petersburg R.R.

Taylor
House

22

Meade and his entourage departed, and the four remaining generals began wrangling over who ought to lead the assault.

Whether the individual division commanders lobbied for or against their respective commands is not recorded, but they covered a number of liabilities. Both Potter's and Willcox's divisions had been roughly handled during the initial fighting, and for most of the time since had occupied the front line. Their men were sorely stressed and fewer in number than Ledlie's. On the other hand, Ledlie's division was in little better morale and was not so near to the point of assault. Several hours would be required to put it in position. No one mentioned that Ledlie's division had made a botch of its attack on June 17, and that many officers in his own command blamed Ledlie's incompetence, cowardice, or drunkenness for the failure. Most likely, Ledlie's incapacity was not the matter of general discussion it later became. Otherwise, Burnside would not have allowed what finally happened.

During lengthy debate, the four kept returning to the same hopeless concensus: the fourth division should lead. It was now about three o'clock in the afternoon, with barely a dozen hours left for placing troops, and they were no nearer a decision than they had been when Meade left. At last, with the same desperate frustration that had driven Meade to order a deliberately uncoordinated attack on June 18, Burnside determined to let the decision fall to chance. Ledlie, Potter and Willcox drew lots from a hat, and Ledlie came up with the odd lot.[19]

Once that issue was settled, Burnside explained to his subordinates what he wanted them to do. Ledlie was to dash around the aperture blasted in the Confederate works and seize what everyone was beginning to call Cemetery Hill, near the historic Blandford Church. Willcox's division would follow Ledlie around the abandoned entrenchments and swing into line on his left, along the Jerusalem Plank Road, to deflect any counterattack there, while Potter would perform a similar function on the right. With the white divisions forming three sides of a protective box, the colored division would then sweep past Ledlie and into Petersburg, much as Burnside had originally envisioned. It was a variation of Ferrero's instructions, set to a larger scale. The differences were that none of the troops involved had carefully rehearsed their roles, and none of the storming party enjoyed the freshness and *elan* that Burnside considered essential to success. Burnside solemnly sent the generals back to their various headquarters to await written orders.[20]

Meade formulated his instructions to Burnside that afternoon, after the two had discussed the new strategy. Grant received a copy of the order of attack, and though he supposedly entertained a poor opinion of Ledlie, neither he nor Meade made any further changes. Perhaps they felt that Burnside's scheme had been disrupted enough.[21]

It was nine o'clock that night before the IX Corps division commanders were handed the written orders for movements intended to begin at dark. The three white divisions formed in the trenches and the covered way leading to the front line, densely packed in the sultry summer night. July 29 was a dreadfully warm day, and when the sun finally fell the mercury did not. The crowding of so many noisome bodies made the breathless air all the worse.

General Potter feared the cramped conditions would breed confusion. His division lay in its accustomed stretch of trenches, parallel to the Confederate line and to the right of the covered way. Because of the darkness and a wrong turn, troops of the XVIII Corps ordered to relieve him did not arrive until too late, so Potter left his men in place. He had Simon Griffin's brigade string out a line of skirmishers to the right of the mine. His other brigade, under the recently-returned Colonel Zenas Bliss, lay on its arms on the open ground behind the trenches, alongside the covered way. Only one regiment was not in line — the overworked 48th Pennsylvania. Potter assigned it to duty as provost guard, to give it a well-earned rest. Colonel Pleasants would have nothing to do with a rest, however, and insisted on serving on Potter's staff as a volunteer aide.[22]

There was another volunteer staff officer in a temporary but important position in the IX Corps that sweltering evening. General Julius White was appointed Burnside's chief of staff sometime before midnight, in place of John G. Parke. Parke, Burnside's perennial right-hand-man for the past two years, had fallen ill with another of the malarial attacks that periodically disabled him, and for the past four weeks Burnside or his assistant adjutant general had been doing Parke's administrative legwork. White had arrived at Meade's headquarters in early July, fresh from a five-month stint as commander of a draft rendezvous in Springfield, Illinois. Meade gave him an unspecified assignment to the IX Corps, and White rather pathetically asked Burnside for any available job. Burnside, who knew White from the East Tennessee campaign, put him in charge of the fourth division late in the month, when Ferrero's commission seemed to be failing Senate confirmation. It was only three days later, near dark on July 29, when news of Ferrero's confirmation arrived. That displaced White, whom no one seems to have wanted: like most men, Julius White was best remembered for his failures, and it was he who had surrendered Harper's Ferry in 1862. Now the IX Corps was about to go into battle with two division commanders who had only the marginal approval of the U.S. Senate, as well as a new chief of staff who might have been characterized as summer help.[23]

The IX Corps troops were not the only men feeling their way through the darkness. The II Corps had been operating north of the James, in company with two divisions of cavalry, and now Hancock was heading back to

24

the Appomattox River to support a division he previously had sent back to take the trenches for Edward Ord's entire corps. With his three divisions of the XVIII Corps and John Turner's second division of the X Corps, General Ord marched south to back up Burnside. He put his first division into Willcox's works in time for Willcox to form behind Ledlie, but Ord's third division — seven Negro regiments — managed to get lost. It was nearly three o'clock in the morning before Joseph Carr could get those black troops up to relieve General Potter, and since the mine was to be exploded at 3:30 Potter said he would make his charge from where he was. Carr held his little division in line just behind Potter, ready to move up when the latter advanced. Ord kept both his second division and Turner's about a quarter-mile beyond the foremost trench, where Burnside had indicated they would be handiest.[24]

The generals were also shifting about. Near the scorched chimneys that marked the site of the Taylor house, behind Taylor's Creek, General Potter's men had been building a huge fort throughout July. It was dimpled with fourteen embrasures, which Potter had filled with artillery on July 26. The earthwork was six hundred yards behind the front lines and offered a wonderful view of the mined Confederate redoubt and the surrounding terrain; it was into this citadel that Burnside moved his headquarters, a few minutes before the mine was to be exploded. There was a tradition developing around Petersburg of naming Union forts after deceased officers, and Burnside christened this one after his lamented engineer, Major James St. Clair Morton, who had been killed in the fighting of June 17.[25]

George Meade shifted his own headquarters from a protected point in the center of the army's rear lines to the knoll behind the Dunn house, near Harrison's Creek, where Burnside's tent was still standing. That placed him three-quarters of a mile nearer the scene of action, though he was still a mile away from the mine, with telegraphic communication stretching to all the corps commanders. The one fault with the location was poor visibility, which disappointed his staff. One aide, Theodore Lyman, complained "you can see nothing from there." Meade's staff arrived just after Burnside's departed for Fort Morton, almost at the appointed hour of 3:30 A.M.[26]

Remarkably, all of these movements were accomplished without arousing the suspicion of the Confederates. It was in order to avoid giving away his intentions that Burnside overlooked a portion of Meade's order that directed him to remove the abatis on his front — the trees that had been felled with their branches pointing toward the enemy. Those obstacles had been shot all to flinders, and would offer no real obstacle to his infantry, and an attempt to destroy what was left of them might very well alert an enemy who already knew about mining operations on that front. Neither did Burnside prepare his parapets to the degree Meade appears to have had in mind. Meade later implied that he wanted them virtually leveled; instead, Ledlie's men only constructed a couple of sandbagged stairways.[27] It is not clear whether the two generals had different notions about the manner in which the troops would deploy, whether Burnside or someone below him misinterpreted the orders, or whether Burnside arbitrarily modified them to preserve the defensive strength of the fortifications, in accordance with his diminishing confidence in the operation.

Burnside had, however, supplied his first three division commanders with a regiment each of acting engineers. The 35th Massachusetts, the 7th Rhode Island, and the 17th Michigan had all been in the service since the summer of 1862, and had lost heavily in the spring campaign. Now, supplied with picks and shovels, they were assigned respectively to Ledlie, Potter, and Willcox, with instructions to reverse the Confederate fortifications or to build completely new ones, as the circumstances of the battle might require.[28]

Few in the Union army got much sleep that night. Meade's staff was in the saddle by 2:30 a.m., after a late night on July 29. The cavalry, the II Corps, and most of the Army of the James was marching all night, and even the V Corps was stirring. Warren stripped his front of all but a skeleton force, gathering his strength on Burnside's left so he could offer support when the time came.[29]

Ferrero's division had pulled out of line at dark and assembled in the open ground in front of Fort Morton. Until late in the evening the blacks expected to do their well-practiced pirouette around the wreckage of the enemy salient; it was not until about eleven o'clock that Ferrero mentioned the change to his brigadiers, who carried the news rather dolefully back to their bivouacs. Not only were the colored troops robbed of their grand opportunity, they also apprehended the difficulties that might be thrown in the way of such a substitution made, literally, at the eleventh hour. Their officers advised them to get a little sleep, and the troops napped for a couple of hours. They were up by three o'clock, nibbling hardtack and salt pork and drinking cold coffee from their canteens.[30]

The white troops of the IX Corps were the most uncomfortable. They endured a nightmare of shuffling and standing in the ovenlike trenches, and from the moment they began to bunch up like stockyard cattle at the loading gate, they were the only troops in the army who were certain to be thrown into the morning's battle. Open battle was no longer the routine expectation it had been in early May. Veterans especially dreaded it in a fashion that might have been considered cowardly a year or two before. What made it all the worse for the leading division was the contempt it harbored for its own general. At least one regimental commander in

Ledlie's first brigade thought Ledlie was totally incompetent, while the general was not even much liked or respected by his own staff. Such opinions rarely fail to filter down to the foot soldier.[31]

At the mouth of the covered way waited the forlorn hope, Elisha Marshall's brigade. In it were two battered little battalions of infantry and a pair of those big heavy artillery regiments. These men had expected to serve in comfortable forts in Washington or on the coast, but in late spring Grant had given them rifles and made them infantrymen. So far, they had not done well. It had been these "heavies," who made up most of the second brigade, whom Burnside had so roundly cursed after the bungled assault of June 17. As he had stated privately, and as a regimental historian would later record, "they had not enlisted for it." Now, these parade-field soldiers huddled in the dense air of the defences, their white cross belts and brass shoulder scales long gone. Gone, too, were many of the men who had signed up with them to polish the big guns and sleep in the wooden barracks. Almost suffocating, their eyes stinging from the dust and fatigue, these demoralized and disillusioned artillerymen were General Ledlie's choice to carry the Confederate works and Cemetery Hill.[32]

Ledlie, the civil engineer, was himself one of those discomfited artillerymen. But for an ill-advised recommendation, he would still be commanding a New York artillery regiment. Now he lingered somewhere near his division in the maze of log-reinforced trenches. He was nervous, perhaps to the point of sickness, as he waited for the unmistakable signal to send in his troops. Burnside would describe him as having been "cheerful" when he left the afternoon council, but no one who saw him in the ensuing twenty-four hours would have used that word.[33]

CHAPTER III

Two Bridges Over the James

In mid-July, Confederate deserters had told Union officers that Richmond was alive with rumors Lee was planning a major offensive. The object of such an offensive, Grant thought, would be to relieve the beleaguered Confederates fighting Sherman in Georgia. Meade and Butler were both alerted, but the expected assault never materialized.

If Lee was not going to launch an offensive effort, Grant decided that he would. Now that Wright's VI Corps had been sent to Washington, Grant supposed Lee might risk sending some of his troops to Georgia, and with Burnside's mine almost ready, Grant determined this was his best opportunity to take Petersburg. To make the thing certain, Grant had to convince Lee to shift as much of his army as possible north of the Appomattox. He chose Hancock's II Corps to lure those Confederates away. With two divisions of Sheridan's cavalry, Hancock would march north against Richmond by way of Deep Bottom, about ten miles northeast of Petersburg. The maneuver could prove advantageous however the enemy responded: if Lee failed to take the bait, the Confederate lines would be so lightly defended that Hancock and Sheridan could plunder Richmond and sever the railroads to the north; if Lee reinforced his defences north of the James River, the lines around Petersburg would be depleted, and the chances of success after the mine explosion would be that much greater.[1]

On July 26, at about 4:00 P.M., Hancock rousted his three divisions out of their camps and started them north. They kept to roads well behind Union lines, to avoid the roving eyes of Confederate signalmen. Each man carried four days' rations and one hundred rounds of ammunition. There was no quartermaster train on this march, just a few engineer wagons carrying entrenching tools and, ominously, twenty ambulances per division. As Major Isaac Hamilton of the 110th Pennsylvania wrote, "we knew desperate work lay before us."[2]

Moving along City Point Road, Hancock's veterans encountered the results of a little military justice — a tandem gallows, from which two members of the 72nd New York were still hanging. Their unit had finished its term of service the day before, and the men had packed their traps for an early-morning departure. But during the night, these two teamsters decided to investigate a local farmhouse that was occupied by the wife of a Confederate soldier who was serving with the army before Petersburg. The two New Yorkers persuaded her to open the door, then seized her, "abusing her person and treating her with shameful violence," as Major

Hamilton phrased it. Satisfied that she would be afraid to report the incident, or that they would be long gone in the event she did, the confident pair slunk back to camp. Morning found the woman at the door of the Union provost marshal, to whom she revealed her horrible story. She remembered the men had had the number "72" on their hats, so the provost marshal trotted out the entire 72nd New York; the woman quickly pointed out the two culprits. There followed a drumhead court martial, and while the rest of the regiment went home the two malefactors were left swinging for all to see — especially the nearby Confederates.[3]

With nearly a full complement of fresh men and horses, General Philip Sheridan also started north, crossing the Appomattox River at Broadway Landing. The two forces groped through total darkness the length of Jones's neck, a finger-shaped peninsula cut by a loop of the James. Hancock's men made their way over difficult terrain, leaving the better roads for the cavalrymen. General Butler eased their journey a bit by providing occasional cavalry pickets to guide the columns, and by building small bonfires along the way to light the unfamiliar landscape. Both the infantry and cavalry arrived at the James River about 2:30 A.M.

Butler had also constructed two pontoon bridges for the crossing: one at the tip of Jones's Neck and a second about a mile downriver. General Robert S. Foster's brigade of the X Corps curled around the end of either bridge, holding them for Hancock. For several days Foster sparred with elements of Kershaw's division of R. H. Anderson's First Corps. He also faced part of Cadmus Wilcox's division, under James Conner, but held his ground until Hancock's arrival.[4]

Hancock's orders were to cross at the upper bridge and move due west to Chaffin's Bluff, to cut off any Confederate attempt to reinforce Richmond. Once he had accomplished that, Sheridan was to lead his two divisions — and August Kautz's cavalry division, borrowed from Butler — over the lower bridge, following an arc that would leave him north of Richmond, where he could cut the vital Virginia Central Railroad. Now came the first hitch in Grant's plan. Hancock rode ahead of his corps to confer with Sheridan and Foster; according to Foster, the Confederates were in great force just beyond the upper bridge, so Hancock decided to cross at the lower bridge. That presented a serious problem, because the land between the far ends of the two bridges was bisected by Four Mile Creek, which served the Confederates as an excellent natural barrier. Hancock would have to swing around the Confederate left to reach Chaffin's Bluff, and that would both remove the element of surprise and delay Sheridan's cavalrymen.[5]

The entire operation depended on rapid movement, but the geography of Deep Bottom precluded this. Crosshatched by the tributaries of Four Mile Creek to the west and Bailey's Creek to the east, the ground here was low and swampy. To the north, the terrain rose gradually to a plateau dotted with broad cornfields and thick woods. It was difficult to move troops except on the three main roads leading northwest to Richmond. New Market Road, closest to the James, was Hancock's route to Chaffin's Bluff; just above that was Darbytown Road (also known as Central Road); the Charles City Road was about five miles farther northeast. Long Bridge Road, running northeast, intersected all three of these routes. New Market Road was by far the most important; Hancock had to hold it to control the central connector, Long Bridge Road. The Charles City Road, passing through White Oak Swamp and leading to the Chickahominy River, was the highway the federal cavalry would have to take to reach the railroads north of Richmond.[6]

Hancock's men preceded Sheridan's horse soldiers over the lower bridge, the hollow echo of their footsteps muffled by a thick veneer of hay. The weary infantrymen crowded behind oak-timber works a few hundred yards from the bridge, hoping to get a few hours' sleep before daylight. Foster's men remained active, both beyond Hancock's troops and on the west side of Four Mile Creek, trying to maintain pressure on Kershaw's divided command so he could not reinforce one wing with the other.

The next morning, when Hancock put his corps in motion, he found part of Kershaw's division behind breastworks along New Market Road. Union artillery opened up in concert with mortar fire from two supporting gunboats, the *Agawam* and *Mendota,* while Hancock prepared to assault with his infantry. These gunboats proved valuable to the Union ground troops both this day and the next. Stationed on the James between the upper bridge and the newly-constructed lower bridge, they lobbed hundred-pound shells into the Southeners at regular intervals. A historian in Kershaw's division recalled years later, "Great trees a foot and a half in diameter were snapped off like pipe-stems. The peculiar frying noise made in going through the air and their enormous size caused the troops to give them the name of 'camp kettles.' They passed through our earthworks like going through mole hills."[7]

DeTrobriand's brigade of Barlow's first division, positioned to the front and right of Mott's division, moved out as skirmishers with the 99th and 110th Pennsylvania in front: the 40th New York covered the flanks and maintained the connection with the river. Regiments from Foster's brigade went along in support, commanded by Colonel Edwin Biles. Biles was directed to probe the woods near the junction of the New Market and Long Bridge Roads, and to link arms with the rest of Barlow's first division, on his left. The 110th Pennsylvania ran into heavy musketry near a large house on its right, and the 73rd New York came up to help. At the same time, Mott's third division slid past Barlow and formed on the Union right. Gibbon's division still stood in reserve, in the woods near the creek

30

bank. While DeTrobriand urged his men on in the face of Confederate fire, Barlow sent part of Miles's brigade forward: the 183rd Pennsylvania, 28th Massachusetts, and 26th Michigan. This contingent went in under the nominal command of Colonel John Lynch of the 183rd, but General Miles was at his elbow. The three regiments quickly worsted the Mississippians of Benjamin Humphreys's brigade, who fell back. Their retreat left Captain Archibald Graham's Rockbridge Artillery unsupported in the open, but the Virginia gunners kept firing, unaware they had been abandoned. Eventually they were forced to retreat, leaving behind all four of their undamaged 20-pounder Parrotts — old U.S. pieces captured early in the war, at Winchester and Harper's Ferry. A frantic Graham begged, to no avail, for muskets for himself and his men, that he might retake his prized rifles. It was too late: artillerymen from the 10th Massachusetts Battery were already hitching their own teams to them. Another Confederate battery opened on the extreme left, but was soon driven off by Mott's men. The entire Confederate line fell back up the New Market and Long Bridge Roads. The fugitives tumbled into some previously-prepared breastworks on the west side of Bailey's Creek, and here the Union advance came to a halt.[8]

Meanwhile, Sheridan's horsemen trotted toward the extreme Union right, in the direction of the Charles City Road. They seized high ground along Long Bridge and Darbytown Roads before the Confederates could recover. As Sheridan's column swung forward, the entire Union line stretched northward, creating a void on Barlow's left that Gibbon's division pulled up to fill. While Gibbon stood firm, Barlow and Mott moved ahead to attack.[9]

The Confederate entrenchments were about a thousand yards west of Bailey's Creek. Before them was open ground, discouraging any Federal frontal assaults. As Grant saw later that day, the Union soldiers were also exhausted from their all-night march and the morning's engagement. Little more could be expected from them in the way of head-on fighting. Barlow and Mott therefore sidled to the right, hoping to find and turn the Confederate left flank. Their men connected with Sheridan's; the combined force of horse and foot continued up the Long Bridge Road but was unable to determine the end of the Confederate line. Sheridan's men probed as far as Fussell's Mill, about four miles above the James River, in hopes of breaking through and gaining the Confederate rear, but the Confederates had refused their left and Sheridan came up against a solid line of battle.[10]

General Grant rode over to Deep Bottom at 3:00 P.M. but could not find Hancock on a front that was now over four miles long. He left a note for the II Corps commander, explaining that he had surveyed the lines and found nothing else that could be done that day. He wanted the cavalry to try to continue its march on Richmond, but without any costly frontal assaults. If the enemy could be doubled back toward Chaffin's Bluff, he felt, the cavalry would have a good chance of completing its mission. Kershaw's Confederates were still supported by the brigades from Wilcox's division, under General Conner: behind the Southern entrenchments were seven brigades, besides men from Richard Ewell's Department of Richmond. Nevertheless, the Yankees' constant northward movement stretched the defenders thin. With the approach of night, troops on both sides started digging in, while their leaders planned for the next day.[11]

Reinforcements began trickling in to both sides during the early evening and kept coming through the night. Hancock learned that the enemy was pulling troops from the south side of the James. Union signal stations reported twenty-nine rail cars, loaded with men, chugging from Petersburg to Richmond. Lee had sent Heth's division to Kershaw, as well as Fitzhugh and W. H. F. Lee's cavalry divisions. General Richard Anderson, commanding the First Corps during Longstreet's convalescence, was on his way to take command of the Confederate forces. General Ewell thought momentarily of calling out the local defence troops in Richmond, but Secretary of War Seddon discouraged that, lest Ewell disrupt the government by taking all the clerks or start a panic among the civilian population.[12]

Late on July 27, Meade passed a message he received from Grant along to Hancock. Grant realized that Sheridan could not continue toward Richmond in safety, for unless Hancock could drive the Confederates back to Chaffin's Bluff the cavalry would be prevented from returning through Deep Bottom. That would force Sheridan to escape down the north side of the Chickahominy to Fort Monroe, robbing Grant of the services of those horsemen for weeks. Grant therefore ordered Sheridan and Hancock to remain together for the moment and try to drive the enemy back to Chaffin's Bluff or Richmond with their combined strength. He still hoped the cavalry could complete its raid, but what he wanted most was for Hancock to keep the growing Confederate presence occupied for another day. He augmented Hancock early on July 28 with the 2,600 men of Henry Birge's brigade, from Butler. This unit had been on its way from Louisiana to rejoin General Emory's XIX Corps in Washington when Grant commandeered it. Hancock sent Birge to relieve Gibbon's men from their advanced position near New Market Road. Sheridan also went under Hancock's official command that morning, his original orders indefinitely postponed.[13]

By dawn of the twenty-eighth, both sides were stronger. Each waited for the other to make a move. About eight o'clock, while fresh troops took their place in line, Lane's and McGowan's brigades of Wilcox's division moved past Kershaw's division. Kershaw's old brigade joined them; under

32

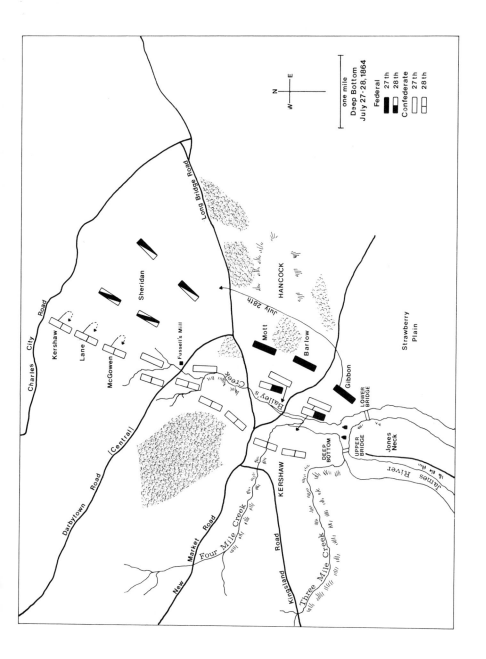

one mile
Deep Bottom
July 27-28, 1864

Federal
  27th
  28th
Confederate
  27th
  28th

Long Bridge Road

Sheridan

HANCOCK

July 28th

Kershaw

Lane

McGowen

Fussell's Mill

Mott

Barlow

Strawberry
Plain

Charles City Road

Bailey's Creek

Gibbon

LOWER
BRIDGE

Darbytown Road (Central)

KERSHAW

DEEP
BOTTOM

UPPER
BRIDGE

Jones
Neck

James River

New Market Road

Four Mile Creek

Kingsland Road

Three Mile Creek

General Conner they all sidestepped north to bolster the Confederate left, above Fussell's Mill, which was held only by Martin Gary's assortment of Southern cavalry. The Union gunboats and field artillery fired so effectively on Conner's column that it had to weave evasively. When Conner's men were in place they reached as far north as the Charles City Road, facing Sheridan's cavalrymen.[14]

It was around ten o'clock when Conner's force attacked Sheridan's front, with Kershaw's brigade on the far left, Lane's in the center, and McGowan's on the right. They advanced through the woods about two hundred yards. As the column crossed a local road, it began to swing to the left. A gap opened in the line when Lane's men bogged down in a marsh, but when McGowan's brigade burst into an open cornfield they loosed a withering fire that repelled the Yankee cavalrymen. The troopers retreated downhill about three hundred yards, where they dismounted and took refuge behind a farmhouse and adjacent outbuildings. Lane's delay left McGowan dangerously advanced, but the mired North Carolinians broke free just in time to react to a devastating enfilade of McGowan's left flank. Though they took the brunt of this fire themselves, with the help of the other two brigades the Tarheels were able to drive the cavalrymen back. Their success, however, was only momentary. As they moved down the hill toward the horsemen they came into ever-more-effective range, and finally the repeating carbines stopped them cold. Gibbon's division was coming on the run to back Sheridan up.[15]

The first of two unfortunate tiffs between two of the Union army's best field commanders had just occurred. Winfield Scott Hancock and John Gibbon, whose relationship had started to sour at the battle of the Wilderness, quarreled bitterly at Deep Bottom. Waiting in reserve a little earlier, Gibbon had received orders to ready his command for a movement to support Sheridan, should he call for help. When the request came, Hancock asked Gibbon whether his division were not already in motion. Gibbon replied it was not, since he had received no final order until that moment. Hancock exploded. "I gave you an order half an hour ago to move it up," he bellowed. Gibbon argued that that order had been only a preparatory one, and the two exchanged hot words. At last Hancock appealed to a member of his staff, who had heard him give the order, but the staff officer manfully corroborated Gibbon's recollection.[16]

As it happened, Sheridan did not need Gibbon's help. Led by Alfred Torbert's division, the cavalry counterattacked and drove the enemy back almost a mile, capturing nearly two hundred prisoners and several stand of colors. The Yankees shot two horses from under General Conner, and Torbert's men boasted of counting 158 Confederate dead on the field. The cavalrymen themselves had only lost about two hundred men altogether. As the Confederates fell back beyond the woods, the antagonists returned to the previous day's positions. Hancock maneuvered to avoid any more such attacks. He ordered Gibbon to hold the approaches to New Market and Long Bridge Roads, while he had Sheridan pull his men back to cover the New Market Road near Malvern Hill: the Confederates were reportedly moving east, in the direction of Malvern Hill, to try to get between the Yankees and the lower bridge. Hancock received a flurry of dispatches warning that the enemy was concentrating to attack him, but nothing developed.[17]

In the afternoon both Grant and Meade came to confer with Hancock. Grant had finally abandoned all hope of sending Sheridan railroad-wrecking north of Richmond. As he had previously reasoned, however, he had achieved his alternate goal by luring half of Lee's army north of the James. Grant ordered Hancock to send Mott's division back to Petersburg that night to relieve the XVIII Corps, while Ord shifted south in accordance with the plan for the mine explosion. Hancock had to hold the line for the rest of the day with his other two divisions and with Foster, Birge, and the cavalrymen.

The next morning the tension between Hancock and Gibbon resurfaced. Gibbon was talking to Sheridan when he heard an angry voice ask, "Is General Gibbon here?" Gibbon turned to see Hancock, who demanded to know who had laid out his division line. Gibbon said that he had, and Hancock shot back that he "would be ashamed of any officer who would make any such line." Gibbon, mortally embarrassed, responded that he knew of no place where it was defective.

"Get on your horse," said the crimson Hancock, "and I will show you where it is defective." Guiding him to a point on the front line, Hancock gestured at a section of trench that was dug "a few inches" too deep, or manned by soldiers who were too short. Hancock ordered the infantrymen to stand up, which they did, and the II Corps commander observed they could not see the field to their front. Perhaps with a note of disgust, Gibbon pointed out that such minor flaws could be discovered on any line, and he directed Hancock's attention to several well-placed batteries, vowing that any enemy assault in this sector could be handily repulsed.

"Well," Hancock snorted, "I will hold you responsible for your line and anything that may happen here." Gibbon quickly replied that he was perfectly willing to be held responsible for any of his command decisions. He added that he wished Hancock had spoken to him in private before insulting him in front of half-a-dozen general officers. Gibbon recalled much later that a somewhat penitent Hancock admitted he had possibly been too hasty, and returned to apologize to the group for his behavior.[18]

Hancock was not the same man he had been before he was wounded at Gettysburg. The constant requirement of riding a horse merely aggravated the pain in his groin and preheated his already-famous temper.

Still, a soldier of the 11th Maine, in Foster's brigade, was much impressed by the man he saw that Friday morning, talking on horseback with Phil Sheridan. "Hancock was a tall, slender officer, with longish light-brown hair, mustache, imperial, and chin-whiskers (*sic*), while Sheridan was short, rotund, darker, and close cropped. Both sat their horses as only perfect horsemen and hard riders can, . . . both seemed flattered and amused by the admiring glances and the not always low-spoken remarks of our men."[19]

Throughout July 29 Hancock demonstrated vigorously before the enemy, hoping to preserve the illusion of a threat against Richmond. But at dusk of that day he, too, marched his troops stealthily back to Petersburg, filing them into works on the Union right, next to the Appomattox River. As these II Corps troops slipped south, another Confederate division from the Petersburg front was just settling into the Confederate defences at Deep Bottom: Charles Field's division had pulled out after dark on the twenty-eighth, and arrived on the Deep Bottom line late on the twenty-ninth.

Sheridan also withdrew from north of the James. His new orders were to circle south of Petersburg and take position on the extreme left of the Union line, beyond Warren's V Corps. Birge, who was allowed to continue his original excursion, made his way toward Washington. Left with only four hundred men at Deep Bottom, Robert Foster still held the bridges. His situation was not so precarious as it may have appeared, however, for Butler's entire army lay nearby at Bermuda Hundred.

Only three Confederate divisions were left in the Petersburg trenches the evening of July 29. By the early hours of July 30, three Union corps crouched opposite them, waiting for four tons of black powder to open the gates to the "Cockade City."[20]

CHAPTER IV

A Forest of Glittering Bayonets

The moonless morning of July 30 was so thoroughly dark that, had he not carried a candle, Henry Pleasants would have noticed no loss of light when he entered his mine. Into the tunnel with him went Sergeant Reese and Lieutenant Jacob Douty, another member of the 48th Pennsylvania. At 3:00 A.M. Pleasants carefully touched off the three separate fuses. There was more than ninety feet of fuse, which he estimated would require thirty minutes to burn, so there was no particular hurry as they departed. Twenty minutes later General Meade wired Burnside that he was concerned about the extreme darkness. Revealing a certain ignorance of the detonating procedure, he suggested ten minutes before the scheduled blast that Burnside could put it off a while, if he chose. Even if Burnside had wanted to postpone the explosion, it was too late, and so he advised Meade.[1]

The appointed hour of three-thirty came and passed. The three Pennsylvanians at the mouth of the mine glanced nervously at each other. At Fort Morton, General Burnside grew uneasy as his pocket watch swept toward four o'clock, and he ordered Major James Van Buren of his staff to find Pleasants and see what was the problem. Two captains from Meade's staff successively trotted into Fort Morton — it was too dark for a faster gait — on the same errand as Major Van Buren. Burnside told them both he did not know what had happened, and then he sent a second officer from his own staff down to the mine. Meade's two men wandered back to their chief, who was now seated at Burnside's old headquarters.[2]

It was still well before four o'clock when Sergeant Reese and Lieutenant Douty offered to go into the tunnel and see what was wrong, but Pleasants would not let them go until he was positive the fuse had failed. At last, about a quarter past four, he allowed Sergeant Reese to crawl in with a lantern. Just about the same time, a dispatch reached Burnside from Meade, who had not yet heard from his staff officers. He wanted to know if there was going to be an explosion. Burnside had no idea, and he did not reply immediately; five minutes later an anxious Meade asked the IX Corps telegraph operator whether Burnside was at his headquarters.[3]

Meanwhile, Reese found the burned end of the fuse and followed it, with understandable apprehension, toward the magazines: faulty fuses might have sputtered out, but there was still an outside chance they were burning abnormally slow and approaching the powder. As it happened,

37

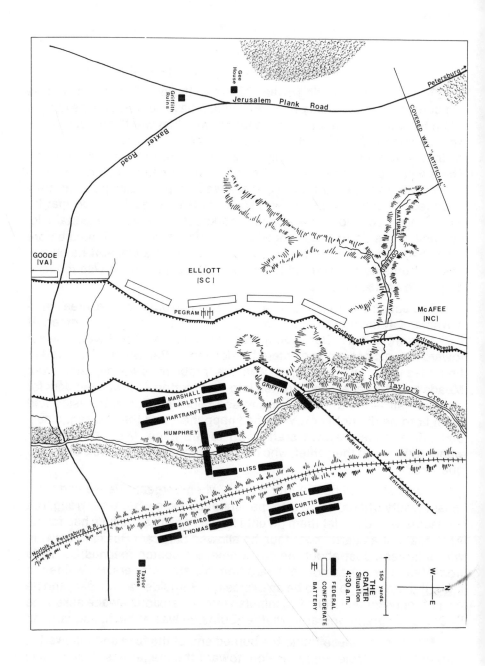

THE
CRATER
Situation
4:30 a.m.

⊞ FEDERAL
☐ CONFEDERATE
■ BATTERY

150 yards

N
W—E
S

38

however, he found all three of the lines extinguished at a splice, a little over halfway to the powder-bedded yoke at the intersection of the lateral galleries. Reese could not relight them without slicing off the wads that had caused the trouble, and when he slapped his pockets he discovered he had forgotten a knife. He was making his way back to the entrance when he encountered Lieutenant Douty. Douty, a thirty-one-year-old boilermaker from Pottsville, had a jackknife with him. Together they cut and lit the shortened fuses and, at about four-thirty, scrambled out of the tunnel. It would take no more than fifteen minutes, they said, and Colonel Pleasants relayed that information to Major Van Buren.[4]

Van Buren had not yet returned to Fort Morton with the news when another frenetic message arrived from Meade. If the mine could not be detonated, he said, something must be done at once. The grey of predawn had not yet relieved the darkness, but it was not far away. Meade said he would wait to hear from Burnside before giving any orders, but he did not wait. In an order headed the same moment as the last telegram, 4:35 A.M., Meade told Burnside to make his assault now if he could not light off the mine. The prospect must have been unnerving to Burnside, who was sufficiently doubtful about the ability of his troops to assault fortifications that had been largely destroyed. The idea of taking those same works intact bordered on preposterous, as Lee discovered the following March in front of Fort Stedman. Major Van Buren soon came and told Burnside the mine would go off about four forty-five, and Burnside hung his hopes on that news. Almost exactly at the specified time — one minute earlier, by most accounts — William Griffith's ravaged Virginia pastures began an ominous trembling.[5]

The danger of a Union assault without the benefit of the mine, even in the wee hours of the morning, was aggravated by the fact that Confederate artillery in this sector was manned day and night. The gun crews served alternate shifts at the embrasures, their guns loaded and the lanyards ready, for they knew something was in the wind. Their own countermines, having found nothing, had lulled them into a measure of security about Union tunneling, but so close were the opposing lines that something seemed bound to happen here. Captain Richard Pegram had been with the four Napoleons of his battery until the evening of the twenty-ninth, when four seven-man gun crews and two lieutenants relieved him. The new shift sat by their guns all night, singing songs and chatting until after midnight. Major James Coit, Pegram's battalion commander, remained at Elliott's Salient with them until about midnight, when he retired to his headquarters behind the front lines. Serving as infantry support in and behind the fort was the 18th South Carolina of Stephen Elliott's brigade. The rest of that brigade stretched to either side of the redoubt, the 17th South Carolina immediately to the left and the 26th beyond that, with the 22nd and 23rd South Carolina regiments on the right. Most of the infantrymen were still sleeping at 4:44 on the morning of July 30. For many, their abrupt waking would be their last.[6]

The sound of the explosion was remarkably muffled. At IX Corps headquarters, where Grant and Meade waited impatiently, it was "dull sounding, . . . like a heavy gun, far away." For those who could see it, it was more impressive. The earth in front of the first division "seemed to swell into a little hill," wrote one of Ledlie's men, "and presently there burst from its summit a huge volume of smoke and flame." A Rhode Islander in Potter's division remembered that the fort was blown straight upward, it and the sulphurous black smoke "slowly mounting into the air to a height of some two hundred feet, and then, spreading out like a fan, fell back again into the excavation made by the explosion." "Earth, stones, timbers, arms, legs, guns unlimbered and bodies unlimbed . . . ascended in fearful confusion and havoc," a Maine man recorded, and the colonel of the 56th Massachusetts watched Ledlie's men recoil and run as this debris threatened to descend upon them. Their officers quickly pushed them back into line, and only a shower of dust and small clods reached them.[7]

Lieutenant A. B. Thrash, a North Carolinian whose company was on picket duty a couple of hundred yards north of the fort, was leaning against the breastworks when the blast ruptured the predawn quiet. In the grey light he could distinguish only two specific objects climbing toward the sky: the carriage of one of the twelve-pounder Napoleons, and the body of a man. The adjutant of a nearby battalion of artillery best recalled the same wreckage as it descended: "hurtling downward with a roaring sound showers of stones, broken timbers, and blackened human limbs, . . . the gloomy pall of darkening smoke flashing to an angry crimson as it floats away to meet the morning sun."

Some three hundred men were unceremoniously rocketed into the air; few of them survived to record their experience. Some men were buried alive. Company B of the 22nd South Carolina, for instance, had about three dozen men on duty. Wilson Moore had just been relieved from guard duty and was sleeping in a ditch behind the trench: everyone else had stretched out lengthwise, so he had only enough room to sleep sitting up. Thus, when tons of yellow clay rained down on the trench, all the others were buried. Moore, half awake, threw his hands over his head, and though the falling soil covered him completely his hands were near enough to the surface for a returning comrade to see them wiggling. This samaritan unburied Moore's face, but could not extricate him until Union soldiers swarmed in to finish the job. The only other survivors of Company B, besides Moore and the private who had come up to rescue him, were Captain George Lake and W. J. Lake, his lieutenant. Both were entombed together, the lieutenant thrown over the captain, and they had but air

40

enough to discuss their apparently fatal predicament. The weight of the earth was too great for them to budge; besides, the junior Lake had a broken leg that prevented him from trying. They fully expected to die, but in a few minutes some of Marshall's heavy artillerymen began digging them out. They, Wilson Moore, and the other man were the only members of Company B left alive. When all four of them were sent to the Union lines as prisoners, the company ceased to exist as far as the Confederate army was concerned.[8]

Of the thirty Confederates on duty in Pegram's battery, the two officers and twenty of the men were killed by the blast. Only the crew of the extreme right gun and one other man survived. That portion of the 18th South Carolina on duty in the fort was almost annihilated. Lieutenant Smith Lipscomb of Company F was the only man in his company to escape death or capture: he was blown to the far side of the works, but recovered himself before the Yankees came. He massaged his arms and legs to see if he was injured; incredibly, he was not. When Union artillery opened on his position he scrambled back to his own side of the works, and with a handful of survivors from his regiment and the 17th South Carolina, Lipscomb took up a musket and prepared to repel the Union assault.

Just north of the explosion, one of Captain Douglas's Confederate engineer sergeants was at work in the gallery of one of the countermines. He had three men below ground with him and five working on the surface. The blast knocked him off his feet while the "gallery heaved and waved as from an earthquake." He found his other five comrades missing when he scrambled outside, but there was already a platoon of Yankees coming toward him — perhaps Potter's skirmishers. The sergeant and his three remaining men bounded for their camp, where they were rejoined by all but one of the other workmen.[9]

General Beauregard later calculated that among the 17th, 18th, and 22nd South Carolina regiments and Pegram's Virginia battery, 278 men had been lost in the explosion alone.[10] What was left of Elliott's brigade tried to draw itself back together to drive away the Yankee horde that was swirling into sight.

With the explosion of the mine, one hundred and ten Union guns and fifty-four mortars opened on the Confederate lines. General Hunt had positioned them to cover more than two miles of the enemy's front, more than a dozen of them ranging in on the Crater itself. There was no response from the Southern guns for some time, and almost no rifle fire. The Union infantry was momentarily impeded by the still-falling debris and the thick dust and smoke that further obscured the twilight, but in a little while Ledlie's division began rushing up the sandbag stairways toward the maelstrom that had been Elliott's Salient. Most eyewitness accounts leaving no more than five minutes between the blast and the beginning of Ledlie's "charge," though some officers tried to stretch the recollected delay to ten or fifteen minutes. Ledlie ordered Colonel Marshall to take in his brigade, and he watched as Bartlett followed, after which he promptly retired to a bombproof hospital belonging to the third division. The general needed a drink. In order to get one he alternately told the surgeons there that he was sick and had been struck by a spent bullet.[11]

For all their supposed disinclination to fight, Marshall's heavy artillerymen led the assault with a cheer that a V Corps captain claimed he could hear over the barrage from two miles away. They spilled out of the works in queues, sprinting individually for the demolished fort without stopping to deploy in columns. What infantry obstacles lay in the way disintegrated in a twinkling, and the rapidly deteriorating organizations of the second brigade were in the Crater before five o'clock. In the van was the 14th New York Heavy Artillery; these men repeatedly faltered when they saw the carnage in the Crater, and the regiment nearly dissolved into a score of rescue parties, digging out their trapped enemies. Lieutenant Colonel Benjamin Barney's 2nd Pennsylvania Provisional Heavy Artillery swept past the New Yorkers and over the far lip of the Crater, which stretched 125 feet up and down the old Confederate works. The Pennsylvanians clambered up the soft sides of the chasm — it was about 25 feet deep — and took position behind the ruins of the fort. There they remained, digging in just as Burnside had feared, while the crowd in the Crater behind them swelled to unmanageable proportions. William Barlett's brigade followed Marshall's into the pit, the peglegged General Bartlett stumbling along beside the middle of the column.

Neither of these brigadiers seems to have been instructed what to do, and conceivably Ledlie never informed them of the plan to rush straight for the crest. Had they done so now, while the sun was not yet up and their position was clouded by smoke and dust, there would have been little to stop them. But in a few more minutes the dazed Confederates raised an annoying if light musketry fire from the flanks. The heavy artillerymen on the far side of the Crater were taking this fire from the rear, and it quickly unnerved them. Stephen Weld, commander of one of Bartlett's black-hatted Massachusetts "veteran" regiments, forced his men out of the Crater to reform in the abandoned works to the north. Colonel Weld had to fight his way, for there were still Confederates in those trenches beyond the first couple of hundred yards.[12]

Major Coit, the artilleryman, was shaken awake by the explosion and knew immediately what had happened. He trotted to the former site of Pegram's battery and found only the divided remnants of Elliott's brigade trying to cover the vulnerable gap with rifle fire. Already the Yankee soldiers were coming, so Coit rushed up the slope leading to Blandford Cemetery; there he had posted Captain Wright's battery of four guns. They had a clear field of fire over the heads of their own men and could safely rain canister on all sides of the Crater. Coit thought Wright's might have been the first Confederate cannon to open.[13]

But other artillerymen were recovering from their shock to the south of the wrecked fort. Only one gun of Davidson's battery bore advantageously on the Crater from that direction, and it was abandoned in the panic following the explosion, though it was over a thousand feet away. Major Wade Gibbs, the battalion commander, scraped together a crew from the First Corps artillery staff officers and one of the eight privates who survived from Pegram's battery. This single gun wrought havoc on the left of Ledlie's division until Gibbs himself was wounded in the neck. John T. Goode, the colonel commanding Wise's brigade, detailed some infantrymen to take over for the disabled Gibbs: Captain Samuel Preston brought his company of the 34th Virginia, which had previously served as artillery, and the deadly one-gun battery went back into action.[14]

Stephen Elliott, meanwhile, was trying to arrange a counterattack with the pitiful fragment of his brigade isolated north of the Crater. He ordered the 26th South Carolina and what was left of the 17th back from the main trench, and formed them beyond the brow of the ravine behind the salient. Young John Haskell, in command of the artillery battalion behind Elliott's Salient, had asked Elliott for some infantry support for his defenceless guns. Elliott responded that his men were terribly demoralized, but it was his intention to clear the Crater with these two little regiments despite the fact there were already a dozen or so sets of Union battle flags in his front. This was not the first time the thirty-two-year-old brigadier had faced long odds: he had defended Fort Sumter for eight months, with a garrison of about 300 men, against most of a Union army and the U.S. Navy.

Fitz William McMaster, Elliott's senior colonel, thought Elliott rash; what Elliott thought of McMaster is condensed in a letter written only sixteen days previously. McMaster, the general concluded, was a "hypocrite .... I suspect that his regard for his hide is paramount."[15] General Elliott and Colonel Smith of the 26th regiment tried to encourage their men to make an assault, but only a handful of dazed Carolinians followed them over the rise. In a few moments Elliott was dropped with a shot through the shoulder.[16]

When McMaster heard that Elliott was down, he revoked the order for the charge. Then he went to his wounded superior's side. Elliott, in great pain but still coherent (the wound would kill him in a year and a half), was not pleased to see his successor. "Not a word from you," he told McMaster, adding somewhat cryptically "If you had obeyed orders, this

43

would have never happened.[17]

Whether Elliott's contempt for the colonel was justified, it was probably for the best that McMaster countermanded Elliott's order. He pulled the 26th and three companies of his own 17th South Carolina behind a "cavalier" trench, near the top of the ridge in the rear of the Crater, where he had them lie down just out of sight. He left Colonel Smith of the 26th in charge, with orders to rise up and fire only if the Yankees made an attempt to advance. These two-hundred-or-so riflemen were the only infantry between the Federals in the Crater and the city of Petersburg. Eventually Colonel Lee McAfee, commanding Ransom's North Carolina brigade on McMaster's left, sent the 25th North Carolina to bolster Smith's last-ditch effort. It was this thin grey line that stopped the Pennsylvania heavy artillerymen and pinned them in the unexploded works just behind the Crater.[18]

Robert Potter's division was working on those North and South Carolinians in the main Confederate line to the north of the Crater. The first wave of Simon Griffin's brigade had gone in almost simultaneously with Ledlie's fragmented assault. Despite the controversial parapets and obstructions later supposed to have prevented proper deployment, Griffin's brigade was lined up in columns of regiments when it advanced just north of the first division. It swept forward into the dust and smoke with far better alignment and cohesion than Ledlie's men. The 9th New Hampshire was in the lead, having been on Griffin's skirmish line, followed by the relatively new but battle-toughened 31st Maine and the decimated battalion of the 2nd Maryland. The first wing of the brigade went in under the colonel of the Maine regiment, Daniel White. His instructions, apropos of the previous afternoon's council of division commanders, were to attack to the right of the Crater and thus protect Ledlie's flank. These orders had filtered down to lower levels much more clearly in the second division than in the first, but in the confusion, poor visibility, and under the mild encouragement of the desperate Carolinians, White's columns veered inexorably to the left, parts of all three regiments falling into the Crater itself.[19]

Sergeant Edward Parsons, who was barely eighteen that day, planted the 9th New Hampshire's United States flag on the ruins of the redoubt almost before the sky had stopped raining dirt. He was instantly shot through the groin and carried away to die. Some of his officers claimed his were the first colors on the fort that morning: that may be, as most of Ledlie's men were still milling about in the bottom of the Crater. Fragments of the first division, however, began mixing with Griffin's men. Stephen Weld's attempt to lead a wing of Bartlett's brigade into the traverses north of the Crater put him into the same works as Griffin, and the commands quickly became confused.[20]

44

Still, Weld's men and Griffin's might have pressed ahead but for the heroic resistance of the outnumbered Confederate infantry. The remainder of the 17th South Carolina still occupied the works north of the Crater, spread terribly thin since the departure of Colonel Smith's contingent. When the head of Griffin's assault came their way some of them broke, bolting up the traverse. Colonel McAfee shifted his command to the right to beef up the remnant of the 17th, sending Lieutenant Colonel John Fleming's 49th North Carolina down the line at a double-quick. The Tarheels came flying down the trenches with their rifles at right-shoulder-shift; they poured into the ravine behind Elliott's Salient and started up the rise, running into the first refugees from the 17th. "Hold on," many of them shouted above the roar of battle. "We are coming!" The North Carolinians jumped into the works just behind and to the left of the erstwhile fort and began loading and firing feverishly at Griffin's men and that part of Ledlie's division beyond the Crater. Men in the front rank fired round after round as loaded muskets were passed forward, while in the rear their officers paced ferociously with drawn swords, chanting persistent encouragement. "Hold them back, boys! Hold them back!" they shouted. "By everything you hold dear on earth, hold them back!" Colonel Fleming fell dead with a bullet in his brain, but the terrible machine he had brought to bear continued to rattle off endless volleys. Crates of ammunition were brought up and broken open, and the cartridge tins were strewn within easy reach along the banquette.[21]

Colonel White's detachment took this fire full in the face. There was, as well, a devastating crossfire of artillery bearing on these Union soldiers from both right and left. Wright's four guns were spraying their front with canister from a distance of five hundred yards. About a dozen mortars previously positioned in an arc behind the salient were lobbing shells into and all around the Crater. White, whose three regiments had a clawhold on a portion of the main Confederate trench, pivoted his line to face the Carolinians, the southernmost of whom had swung their flank back into the safety of what had once been their covered ways. What White was trying to do was sweep up the enemy lines as Potter had planned. He advanced less than two hundred yards. His thick blue ranks withered before the fierce rifle fire and the Southern guns; he sent a man back to ask Griffin what was going on. "How are our lines doing on the right and left?" he wrote. His men were beyond Ledlie's already, and his flanks were taking a beating. The fight was so fierce that ammunition was already running low. Griffin wrote back that Ledlie was finally advancing, and all should be well. White tucked the message in his pocket, where he carried it through many months as a prisoner of war. Griffin did not mention that the Union infantry on their right were doing nothing, or that White was now, for all practical purposes, himself the right of the army. Neither was Griffin aware that the order to advance the first division reached Ledlie in the same hospital bombproof where he had earlier retired, nor that Ledlie declined to leave his musty little den to relay the command. Instead, he sent a staff officer.[22]

Once the last of Ledlie's division had cleared the main Union trench and the covered way, Orlando Willcox began tumbling his division onto the field. Part of John Hartranft's brigade sprang up behind Ledlie, but when the men of the first division balked at the Crater, they brought Hartranft up short. The head of his brigade huddled on the exposed front of the abandoned Confederate line, the tail was back in the choked-up covered way, and the rest was strung out between. His orders had directed Hartranft to wait for Ledlie to advance, and there he waited. Eventually though, Burnside sent a directive to Willcox to push forward at once for the hill. Willcox got the message nearly an hour after the explosion, whereupon he tried to unfold his original plan for protecting the left flank. The lead regiment, the 27th Michigan, veered left to clear the trenches in that direction, both to give the brigade more room for deployment and to minimize resistance from Confederates to the south.

The opportune moment had passed. When the Michigan regiment swung left it encountered a solid sheet of flame that leveled its commander and threw the intended guardians of the left flank into confusion. They could advance no farther for the moment, and Hartranft's brigade began bunching up again in the short length of trenches they occupied south of the Crater.[23]

The troops the 27th ran into were the 26th and 59th Virginia, sent by Colonel John Goode to shore up the breach. These two regiments had taken position in traverses perpendicular to the assailants' flank, and with the help of the 23rd South Carolina and the survivors of the 22nd they spent the early moments of the battle worrying the left of the first division. When the harbingers of Willcox's assault appeared before them, this makeshift brigade stunned them and stopped them cold.[24]

Back on the right, Simon Griffin brought up the rest of his brigade to support Colonel White. Upon his arrival on the embattled works he found the left of his brigade badly snarled with Ledlie's men. Down in the Crater there was a perfect Babel of contradictory commands but almost no firing. Having just received the same peremptory order to advance on the hill that had sparked Willcox, Potter ordered Griffin to disentangle himself and advance regardless of what Ledlie's men did.[25]

Burnside's latest order, which seemed to transform the plan of a movement by protected flanks to a headlong rush for the hill by the entire corps, had come under pressure from the distant command post where Meade and Grant were standing by the telegraph. Down at the Crater, Burnside's inspector general had sent him a dispatch warning of the disinclination of Ledlie's men to advance. They were mostly cringing

46

under the ever-increasing crossfire; a few regiments under Weld were sparring manfully alongside Griffin, but nearly an hour after the explosion most of the first division was still under cover in the Crater or in the surviving works immediately behind it. Colonel Loring, the inspector general, entrusted the dispatch to a courier who did not know General Burnside was at Fort Morton: he carried it all the way back to the customary headquarters of the IX Corps, where Meade opened it. Disgruntled, Meade telegraphed Burnside that he had learned of the delay and wished him to push in all his men at once, and directed him to call on Ord to advance as well. Perhaps perplexed that the news had reached Meade before himself, Burnside nevertheless dutifully ordered Potter, Willcox, and Ferrero to give it all they had.[26]

Unlike Willcox, who had perceived this order as a more vigorous repetition of the verbal orders he had received the previous afternoon, Potter interpreted it as a radical change, and when he directed Griffin to push ahead he largely ignored the earlier decision to use his division to protect the right flank. He did order Zenas Bliss to follow with his brigade, though, and to keep an eye on that flank.

Bliss found the front crowded. He could squeeze only three regiments into line behind Griffin's last battalions as they struggled forward. The 4th Rhode Island led the way, followed by the ten dozen officers and men of the 45th Pennsylvania. The 58th Massachusetts trailed them, marching by the flank, but the rearmost half of that regiment took a wrong turn, and the two wings became separated. Bliss had previously been expected to swing these regiments obliquely to the right; in light of Burnside's new order he faced them to the front. Thus there developed a dangerous gap between the extreme right of these regiments and the left of his other two, the 51st New York and the 2nd New York Mounted Rifles (who were not now mounted). These last two he threw against the trenches still defended by McAfee's 49th and 24th North Carolina, well to the right of Griffin's assault.[27]

The objective for which General Griffin now strove was the Jerusalem Plank Road, less than five hundred yards to the west. All that stood between that thoroughfare and the slowly-materializing Union line were Colonel Smith's few hundred Carolina riflemen and Henry Flanner's North Carolina battery. Beyond the fieldpieces was the Gee house, which etched itself in the memories of many Union soldiers as a barn. In the second story of that house the anxious Confederate leaders waited. Before long General Lee would be there, and Beauregard, and Bushrod Johnson, whose division held responsibility for the vicinity of the Crater. Capturing that house was of greater significance than any of the Union officers recognized, but it was not quite within their grasp.[28]

The entire front of Griffin's assault was raked diagonally by Wright's

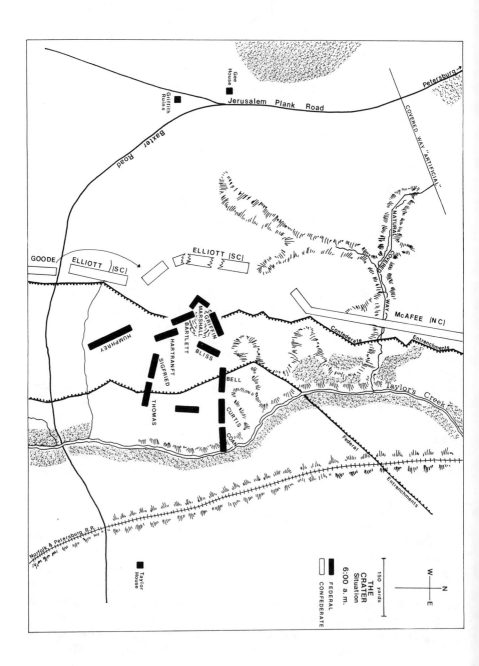

Petersburg

Gee House

Griffith Ruins

Jerusalem Plank Road

Baxter Road

COVERED WAY "ARTIFICIAL"

NATURAL

COVERED WAY

GOODE

ELLIOTT (SC)

ELLIOTT (SC)

ELLIOTT (SC)

McAFEE (NC)

Confederate

Entrenchments

GRIFFIN
MARSHALL
BARTLETT
BLISS
HUMPHREY
HARTRANFT
SIGFRIED
THOMAS
BELL
CURTIS
COAN

Taylor's Creek

Federal

Entrenchments

Norfolk & Petersburg R.R.

Taylor House

THE
CRATER
Situation
6:00 a.m.

FEDERAL
CONFEDERATE

150 yards

W — N — E

48

battery, on the slope near the cemetery. In addition to this, parts of two more batteries eventually opened beyond Wright's. Nevertheless, Griffin finally extricated his brigade and the leading regiments of Bliss's from the writhing mass of the first division, and with these ten frayed regiments he started into the firestorm.

All the while, Ferrero's Negro division was stalled in the covered way. Colonel Loring, finally deducing that General Burnside had not received his dispatch about Ledlie's failure to move, ordered the black troops kept in the covered way despite the orders to advance. Then he went looking for Burnside, to warn him how crowded things were.[29]

Others had sent him the same information, however, so when Meade asked if Warren's V Corps ought to go in Burnside said no. Warren's force should be concentrated and made ready to attack, he suggested, but it should be held at bay for the moment. Meade angrily retorted that Warren had been prepared to move since before the explosion. What, he demanded, was holding up Burnside's advance? If the crest was not gained soon, all would be lost.[30]

Burnside decided he needed a closer look. Climbing down from the embrasure where he had been observing the progress of his attack, he ventured down the covered way in company with General Warren. They shouldered through the crowded regiments of John Turner's division and Ferrero's two brigades: here Loring finally found his chief, learned the order to advance was Meade's and not discretionary, and started the column moving again. When they arrived at the extreme front trench the generals saw Griffin's tortured line billowing like a ribbon in the breeze, one regiment advancing while another was falling back; still another advancing again. Obviously, the enemy artillery was the greatest difficulty. All those guns to the right enfiladed the column, and the single gun manned by infantry volunteers was butchering Griffin's left. Satisfied they knew what needed to be done, the two worked their way back through the tedious passageway to their respective commands. Warren wrote Meade that the one-gun battery ought to be silenced, after which the hill could easily be taken. He urged the commanding general to come have a look for himself, from Burnside's vantage point. Warren had told Burnside he would report to Meade, so Burnside did not feel it necessary to answer Meade's earlier telegram.[31]

Griffin continued to drive the better part of Potter's division toward the low crest near the Gee house. At one point the 45th Pennsylvania seemed to have it within reach, but the artillery to the north showered canister and case shot uninhibited. One slug struck a Pennsylvania lieutenant on the left cheekbone, carrying away his eye and the side of his face; a captain wrapped the wound in a handkerchief and pointed him to the rear, and when the captain was released from prison months later he was dumbfounded to learn the man had survived the terrible wound. An orderly sergeant of the 4th Rhode Island dropped to the ground, and two of his men tried to drag him to the rear: Hugh McInnes's grip was broken by a ball that shattered his wrist, splintering the radius and ulna and leaving the soon-to-be amputated paw dangling. Two comrades in that regiment sought shelter from a volley of canister in the same furrow left by a bounding shell, fighting each other for the bottom. When the man on top was wounded he cried out, but his friend heartlessly replied, "Go to the rear then, where you belong." The colonel of the 32nd Maine was shot twice in this assault. At last the valiant efforts ceased to gain ground. Griffin's brigade and the three regiments orphaned from Bliss's could barely hold on where they were, a hundred yards beyond the Crater.[32]

The two other regiments, off to the right, made some progress toward Wright's battery. They hit the Confederate trenches endwise, straddling them in the manner Burnside had planned, the 51st New York working its way up the inside of the works and the Mounted Rifles coming up on the Union side. For a time this was effective in suppressing the fire of McAfee's North Carolinians, but the void between the two isolated regiments and the main body left them vulnerable — especially the 51st, the command of which devolved on Walt Whitman's brother when a solid shot knocked the major down. In the end, while Griffin was still holding grimly to his advanced position, these two New York regiments had to fall back.[33]

When General Burnside had returned from inspecting the situation at the front, he found the sarcastic note from General Meade. Assuming Warren was telling Meade the need to subdue the enemy artillery, he made no mention of putting in the V Corps, and because of his jaunt down the covered way he was late in answering the commanding general. His fill-in chief of staff, Julius White, seems not to have made any effort to supply Meade with information in Burnside's absence, so when Burnside wrote that he was doing all he could to push the troops forward — but it was hard work — Meade was already boiling. Frustrated by the apparent inability to get frequent, accurate reports from Burnside or his staff, Meade fired off a terse dispatch: "What do you mean by hard work to take the crest," he asked, adding rather unfairly, "I understand not a man has advanced beyond the enemy's line which you occupied immediately after exploding the mine." He questioned whether Burnside's troops were obeying him, and though he probably meant nothing offensive by it, he tactlessly finished with, "I wish to know the truth; and desire an immediate answer."

An immediate answer is precisely what he got, from a man fully as tired and frustrated as he. Burnside was growing sensitive to the continued prodding of his absent chief; he reared indignantly at this perceived assault on his truthfulness. Potter's division, he wrote, was beyond the Crater; his men were not disobeying orders, but they were struggling under stiff resistance; and General Burnside was not in the habit of reporting anything other than the truth. He ended the message with the ill-advised observation that, "were it not insubordinate, I would say that the latter remark of your note was unofficerlike and ungentlemanly." Regardless of the qualification, he had said just that, and indeed it was insubordinate. Ominously, Meade requested a copy of the message that had sparked Burnside's ire, explaining that he had not kept a duplicate because he had intended it to be confidential. "Your reply," he said, "requires I should have a copy."[34]

The single gun of Davidson's battery was still spewing canister south of the salient. Captain Preston had been shot through the head and carried away, mistakenly assumed to be dead, but another officer took over and the former artillerymen of the 34th Virginia continued to ram charges down the throat of their sizzling piece. Though General Wise was present on the field, Colonel Goode retained control of the infantry in this sector. He wrote General Johnson, urging him to visit the front and review the disposition of troops, but, like Union General Ledlie, the Confederate division commander merely sent an aide to congratulate Goode on a job well done and to order him to defend his position at all hazards — a position which, it later appeared, Johnson had misapprehended by a few hundred yards. "That was the last I heard of him," Goode explained, "until the battle was practically over."[35]

In order to silence the single gun and disperse Goode's refused left, General Willcox lined up his other brigade in the no-man's-land to the left of the Crater. Colonel William Humphrey had seven regiments in this brigade. On his extreme right he placed the 1st Michigan Sharpshooters, Company K of which was composed of Chippewa Indians. The sharpshooters numbered about a hundred men. To their left was the 2nd Michigan, then the 20th Michigan, which was a little larger than the 1st. Beyond the Michigan men were the 46th New York and the 50th Pennsylvania. To strengthen his vulnerable left flank, Humphrey backed up these last two units with the 60th Ohio and the dismounted 24th New York Cavalry. When Humphrey's line swept forward Goode's two left regiments, the two stranded South Carolinia regiments, and the one-gun battery pivoted to face it. The rest of Goode's brigade fired obliquely into Humphrey's left, so shredding it that the 46th New York broke and ran, taking with it the 50th Pennsylvania and the big new regiments behind it. The three veteran Michigan regiments carried the works despite the disintegration on their left, presently sending three or four dozen prisoners back toward Union lines.[36]

For a time things looked bleak for the Southerners in this

neighborhood, and those south and west of the Crater began to get a taste of their own canister. When Pegram's battery was exploded, more than half of the redoubt was demolished — his left Napoleon was blown twenty yards toward the Union lines; the next one went forty yards. The two right guns were relatively undisturbed, though, as was about thirty yards of the southern part of the fort. When they had finished rescuing half-buried Confederates, a few heavy artillerymen of the 14th New York began brushing off those two smoothbores. Sergeant Wesley Stanley was assigned a detail to dig for the magazine suspected to be nearby, and when he found it he had the men pull the guns into an advantageous position. He assembled two crews from his own regiment and from some volunteers from General Hartranft's brigade, gave them a crash course in loading, and began firing toward the Virginians and South Carolinians in the trenches to the left.[37] When Humphrey's Michigan men took those works, the two guns began ranging elsewhere for targets.

After much confusion and contradiction, General Ferrero's black troops finally deployed. They had stood at the brink for an hour when General Grant appeared among them with an aide and a single orderly. He asked Colonel Henry Thomas about the delay in committing his brigade, and Thomas pointed ahead to Sigfried's brigade, standing idle. "My orders are to follow that brigade," he explained. He asked if Grant would give him orders to go in, but Grant demurred, not wishing to disrupt the chain of command. He rode on, while the Negroes stood waiting. Ferrero, meanwhile, had been couched with Ledlie in the hospital bombproof, sharing a couple of snifters of rum. For some time he had been under orders to advance again, but he had fallen back on the excuse that his way was blocked by other troops. Each time the orders came he repeated this, without once investigating whether it was still true, and whenever he reiterated that excuse Ledlie would guiltily dispatch an officer to tell his own men to get moving. This comfortable interview came to an end when Burnside's peremptory order came into the bunker for Ferrero to push ahead, regardless of interference from others. Reluctantly, the beefy dancemaster bustled outside into the covered way, where his two brigades stood, sweating and justifiably nervous.[38]

The officers of colored troops tended to be of two extremes — incredibly negligent and incompetent, or extremely conscientious and able. A number of scapegraces in white regiments had finagled commissions in Negro regiments: however, many of these survived only briefly. The more common variety was the officer who struck the delicate balance between benevolence and discipline: In 1864 it took a certain liberal attitude to admit that Negroes could equal white men in combat, but it would never have done to forget these black soldiers were only a few cultural steps removed from draft animals, and required a stronger rein than their white counterparts. These officers needed a greater degree of personal courage, too, for their chances of surviving capture were poorer. When the first Negro troops had been raised, the Confederate Congress had promised to execute their officers taken prisoner, on the grounds they were guilty of the old capital crime of inciting a slave revolt. Though the sentence was never formally invoked, the previous April Bedford Forrest's cavalry had reportedly butchered a colored garrison at Fort Pillow, Tennessee. The full story was not then available, but Negroes and their white officers were said to have been slaughtered alike, with few prisoners taken.[39]

It was not only with apprehension for their safety that Ferrero's officers led their men down the covered way and into the abandoned trenches. This was to be the bloody baptism of their new men, and they were determined to see that they performed well.

The first of the colored troops shouldering down the trenches encountered John Turner, the X Corps division commander temporarily under Ord's orders. He was just returning from the Crater — the only division commander to see the inside of it — on a reconnaissance for his planned advance in support of Burnside. Turner rushed back to his lead brigade, under twenty-seven-year-old Colonel Louis Bell. He told Bell to have a try at the trenches north of the Crater, where Bliss's two New York regiments had been repulsed. While Colonel Bell moved ahead parallel to Ferrero's covered way, Turner continued on to fetch his other two brigades. William Coan's four regiments followed Bell and sidled even farther to the right, while Colonel Martin Curtis filed the last of Turner's division into the original Union works, alongside a couple of overlooked regiments from Zenas Bliss's brigade.[40]

The extreme right of the Confederate army was very thin just now. Bushrod Johnson's division was concentrating on the Crater, with Goode's brigade fully engaged and Alfred Colquitt's stretching to the north to cover ground Goode had had to abandon. The only other troops beyond Colquitt were the five brigades of William Mahone's division, more than half of which was now on its roundabout way to the Crater.

Mahone's troops had not begun to move until shortly after six o'clock. News of the explosion had reached General Lee by way of a colonel on Beauregard's staff, who was at his Petersburg home when the detonation jarred him from sleep. He had immediately ridden to notify Beauregard, who sent him to Lee. General Lee was just sitting down to breakfast when he heard the report, and he dispatched one of his own staff to Mahone, who commanded the component of the Army of Northern Virginia nearest Elliott's Salient. Colonel Charles Venable vaulted into the saddle. Lee told him to ride straight to Mahone: there was no time to observe the niceties of the chain of command, and a detour to A. P. Hill's corps headquarters would take Venable too far off course. Lee instructed him to have Mahone send two brigades to Blandford cemetery. Venable leaned over his horse's neck and flew south at a dead gallop.[41]

Venable found Mahone encamped on the Wilcox farm, near Lieutenant Creek. The general was a wiry little fellow with a long, lank beard. A graduate of Virginia Military Institute, he had been chief engineer of the Norfolk and Petersburg Railroad, which bisected the Union position; he was, therefore, better acquainted with the terrain than the other commanders in the vicinity. His division was fanned out in an arc before Warren's V Corps, and his troops were an average of two miles away from the Crater. The two brigades he chose to send, his own Virginians under David Weisiger and Wright's Georgia brigade, temporarily commanded by Lieutenant Colonel M. R. Hall, were on the far right of his lines. They had the farthest to march, but it could not be helped — his left was too near Warren's front, and the removal of those brigades would alert the V Corps.[42]

Mahone rode back with Colonel Venable for a way, listening to the colonel's explanation of the crisis. The general noticed his men were marching with their knapsacks; he halted the column to make them strip off everything but their cartridge boxes and canteens. While the men were throwing off their excess baggage in a peach orchard belonging to a Mr. Ragland, Mahone was stricken with a pang of affection for his troops, particularly for the brigade he had formerly commanded. He twisted in the saddle to face Colonel Venable.

"I can't send my brigades to General Johnson," he said. "I will go with them myself." Venable rode away to inform Lee, and Mahone cantered ahead to have a look at the battle. He left instructions for the Virginians and Georgians to march over a crosscountry route that would screen them from Union signalmen in their lofty towers.[43]

Mahone stopped at Bushrod Johnson's headquarters, where he expected to find A. P. Hill. His corps commander was not there. He did meet Beauregard, however, whom he told of the two brigades that were following him. Beauregard expressed satisfaction, and suggested to Johnson that he give Mahone any of his "outlying troops" for a counterattack. Johnson, who seemed unconcerned with any emergency except his tardy breakfast, agreed. Mahone questioned Johnson about the extent of the breach, then asked him to take him to a spot from which he could see the action. Johnson, perhaps too hungry to comply, detailed a staff lieutenant to escort General Mahone.

Mahone and the lieutenant hurried down the Jerusalem Plank Road beyond the cemetery. A covered way had been dug east of the road, and the two followed it a couple of hundred yards, until it emptied into the natural protection of the deep swale behind the Confederate entrenchments. The lieutenant stopped and pointed to the high point of that swale leading to the noise of battle. "If you will go up that slope there, you can see the Yankees," he said, but he did not offer to lead, or even follow, so Mahone sprinted up the rise. He was stunned to find himself face-to-face with thousands of Union soldiers teeming in the Crater and in the many traverses behind the salient. It was, as one Confederate described it, "a forest of glittering bayonets." He counted the flags of eleven regiments in a single hundred-yard section; his first reaction was to send back to the Wilcox farm for a third brigade — J. C. C. Saunders's Alabamians.[44] The Federals were obviously disorganized, but there were too many of them for the fifteen-hundred-or-so men he had coming now.

While Mahone was weakening the Confederate right, his remaining two brigades spread out to cover the gap. There were now only three depleted Confederate brigades on Warren's entire front — fifteen emaciated regiments. Union signalmen reported the abandoned trenches to Meade, who asked General Warren about attacking that flank, at least as a diversion, but before he followed Burnside down the covered way Warren had suggested waiting for one of his division commanders to complete a reconnaissance in that area. Just as Mahone sent for his Alabama brigade, Warren's division commander made his report: no such attack was practical at that point, he said, though Warren could have thrown two divisions with twenty-six regiments against those thinly-defended works.[45]

The Federal signal officers could detect empty works, but they never saw Mahone's brigades filing toward the Crater until they crossed the Jerusalem Plank Road. The column trotted off the road to the shelter of a ravine cut by Lieutenant Run, following that and other drainage swales until it could take advantage of the covered way. The troops were excited; from the moment they had shucked their packs they knew they were in for a fight. Henry Hunt's massive accumulation of artillery still punished them, though the gunners could not see them, and while they were placing guards over their jettisoned equipment a few shells fell in the orchard. One exploded near a private of the 41st Virginia, tearing away his leg. The regimental surgeon knelt over the dying youth; as his comrades lined up to shuffle away they could hear him wailing, not for himself but over the fate of his widowed mother. The shot and shell kept coming as the column moved, the Yankees still firing blindly but occasionally striking a blow. As the 12th Virginia crossed the levee of an artificial pond one round buried itself in the water, a step or two away.[46]

The Virginia brigade had a personal stake in this fight. By now, word had drifted down the column that the Yankees had broken through and captured some of the lines near the cemetery. Many of the men in the 12th Virginia, and some in the other regiments, came from this very place;

some of them had homes within range of those Union cannon. The officers had to do little prodding to hasten their pace.

Back at the Crater, the attenuated Confederate line was in trouble. Haskell's battalion and other artillery still held Griffin's assault in check, but the infantry support was melting away. Already, three Union divisions were engaged and two others were coming into line, while not quite all of three Confederate brigades opposed them. The 61st North Carolina, of Clingman's brigade, marched south from its position north of Gracie's Salient to reinforce the diminishing stopgap under McMasters. His impromptu brigade of North and South Carolinians was under great pressure, and that pressure was increasing.[47]

Joshua Sigfried's brigade of U.S. Colored Troops led Ferrero's division onto the field. Coming down the same covered way Ledlie had chosen, they were forced to use the two sandbag stairways in that section of the trenches. First, with a chilling clatter and clank, they fixed bayonets. Then the lead regiment, the 30th U.S.C.T., went in by the flank with battalions side-by-side, four men at a time skipping up the passageway toward the Crater. The entire front was swept now by both artillery and musketry, so there was no time to form in columns of attack. Their best chance was to dash for the enemy's works as rapidly as possible. Colonel Delevan Bates, the young New Yorker in command of the 30th, veered his regiment away from the Crater, but rifle fire persuaded some of the column to pour into it. Bates took his men into the Crater, then, and out the other side, running through the huddled throngs of Ledlie's division. The 43rd regiment, just behind Bates, was not so fortunate. The occupants of the Crater, perhaps startled by the sudden rush of the first regiment, were milling so haphazardly that the rest of Sigfried's brigade could get through only at the sacrifice of its formation.[48]

Bates halted briefly in the shelter of the Crater, listening to the devastating volleys that were raking the ground outside. He tried to work his regiment toward the enemy through the maze of traverses behind the Crater. These were filled with the survivors of Griffin's nearly-stalled attack, but in the smoke the Negroes could not distinguish the Federal uniforms. Many of them fired into the smoke, thinking they had already come upon the Confederates. Captain Andrew Jackson Hough, commanding the 9th New Hampshire, courageously leapt upon the intervening trench and waved the United States flag. Someone in the colored brigade finally saw the mistake, and Bates turned the head of his column back to the top of the enemy parapet, leading it to the right until he was beyond the main body of Griffin's force. He was able to use the top of the embankment only because of the X Corps troops who were keeping McAfee's North Carolinians busy on his right. His regiment had already suffered quite a few casualties before it was in position to advance; Bates compared it to autumn leaves falling in a gale. Among the first killed was his color sergeant, whose brains were splattered over the flag. A corporal happily took up the standard and carried it on.[49]

Henry Thomas's brigade came in next. Thomas guided his men to the right of the Crater but some of them also fell in with Ledlie's troops. Sigfried's brigade had passed to the right, and Thomas was supposed to link on his left, but some of Bliss's men were still between them. These three regiments were fighting under Griffin, for Bliss never set foot on the field. Griffin had most of his own brigade on Thomas's left, though the Negroes were mixing in and confusing Griffin's troops. Still enduring that fearful artillery crossfire, the colored brigades reorganized their formations. Griffin tried to put his bloodied regiments in position to help. Since he had been making some progress through the labrynthine traverses and bombproofs, it seemed logical that the additional muscle of the fourth division would turn the tide.

Colonel Thomas had difficulty getting his own men together. Two full regiments were still trapped in the crowded Crater when he made his first attempt to advance. Before the white troops on either side of him were ready he ordered a charge: it went nowhere. One regiment had already lost so many officers the men were demoralized, and still more officers were shot down trying to coax their companies ahead. Thomas himself led the assault. He and two staff officers stepped up from a trench, followed by four white orderlies. Lieutenant Colonel William Ross followed, as well as some of his 31st U.S.C.T.; half of those who climbed out of the traverse tumbled to the ground. Ross was one of the first to fall, and one of his captains landed on top of him. Two of the white orderlies were shot, and the other two fled. Lieutenant Christopher Pennell, the surviving staff officer, took up the guidon one of the orderlies had dropped and ran out on the open ground in front of the brigade. He raised both the flag and his sword and tried to encourage the black men to follow him. The 31st regiment and two others responded, at least in part, but they and some of the white troops were momentarily distracted by Pennell's spectacular death. They had watched him for some moments, so impressive was his audacity, but the Confederates saw him too. Carolina marksmen — the men McMaster had reserved against just such a contingency — leveled a volley at him. Pennell, still waving the sword and flag, spun from one wound, then took another and reeled again in the same direction. As bullet after bullet struck him he refused to fall, as though afraid it would dishearten the men, and he continued to stagger in that ghastly pirouette until he keeled over head foremost, perhaps already dead. His body lay where thousands of bullets would reduce it to an unrecognizable pulp. The fire he had drawn also shattered the ranks of the 31st regiment behind him, men Thomas said were "mowed down like grass." That was the end of the second brigade's first attempt. Of the headquarters detachment, only Thomas and one staff officer reached the safety of the traverse.[50]

Sigfried had better luck, though. Two of his regiments found themselves stymied by coming in behind white troops, but the 30th and 43rd U.S.C.T. made a rapid advance on the last Confederate trench before the ravine. As the colored troops approached, Confederates heard them shouting "Remember Fort Pillow!" before they dove into the trench, and the Carolinians were enraged to see they were compelled to fight Negro troops. One Confederate captain refused to surrender and shouted "Kill 'em! Shoot 'em! Kill the damned niggers!" until his wrath was silenced by a bayonet. As the 30th jumped into the midst of McMaster's men, Colonel Bates was shot through the head, the bullet traversing his cheekbones. His major took a round through the chest and began coughing blood, and two captains and lieutenants fell wounded, as well as scores of privates. The commander of the 43rd had his right arm shattered, and his adjutant was also shot through the chest. The Negroes secured this section of the cavalier trench, however, and they sent over a hundred and fifty prisoners to the rear. A captain of the 43rd regiment personally took five prisoners and a battle flag. The mine had exploded over three hours before, but it finally looked as though the breach could be made complete. A message came to Thomas from the invisible Ferrero, ordering him to move up abreast of Sigfried and take the crest with the house on it.[51]

Courtesy: Miller's "Photographic History"

The trenches at Petersburg.

Courtesy: Miller's Photographic History"

"The Dictator," 13" Seacoast Mortar

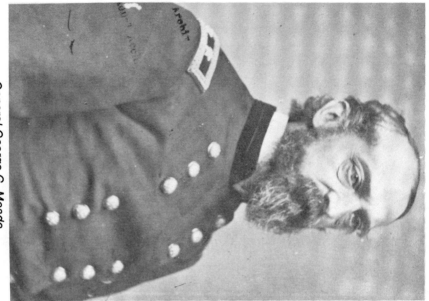

General George G. Meade

Courtesy: Library of Congress

General Ambrose E. Burnside

Courtesy: Library of Congress

Colonel Henry Pleasants

IX Corps badge made from the clay in the tunnel.

Digging the tunnel.

IX Corps Division Commanders

Courtesy: Dave Charles collection

James H. Ledlie

Courtesy: USAMHI

Robert B. Potter

Courtesy: Dave Charles collection

Orlando B. Willcox

Courtesy: Dave Charles collection

Edward Ferrero

IX Corps — First Division

William Francis Bartlett

Elisha G. Marshall

IX Corps — Second Division

Zenas R. Bliss

Simon G. Griffin

IX Corps — Third Division

John F. Hartranft

William Humphrey

Courtesy: Dave Charles collection

Courtesy: USAMHI

IX Corps — Fourth Division

Joshua K. Sigfried

Henry Goddard Thomas

Courtesy: USAMHI

Courtesy: USAMHI

Black soldiers in the Petersburg trenches.

X Corps — Second Division

Courtesy: C. W. Library & Museum

John W. Turner, Commanding

Courtesy: Miller's "Photographic History"

Newton M. Curtis, 1st Brigade

Courtesy: C. W. Library & Museum

William B. Coan, 2nd Brigade

Courtesy: C. W. Library & Museum

Louis Bell, 3rd Brigade

Courtesy: C. W. Library & Museum

Courtesy: National Archives

Winfield Scott Hancock

Phil Sheridan

Courtesy: Harper's Weekly

II Corps crossing lower bridge into Deep Bottom.

Joseph B. Kershaw, Kershaw's Division   *James Conner, Commanding Wilcox's Brigade.*

Graham's Rockbridge Artillery overrun.

Carrying in the powder

Pleasants supervising placing of the powder.

69

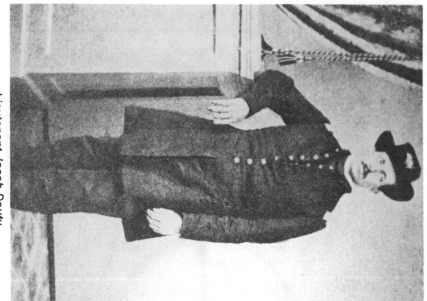

Lieutenant Jacob Douty

Courtesy: Gould: "48th Penn."

Sergeant Harry Reese

Courtesy: Gould "48th Penn."

"Explosion Of The Mine Before Petersburg" By Andrew McCallum

Army of Southern Virginia and N.C.

P. G. T. Beauregard, Commanding

Bushrod R. Johnson, Johnson's Division.

Stephen Elliott, Jr., South Carolina Brigade.

Alfred H. Colquitt, Georgia Brigade

72

Blandford Church — Cemetery target of Union forces.

Union officers trying to rally their men. Sketch by Andrew McCallum

"Lee Hastening To The Crater" by Henry Kidd

Courtesy: Henry Kidd, Colonel Heights, Va. — © 1988

Jerusalem Plank Rd. looking north. Marker at entrance to the Covered Way.

John C. C. Saunders, Alabama Brigade

David A. Weisiger, Mahone's old Va. Brigade

William Mahone

Victor J. Girardey, Mahone's Aide

John C. Haskell, Confederate Artillery

E. Porter Alexander, Confederate Artillery.

Confederate Coehorn mortar from Capt. Lamkin's Battery used at the Battle of the Crater. Now located on the Courthouse Green at Amelia, Va.

76

Battle of the Crater by Tom Lovell

Battle of the Crater by John Elder

Confederate K.I.A. at the Crater

Lt. Charles E. DeNoon, 41st Va. Infantry

Lt. Col. John A. Flemming, 49th N.C. Infantry.

Lt. Winfield Scott Gee, 41st Va. Infantry.

79

Union K.I.A. at the Crater

Lt. John K. Knowles, 4th R.I. Infantry

Col. Jacob P. Gould, 59th Mass. Infantry.

Capt. Adam C. Lipcomb, 23rd U.S.C.T.

David E. Proctor, 30th U.S.C.T.

Engraving on Proctor's sword

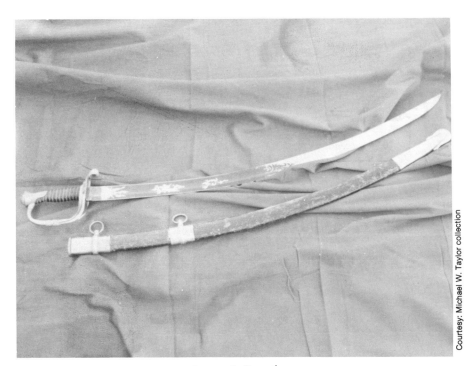

Proctor's Sword

Crater area — Confederate lines on left facing Union line. Note skulls on ridge Circa 1865.

Visiting the Crater in 1867.

Confederates reestablish lines in the Crater.

Hancock court of inquiry at the Jones House in Petersburg.

Veterans of the 58th Mass. at a tablet marking their advanced position. House probably Griffith's new home near Crater.

General Mahone with group of veterans.

CHAPTER V

Hell is Busted

Apparently General Ferrero had abandoned his comfortable bomb-proof long enough to watch, from a safe distance, while his two brigades made their attack. From the wording of his order to Thomas, referring to the capture of the crest, it appears Ferrero could not distinguish the ravine that lay between Sigfried's captured trench and the Gee house. He had no idea that Confederate reinforcements had arrived.

That fact did not, however, escape Captain Jedediah Paine. From his crow's nest behind IX Corps lines, that signal officer trained his binoculars on the Jersualem Plank Road, just where the covered way crossed it. He saw the head of Mahone's Virginia brigade streaming over the road and counted the flags. Then came Hall's Georgians. Paine scribbled a note to Burnside, warning him of the fresh enemy troops and accurately judging that they had come from the Confederate right flank.[1] It was some time, though, before Paine's courier could climb down from his perch and find General Burnside, and he was too late to allow for a message to reach Griffin, Thomas, and Sigfried.

Colonel Thomas attempted to reform his brigade and comply with Ferrero's order. He disentangled his last two regiments from the first division troops, put one of them in advance of the dispirited 31st regiment, and started them forward. Lieutenant Colonel John Bross of the 29th U.S.C.T. led the advance with the regimental colors in his own hands.[2] Sigfried had two regiments well to the front and two more still blocked by white troops, but the two lead regiments were boiling with enthusiasm over their little victory. They gamely put the colors in front and dressed ranks as effectively as they could in the hail of canister. Griffin's men had hardly recovered from the disruption of having the Negroes fire into them and crash through their ranks screaming wildly, and for that reason neither Griffin nor the regiments from Bliss's brigade were able to assist in the advance. Besides, the white troops had been so long under fire that many of their regimental commanders were dead or disabled who had not been properly replaced. Nevertheless, disjointed fragments of the white regiments moved out with their black comrades.[3]

General Mahone was still standing on the rise where the covered way met the ravine when Colonel Weisiger came down the trench with his old Virginia brigade. Mahone directed him into the swale, ordering him to form for an attack, and Weisiger led his command in by the flank. The 6th Virginia filed in first, and thus had the honor of taking the right of the for-

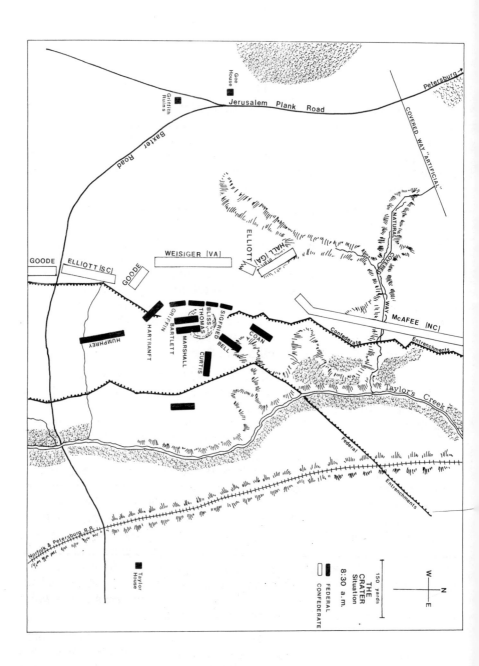

Gee House

Griffith Ruins

Jerusalem Plank Road

Petersburg

COVERED WAY "ARTIFICIAL"

Baxter Road

NATURAL COVERED WAY

WEISIGER (VA)

ELLIOTT

HALL (GA)

GOODE

ELLIOTT (SC)

GOODE

McAFEE (NC)

HARTRANFT

GRIFFIN

BARTLETT

MARSHALL

BLISS

THOMAS

CURTIS

SIGFRIED

BELL

COAN

HUMPHREY

Confederate

Entrenchments

Taylor's Creek

Federal

Entrenchments

Norfolk & Petersburg R.R.

Taylor House

N
W—E
S

150 yards

THE
CRATER
Situation
8:30 a.m.

FEDERAL

CONFEDERATE

mation, followed by the 16th, 61st, 41st, and finally Weisiger's own 12th Virginia with its anxious collection of Petersburg boys. Coming over the rise at them were some of Colonel Smith's demi-brigade — refugees from the cavalier trench. The Virginians made fun of their wide-eyed flight, but one of them paused long enough to tell them there were "niggers" on the other side of that little ridge who were offering no quarter. General Mahone tried to stop another fugitive to ask what had happened; the man only said "Hell is busted back thar," and never lost a step.[4]

As the various regiments passed him, Mahone took their commanders aside and gave them a verbal sketch of the situation. He told each to have his men fix their bayonets and withhold their fire until they closed with the enemy. Colonel Weisiger faced his brigade to the left, and took a position where he could just see above the shallow lip of the ravine. The commander of the 61st Virginia counted seven Union flags in the immediate front, then ducked back down to tell his men "We must have those flags, boys." Officers up and down the line stepped out to make the little speeches that usually preceded a charge. Aides from Mahone's and Weisiger's staffs repeated the orders to reserve their fire until they actually reached the cavalier trench, and bayonets went over the muzzles of eight hundred rifles.

Hall's Georgia brigade was shouldering its way toward the swale now. Mahone ordered Colonel Hall to form on Weisiger's right, hoping to extend his line far enough to cover the entire length of captured works. The Georgians tramped across the sunburnt grass behind the Virginians.

Captain Victor Girardey, one of Mahone's acting staff officers, wandered to the right of the Virginia brigade to confer with Colonel Weisiger. As he did, a private in the 61st Virginia directed his own colonel's attention to some movement in the Union lines. Weisiger simultaneously saw Colonel Bross of the 29th U.S.C.T. step out with the Stars and Stripes in his hands and told Girardey they ought to charge now, without waiting for the Georgia brigade.[5]

Captain Girardey, himself a Georgian, had been on the staff of Ambrose Wright's Georgia brigade — the one passing behind the Virginians — since the early days of the war. He was an able battlefield commander himself: during the retreat from Gettysburg he had taken control of his brigade in a skirmish, when the senior colonel was wounded. Now, he ran back to the left of the formation to warn Mahone of the Union assault. When he was about midway of the brigade he shouted to Mahone, "General, they are coming!"

Ignoring both the Georgians and the rules of grammar, Mahone called back "Tell Weisiger to forward." Under the pressure of time Girardey said nothing to Weisiger. Those men who had heard Mahone expected to receive some preparatory commands, but the bearded young staff officer simply drew his own sword, waved his hat, and yelled "Forward! Charge!" He led the brigade himself, a Confederate Pennell bound for victory or death.[6]

The Virginians moved out with their weapons at trail arms. One of the Petersburg citizens noticed that the flanks were slightly advanced, so the formation was perceptibly curved like the blade of a scythe. As they topped the rise they began yipping that eerie Rebel Yell, drawing the attention of everyone on the battlefield. The last assault of the colored troops ended in petrified astonishment. The remains of Colonel Smith's impromptu rear guard, elements of the 17th and 26th South Carolina and the 25th North Carolina, attached themselves to the left wing of the Virginia brigade and swept forward with them. The 61st North Carolina had finally arrived from Clingman's brigade, and went in behind Weisiger.[7]

The Confederates swooped down on their assailants with redoubled fury when they saw it was really Negroes who faced them. The Virginia brigade, as directed, emptied its guns into the faces of the black Yankees. Colonel Bross was riddled, his flag captured. The Southerners leaped recklessly into the cavalier trench and began clubbing and stabbing everything in blue. Whether it was true the blacks had threatened no quarter or not, the Confederates believed it and they were willing to offer none now. Orderly Sergeant Emmett Richardson of the 12th Virginia was remembered by his comrades for shooting one of the Negroes, bayoneting a second and, when his bayonet came off in the dead man's body, clubbing a third to death. Some said he killed five Yankees that day; some counted seven. A Petersburg man in the 41st Virginia saved his major, who was beset by three Yankees at once, and went on to kill as many as fourteen men in the course of the day.[8]

One captain in the 30th Colored Troops was wounded in the knee and was unable to fall back. He emptied his revolver into the swarming Virginians, refusing to surrender. He was shot and bayoneted; finally a rifle butt came down and brought the darkness. Everywhere, the colored troops were driven back. The cavalier trench was soon in Confederate hands again, and its captors climbed out of it to chase the retreating enemy. The Negroes, green at this sort of work and astonished by the Confederates' ferocity, began to panic. Many of them just threw down their arms and fled, while others followed them with some vague notion of making a stand in the many traverses before the Crater. The Confederates picked up the bayoneted muskets they abandoned and began throwing them like spears into the dense masses trapped in those confusing works.[9]

To escape the wrath of these grey-clad demons, the fugitives jumped from one traverse to another, crowding back on the white troops Griffin still commanded. They flung themselves headlong into these white allies, wounding them with their bayonets and knocking them over, trampling them underfoot. Corporal Newell Dutton, a color bearer in the 9th New Hampshire, described "a mass of worms crawling over each other." Then Mahone's men came to the very edge of those traverses and poured a volley into them. Corporal Dutton was enough of a veteran to see what was bound to happen: the color sergeant of the 32nd Maine was wounded, and both he and the flag captured; a private in the 6th Virginia grappled with the color sergeant of the 11th New Hampshire, and took the shredded remnant of that flag; a corporal of the 61st Virginia similiarly wrestled for the flag of the 31st Maine, and likewise tore it to pieces before taking it. Dutton clutched his New Hampshire state flag to the staff, boldly vaulted from the traverse, and raced down the embankment alongside it to the temporary safety of the Crater. Inside, he found a lieutenant from his regiment who had saved the national flag in the same manner.[10]

To the north of the Crater, the havoc was even greater. Colonel Weld, in nominal command of the right wing of Bartlett's brigade, actually had control over no one. The charge of Sigfried's troops into and through his troops had utterly disintegrated their formation, and their wide-eyed return flight secured disaster. Once the blacks crammed themselves into the already-crowded traverses escape was impossible, because no one could move. Weld could not even raise his arms from his sides. At one instant he saw a Confederate flag hanging over the parapet about four feet away; in the next he saw the yawning muzzles of scores of rifles, which blazed into the teaming, defenceless mass. Those who were trapped in this network were forced to surrender, if they could lift a hand with a scrap of white linen. Then the Virginians prodded their prisoners out of the traverses under a heavy fire of their own artillery, and as the dejected mass streamed over the top the Confederates took revenge on the Negroes. Weld said he heard someone shout "Shoot the nigger, but don't kill the white man," and two Confederates ran up to a black soldier beside him. They turned their rifles on the Negro and killed him at pointblank range. Another of Sigfried's blacks was staggering along in front of Weld, already wounded in two places. Two Virginians successively dashed up to put a couple more rounds into him, and the fellow dropped dead.[11]

Still farther to the north, routed elements of Sigfried's brigade disrupted the efforts of Louis Bell's brigade to neutralize Lee AcAfee's North Carolinians. They bolted blindly into his men, stabbing many with their bayonets and carrying them away, offering McAfee's brigade an uninhibited field of fire that further accelerated the rout of black and white alike. "I . . . was among those who were run over by the panic stricken negroes," Colonel Bell wrote. "We used our sabers freely on the cowards but could not stop them and were all driven back — pell mell." The runaway blacks dropped into the covered way behind the Union lines, crashing through Martin Curtis's oncoming brigade. There they met Ferrero and washed him back in their irresistible tide, "grabbing and clutching like a cat on a fence on a windy day." When New Yorkers blocked their flight, the Negroes tried to scale the eight-foot walls of the passageway.[12]

Without the shield of Bell's brigade, McAfee's men lay a devastating fire into those troops remaining in the trenches north of the Crater. Soon every Union soldier in that sector drifted back into the Crater itself.

The IX Corps observers at Fort Morton could readily see the repulse of Ord's and Ferrero's men, but they were getting encouraging news from Captain Paine's signal station perch. Paine overestimated Mahone's two brigades as a division and a half — not so great an error, considering the IX Corps divisions were all composed of paired brigades — and he surmised that these troops had all come from the Confederate right. General Burnside was down on the parapet of the old front line, conferring with Potter, when this message arrived. Some time later Paine sent another note with the exhilarating but incorrect information that a force of several hundred Union soldiers had penetrated as far as the house on the Jerusalem Plank Road. The signal officer soon corrected himself — the troops he had seen were indeed Union, and were passing as far as the Gee house, but they consisted of prisoners. Still, Paine noticed what he thought were two more brigades of Confederate infantry coming toward the battle from the enemy's right. These must have been Saunders's brigade of Alabamians. Paine was inadvertently exaggerating again, and these reinforcements were still some distance away, but the gist of his information was accurate. Lee was stripping his right to plug the Crater gap.

When Burnside returned to his command post and found these dispatches, he wired Meade that now was the time to send in Warren. In his haste he failed to include Paine's sightings, instead mentioning only that the IX and XVIII Corps troops were falling back.[13]

The Virginia brigade suffered terribly for its audacious charge. These men had the advantage of never having grown accustomed to earthworks in battle; compared to the Yankees they were absolutely reckless. The colonel of the veteran 6th Virginia noticed this difference, and it cost many a rash Confederate his life. The 6th had fewer than one hundred men in it when it came over the rise (half the regiment had been left on the picket line, bluffing Warren); eighty fell that day. Entire companies were wiped out. One private in Company K who remained on picket reported the rest of his company went into battle with three "conscriped" officers and twenty-one men, and it came out with one officer and two men. The 16th Virginia lost just half of its ninety-six men. The carnage was equally great in the 61st and 41st regiments. Colonel Stewart and Major Etheridge, commanding those units, were forced to take men out of the firing line for a detail to clear the captured trenches of bodies — black and white, Union and Confederate. Until they did, the brigade was unable to move laterally. Blood pooled in the trench deep enough to soak the uppers of the combatants' brogans. Colonel Weisiger himself was wounded in the side, and turned over command to Colonel George Rogers of the 6th Virginia under the impression that he was dying. Rogers was momentarily captured a few minutes later, only to be rescued by his fellow Virginians. Weisiger leaned on a private and worked his way back to the Gee house, where he ran into Beauregard. The Creole bowed low in a style as moribund as his cause, and told Weisiger "Colonel, you have covered yourselves with glory." The valor of the Virginians won three promotions that day: Mahone's to major general, and both Weisiger's and Girardey's to brigadier. In the only instance of its kind during the entire war, Girardey rose in a single step from captain to command of the Georgia brigade. He would die at the head of those Georgians barely a fortnight later.[14]

Even with the help of Colonel Smith's North and South Carolinians, the single Virginia brigade could not clear the Crater. John Haskell, the Confederate artilleryman, directed Captain James Lamkin to move a section of his mortar battery up from the plank road, placing the pieces among the infantrymen of the 16th Virginia. From there he could lob shells into the Crater with as little as an ounce and a half of powder. Lamkin put the two Coehorns right into the recaptured trenches. This proved rather dangerous, as the traverses were still full of straggling Yankees. Haskell himself was rounding one reach of the zigzag trenches with a borrowed pistol when he flushed a white officer and two Negroes. The Union officer told his men to fire, but Haskell dropped him with the revolver and called on nearby Confederates to charge over the works. These Southerners came back with more than a dozen black prisoners. Periodically, other Yankees would leap over the intervening parapets and surrender, shelled beyond endurance by the mortars.[15]

Now Mahone wanted to bring in Lieutenant Colonel Hall's Georgia brigade, which he hoped could sweep Willcox's Michigan troops out of the trenches south of the Crater and, perhaps, bag the entire crowd. Mahone might have saved the Georgians a thrashing, for the remnants of Willcox's division were already pulling out of those trenches.

So precipitate had the flight of Ferrero's division been — like a tidal wave, sweeping all the white troops back with it — that General Hartranft had called on the 20th Michigan to come back into the undestroyed portion of the fort to help stem their rout. The 20th, Willcox's leftmost regiment on the front line, was the last Union force in those works. When they sidled to the right they found the 1st Sharpshooters and the 2nd regiment already in the remaining ramparts. Confederates from Goode's Virginia brigade and the last two South Carolina detachments closed in still more, taking up the abandoned stretch and building barricades.[16]

General Warren was watching this sidelong shift from V Corps headquarters. He had finally gotten authorization from Meade, who ignored Warren's invitation to come look at things, to assault the single gun of Davidson's battery on the left of the Crater. Warren had this dispatch in his hand when he saw the last of the Michigan men disappear into the Crater. Straining his eyes through the smoke and the distance, he detected a Confederate battle flag in the same spot where Willcox's men had been only a few minutes before. "All our advantages are lost," he told Meade, and declared he could no longer take the position. This unfortunate communication reached the commander of the Army of the Potomac about the same time General Grant returned from his personal reconnaissance of the front. Grant, too, had seen the repulse of Ferrero's assault and the panic it had caused, and he felt the day was lost. At 9:30, therefore, a message came to Burnside from Meade, directing him to withdraw his troops unless he felt there was some advantage still to be gained.[17]

Burnside felt there was most definitely something to be gained. According to his information the Confederate right was dreadfully weak. For all the inflation of Captain Paine's estimates, that was correct: deducting the troops occupied by the IX Corps, the entire front originally assigned to Mahone was guarded by eight scrawny regiments from Mississippi and Florida. But Meade would listen to no such argument. At 9:45, when Warren could have crushed Lee's flank with only two of his divisions and the available cavalry, Meade sent orders out to Hancock, Warren, and Ord to cease all offensive operations. These orders carried the authority of Grant himself. Hancock was to stay where he was, Warren to put his troops back in the trenches, and Ord to bring his divisions back to some safe place behind the IX Corps. Thus deprived of any diversionary assistance, Burnside was ordered to disengage and withdraw to his old trenches.[18]

Already exasperated with Meade, Burnside turned perfectly livid. With all the control he could muster, he left his temporary chief of staff in charge at Fort Morton and rode back to his old headquarters to see if Meade would countermand the withdrawal. Ord went with him. Burnside's face was crimson when he dismounted and confronted Meade; he let fly a salvo of language that one of Meade's staff considered "extremely insubordinate," and insisted further assaults would break the enemy's line. Ord disagreed, however, and Meade said the order stood. While they were there a telegram arrived from Julius White, suggesting that the Crater ought at least to be held and incorporated into the permanent siege fortifications. Meade would not permit it. When Burnside told Meade of the vicious crossfire behind the Crater, the army commander agreed he could hold his present position until nightfall if necessary, but no longer. Burnside relayed that qualification to White and prepared to go back to the front.

When he stepped out of the tent, Burnside turned to Ord and commented on the fifteen thousand Union soldiers concentrated around the Crater. "It is strange if you cannot do something with them," he said. The white-haired Ord responded defensively. "If you are held by the throat" he said, throwing up his arms, "how can you do anything?"[19]

While the generals argued a mile away, the men in and around the Crater were about to be put to another test. They had been cleared from the trenches everywhere now: the refuse of the entire IX Corps was trapped either in the Crater itself or in the surviving redoubt where Hartranft was marshalling both his own and Humphrey's brigades. Several thousand men confined to a front less than a hundred yards wide were in poor position to defend themselves, and what organization they had was altogether makeshift. On the left, Hartranft assumed the role of acting division commander, while Sergeant Stanley of the 14th New York served as his chief of artillery; in the Crater, Simon Griffon was the *de facto* commander of everyone else. The only other general officer, William Bartlett, was out of action. His cork leg had been smashed by a clod of earth when a shell exploded, and he could no longer move.[20] Now, William Mahone decided to send Hall's Georgians down on them.

Hall's instructions were to chase Hartranft's men away from the left of the demolished fort. His men came out of the protective swale with the same enthusiasm but less success than Weisiger's. Hartranft put every man with a rifle in line, and Sergeant Stanley loaded both captured Napoleons with Confederate canister. In the Crater the veterans, particularly from Potter's division, dug footholds along the rim to meet this new assault. They poured a steady stream of lead and iron into the advancing Georgians, who had come into sight with their line swiveled to the north. Their flank was exposed to this defensive fire, and the attackers suffered severely. Sergeant Stanley unloaded bucket after bucket of canister, doing yeoman service on this last day of his life, and Hall's regiments were forced to take cover in the network of traverses and bombproofs that were impeding their progress. Eventually they were driven away from these, too, taking cover behind the Virginians. Some of Hall's men retreated back over the edge of the swale; a few others threw up their hands and darted into Hartranft's little Alamo as prisoners.[21]

Undaunted, Mahone met with Bushrod Johnson in the safety of the ravine, from which Johnson seemed disinclined to venture. A native of Ohio, Johnson has been forced out of the U.S. Army during the Mexican War after offering a superior officer a bribe to aid him in some illicit speculation. This was Johnson's first journey to the battlefield this morning, and he was not impressing his fellow officers either with his competence or his courage. Nevertheless, Mahone conspired with him to close the trap on the Yankees. If Johnson would have his troops south of the Crater drive at the left of the Union position, and have Colquitt's brigade lay a thick crossfire behind it, Mahone would send Saunders's Alabama brigade against it from the southwest. From there it could avoid those troublesome traverses. The flank fire of Goode's brigade would also hamper the crews of the two Napoleons, which would further facilitate Saunders's advance. With simultaneous pressure from Colonel Rogers and the survivors of Weisiger's brigade, as well as a gale of musketry from McAfee to discourage retreat, they should succeed not only in retaking the original lines but in capturing most of Burnside's men. They fixed one o'clock as the time for the start of this final assault, which was predicated on the timely arrival of Saunders. Meanwhile, they would maintain the leaden gantlet over no-man's-land, to prevent the prey from getting away. And the mortars could move in still closer, to shell the Yankees to a frazzle.[22]

Hartranft's men were running out of ammunition after their heroic effort. A fortunate courier managed to carry word of the shortage to Willcox, who had already stockpiled numerous cases of cartridges near his front. Appropriately, General Willcox detailed members of the 51st Pennsylvania — Hartranft's original regiment — to carry ammunition across. They counted off in teams of four and dumped as many cartridge tins as they could carry in the center of a shelter half, then picked up the corners and raced through the fusillade. Some of them did not make it, but eventually ten thousand rounds were transported into Hartranft's bastion.[23]

Now began the worst part of it all. From three sides, Confederates dropped mortar shells into what had been their own fort. Lamkin brought his two little Coehorns up again, to the very base of the slope outside the Crater. Sharpshooters, companies of whom were attached to certain brigades, posted themselves where they could keep the Yankees' heads down and lower the odds that any of them could escape. Confederate infantry around the Crater grew bored when minutes passed without a target, so they retrieved more abandoned muskets and sent them sailing over the rim, bayonet-first, into the writhing mass of humanity.[24]

Inside, the slaughter was pitiful. The trapped Yankees quickly learned to distinguish the hollow thud of the mortars just outside, and many of them would keep watch overhead for the shell, so as to dodge it. The method was not foolproof, though; while some jumped the right way, in time, others were either too slow or too poor a judge of the missles' descent. Both these and the inattentive were either crushed by the shells or mutilated when they exploded. Sometimes the rounds buried themselves in the clay or in a mound of bodies without exploding, and sometimes they blew arms, legs, or entire bodies several feet into the air. Terror swept

94

through the throng, and any semblance of cohesion that had existed was gone now.[25]

Along the lip of the Crater a fringe of free-lance Federal riflemen held on, ignoring the mortars from which they were largely immune. They simply loaded and fired mechanically or took loaded rifles from the men below. Sergeant James Lathe, a rugged Granite Stater who had gone into the fight in command of his company, was careful to watch the effects of his shooting and to keep score. Cheering at each shot, he killed or wounded five Southerners that day, one of them an officer. His marksmanship came to an end when a bullet clipped off two middle fingers and ripped his hand in half, all the way to the wrist. Screaming in pain, he dropped into the bottom of the Crater and made for the rear. In the last instant before he dashed across the bullet-swept path to his own lines, Lathe met a lieutenant from his regiment. That officer, who would be killed an hour later during his own attempt to escape, bound the rent hand up in a handkerchief. Tenderly cradling his bloody claw, Lathe burst into the open and ran for his life.[26]

The 1st Michigan Sharpshooters — particularly the Chippewas — also kept up a slow, accurate fire, conserving the ammunition so perilously provided. As these courageous sentinels fell along the ragged edge of the Crater, the shellfire increased. Confederate artillerymen found a good target where the trenches opened into the Crater on the north; through these slots they could cut a swath across the entire crowd of Union soldiers. Driven to a new level of panic by this fire, the Yankees began to mill helplessly until General Bartlett ordered some black soldiers to build a breastwork across the openings. There was no lumber available; there were no rocks. The Negroes propped up a few clods of loose earth, but it was slow going and the canister just plowed through it. At last someone shouted above the roar, "Put in the dead men." The words were hardly out of his mouth before the first limp body was dragged into the apertures. Some of the marksmen on the edge of the Crater actually rolled bodies up on the rim, then scooped hollows in the clay below them and continued sniping at the enemy from the relative safety of these grisly loopholes.[27]

Still the shells came looping in. A Maine major was struck by a mortar round that blew his head to fragments and left his decapitated and bloodless body draining upside down on the interior slope. A seventeen-year-old New Hampshire soldier found himself covered from head to foot in the gore and brains of men who had been blown up around him. Nor were the mortars the only danger. A Maine lieutenant, also only seventeen, stood momentarily on a prominence in the Crater to see why the enemy musketry had diminished. In that instant someone from Colonel Goode's front drew a bead on him and fired. The bullet entered the boy's left temple and came out the bridge of his nose, destroying his left eye in its passage and damaging his right. Blinded as he was, it was the young lieutenant's extreme good fortune to be able to hobble safely to the rear.[28]

Captain Hough, the New Hampshire officer who had had to wave the flag to stop the colored troops from firing into his men, fell victim to a worse piece of luck. A nervous private beside him was putting a percussion cap on his loaded rifle when his thumb slipped: the hammer fell, the rifle discharged, and Captain Hough was struck in the back of the head. He fell face down, with the gaping hole visible for all to see, and everyone who noticed him thought he was dead. His obituary appeared in the hometown paper a few days later, though he was to survive both the wound and Libby Prison.[29]

The need for water had reached critical proportions inside the Crater. Men were drooping, stumbling, and collapsing from heat exhaustion. One eyewitness remembered a fog that rose from the Crater to moisten the battlesmoke — a mist created by the collective respiration of this confined multitude. The wounded cried for water with even greater pathos than usual, and men moistened their lips so frequently it seemed their tongues hung from their mouths.[30]

A private from General Griffin's original regiment approached him for permission to fetch water from the Union lines. The crossfire from Colquitt's and McAfee's infantry and Wright's artillery made it almost certain death to traverse the slope behind the Crater, but Griffin told the man he could try it if he took enough canteens to make it worth the hazard. As he watched the fellow bound onto the bullet-swept plain laden with dry canteens, the general thought he might not return if he once landed safely in the old trenches. His courage would probably fail then, Griffin surmised, and he could hardly blame him. When several other men came to him with the same proposal Griffin was sure they were merely angling for an honorable means to escape the bloodbath. Sympathetically, he allowed every man to go. It was therefore with a good deal of surprise that the general saw the first man lumber back across the wasteland with all his canteens filled. Bullets perforated a couple of them, but that mishap simply lightened his burden and propelled him all the faster. He waddled almost comically past the bodies of some who had never made it through the first dangerous lap, finally clambering up the rear slope of the Crater and flinging himself inside. The canteens circulated away from one set of clutching hands to another as a second man climbed the Union parapet and burst into view with more water. Just past the point of no return he fell dead, but so precious was his cargo that someone else darted from the Crater to finish his mission. This young man was also shot, but he regained his feet and came over into the inferno to distribute the priceless liquid. Until the very end a dwindling handful of these nameless heroes kept a trickle of water moving into the steaming cauldron, but for all their gallantry it was not nearly enough.[31]

In all of this confusion came Burnside's reluctant order to retire. He instructed General White to ask the division commanders to endorse it and decide upon a common time for the withdrawal, but no division commander ever signed the actual order. It went instead to the acting division commanders in the Crater. Hartranft got it first, and suggested all the Union batteries should bear on the artillery that was punishing them from the Baxter Road — Davidson's and Flanner's, presumably. The circular next went to the hobbled Bartlett, who thought they could never get the troops out safely in the daylight. They were, he said, "a rabble." They were going almost crazy from thirst, as well. Hartranft and Griffin finally agreed that a daylight retreat could only be accomplished if the troops on either side made a diversionary assault. Since there was effectively no IX Corps left except for the men in the Crater, they could only have been referring to the II and V Corps. Burnside had no authority over those troops, however, and Meade had essentially ordered them to bed.

General Willcox attempted the impossible, putting some of Ferrero's escaped troops to the task of digging three covered ways to the Crater. Frantic men inside the Crater itself saw the picks and shovels flying and began digging back with bayonets and bare hands to meet them. A man with the luxury for calm reflection might have told them there was no hope of completing a trench eight feet deep and four or more feet wide, over four hundred feet of embattled ground, in less than a couple of days.[32]

By now J. C. C. Saunders's brigade was coming down the serpentine covered way that dumped into the swale. Mahone himself came back to meet it. In a brief consultation with the senior officers he described the situation again and made his plans known. So thin was the Confederate right that these five regiments were the last men Mahone could hope to put into the fight. From here on it was a game of table stakes, and there were by actual count only 632 riflemen in Saunders's command. Many of them were already falling victim to the heat. If they could not dislodge the several thousand Yankees in the destroyed fort, there was no hope of getting any more troops down from the James River in time to fill the gap; it was still possible for the enemy to break through, though he seemed to have slackened his effort. But Mahone had no way of knowing that George Meade had long since given up.

As he explained it to the three captains and two colonels in command of these five regiments, it was in their best interest to creep as close to the lip of the ravine as possible, then lurch forward at a lope, without firing. Perhaps silence, combined with the smoke and dust, would buy a few moments' reprieve from the punishing Union artillery. Unlike the Georgia brigade, the Alabama men would strike from the relatively unbroken ground southwest of the Union position, and once the first volley of rifle fire had been drawn Saunders was to drive his men at a double-quick, so as to get rapidly under the brow of the Crater wall, where neither artillery nor musketry could do them much damage. The appointed time was approaching for the synchronized assistance from Johnson's troops on either side of the Crater.[33]

In the last remaining moments Mahone sauntered up and down the waiting ranks. Again he reminded those Southerners there were Negroes in the pit who had sworn to give no quarter. While a detail of privates prudently filled the brigade canteens, Mahone pointed to the Gee house and told the devoted soldiers that General Lee was watching them. A staff officer shouted to Saunders that if his brigade did not carry the Crater on the first try, it would have to be reformed for another attempt; in that case General Lee would lead the charge personally. The threat had the desired effect: "If the old man comes down here," said one of the privates, "we will tie him to a sapling while we make the fight."[34]

Fired by this image of General Lee, the six hundred fixed their bayonets and stooped low, trotting to the top of the ravine and over, into the wreckage of three Confederate brigades and four Union divisions. As they arrived they were joined by men they passed over, including a blackened South Carolinian who had barely survived the morning's explosion. At last the defenders in the Crater saw them and sputtered a fragile but defiant volley that injured almost no one. With the taste of victory in their mouths the Confederates hurtled onward, leaping the traverses and bombproofs and raising once more the shrill staccato of the Rebel Yell. Inside the Crater many Yankees who could not see the charge could hear that fearful cry, and their blood fairly gelled at the sound. Among those who stumbled over the nearly solid layer of dead and dying men who veneered the Crater there arose a palpable panic. White men turned on their black comrades in blind fear that the Confederates would execute anyone captured with them. Negro soldiers began to fall here and there, bayoneted or shot by other Union soldiers; one officer who survived wrote home that "the men was bound not to be taken prisoner among them niggers."[35]

Up along the rim of the Crater, bolder souls kept up the fight. The Alabamians crawled fitfully up the sides of the Crater while their compatriots poured in the promised covering fire, and soon the crippled General Bartlett saw a Confederate flag peeking over the parapet at him, only six feet from his own guidon. The attackers tipped their rifles over the edge to fire, or sometimes jumped up for a quick shot, and courageous defenders responded in kind. Again came the javelinlike flurries of bayoneted muskets, which the cartridge-poor Yankees collected and threw back. Generals Griffin and Hartranft could rally almost no one among the thousands of intermingled soldiers; the motley rear guard of one or two hundred was all that could be mustered to hold back the enemy. Thanks to the withdrawal of Warren's and Ord's corps, surrounding Confederates were able to give their complete attention and firepower to the doomed contingent, so the string of defiant men on the parapet was fast being cut to pieces. Even the Michigan marksmen had been silenced: a group of wounded Chippewa sharpshooters huddled in the southern part of the fort, their shirts draped over their heads while they chanted their death song.[36]

The melee continued longer than anyone expected, with nothing between the opponents but the ridge of earth thrown up by the explosion. With no thought of holding until dark any longer, Griffin and Hartranft sent their staffs through the throng with orders to withdraw on the signal. The signal would be the opening of all the Union artillery on the Confederate lines north and south of the Crater; another staff officer had been sent back to arrange for that protective barrage, carrying with him the deceptively calm endorsements on Burnside's circular order to withdraw.[37]

It was about two o'clock when the dispersed fragments of Mahone's division drew together around the Crater, like fingers tightening around a throat. Finally, the Confederates decided the time had come.

The two separate magazines in the mine had left two distinct cavities in the Crater, divided by a narrow diaphragm of clay. In the larger of these, to the north, Lieutenant Freeman Bowley of the 30th U.S.C.T. waited with the only man left in his company, a Negro sergeant. He heard a voice on the other side say "Every man get his gun loaded, give one spring and go right over." A few moments later Bowley heard the same voice shout "Forward 41st!" The lieutenant cocked his revolver, and the first man he saw surmount the parapet was a big Confederate major, William Etheridge of the 41st Virginia. A Virginia sergeant pointed his rifle at Bowley's head, and cries of "surrender" rose all around. At first most of the Yankees near Lieutenant Bowley complied, but the captors began shooting and bayoneting Negro prisoners, including Bowley's sergeant. Other blacks took their arms back up and the hand-to-hand conflict continued.[38]

At the adjacent quadrant of the Crater, the Alabama troops stormed over the top at the same moment. Here, too, the bayonet and rifle butt did most of the work, though Colonel Saunders shot it out toe-to-toe with a big Negro soldier. Saunders, who had barely three weeks to live himself, went unscathed. The adjutant of the 14th Alabama and a lieutenant in the 11th were killed by Negroes; a sergeant of the 9th Alabama was shot through his open mouth as he leaped into the Crater, and fell stone dead on the inside slope. Two lieutenants of the 11th Alabama dove into the brawl together, one of them carrying the regimental colors. The other officer, P. M. Vance, was shot through the leg as he sprang. The bullet grazed his thighbone and numbed his leg for a few critical moments, but he fell upon his Negro assailant. The black drew a knife, and they grappled in the confined bottom of the pit. Vance could not find room to use his sword, and had no pistol, so he grabbed his opponent in a bearhug and waited for someone to come to his assistance. Just as he was about to faint from loss of blood his men came to bayonet and bludgeon the Negro to death.[39]

The Confederates were sorely outnumbered when they threw themselves into that cauldron. Even if all of Mahone's surviving troops had gone in they would have faced more than twice their number in blue uniforms, and there was not enough room for all three of his brigades. But the Union soldiers were utterly demoralized. At last, with their two ambulatory generals pointing the way, the remainder of Burnside's corps bolted for the rear. They crammed into the rough beginning of the covered way and spilled over the rear rampart, surging into the deadly fusillade that separated them from their own works. Scores of them fell in the retreat as uninhibited rifle fire ripped through the dense mass. One Rhode Islander who had been trampled and badly injured in the rout of Ferrero's division ran instinctively with the mob, unable to see or care how many dead or wounded he trampled in turn. He catapulted himself over the breastworks into his own lines, mumbled a prayer of thanks, and collapsed. A comrade had to drag him out of the path of following troops. A New Hampshire private whose brother was starving to death in a Confederate prison was not about to be captured, and he sprinted over with the swarm of refugees despite a bullet in his knee.[40]

Hundreds of the men in the Crater did not follow. When the bulk of the troops had fled toward Union lines their herd psychology failed them. As the flight deteriorated to a few scattered groups here and there, Confederate fire became more effective again. Those who might have run three minutes before could not bring themselves to do so now; and when they turned to look at the Crater again it was filling up with soldiers in different shades of grey.

The killing continued. The Confederates, forewarned that no quarter would be given them and enraged by the deployment of Negroes against them, stabbed and bashed everywhere. General Bartlett, stranded on a clay throne, had wished to surrender the Crater as soon as the Confederates clambered over, but the mutual assumption of the Black Flag kept every man fighting for his life — especially the Negroes.[41]

Ultimately appalled and exhausted by the carnage, Adjutant Morgan Cleveland of the 8th Alabama cried out "Why in the hell don't you fellows surrender?"

"Why in the hell don't you let us?" answered a Union colonel. Presently a Lieutenant Kibby of the 4th Rhode Island tied his once-white silk handerchief to his sword. When he held it up, the firing quickly subsided around him. Gradually this silence reached all over the Crater, and the

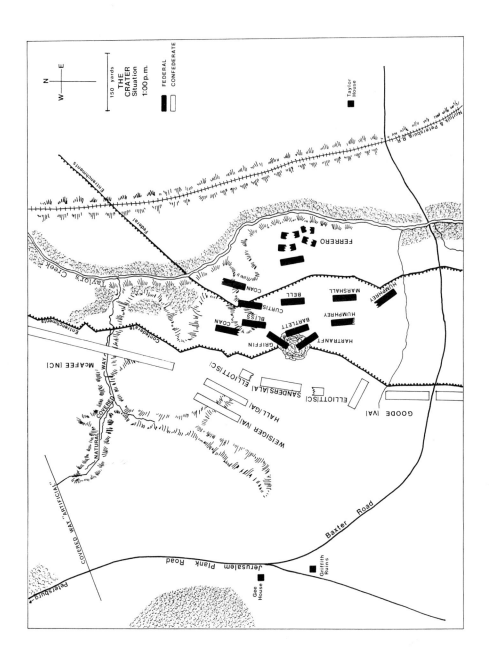

THE CRATER
Situation
1:00 p.m.

FEDERAL
CONFEDERATE

150 yards

Taylor House

Norfolk & Petersburg R.R.

Entrenchments

Federal

Taylor's Creek

FERRERO

COAN

BELL

CURTIS

MARSHALL

BLISS

HUMPHREY

COAN

BARTLETT

HUMPHREY

HARTRANFT

GRIFFIN

Confederates

Entrenchments

McAFEE [NC]

COVERED WAY

NATURAL

SANDERS [ALA]

ELLIOTT [SC]

HALL [GA]

ELLIOTT [SC]

WEISIGER [VA]

GOODE [VA]

COVERED WAY "ARTIFICIAL"

Petersburg

Baxter Road

Jerusalem Plank Road

Gee House

Griffith Ruins

101

Union men dropped their guns as Mahone and other Confederate officers moved about guaranteeing their safety. The Southerners pointed gory bayonets while the Yankees slipped off sword belts and cartridge boxes. While the wounded leaned on each other, and a couple of men got on either side of General Bartlett, Mahone's men went about exchanging their perforated hats for those of the Union officers. These black hats, and sometimes even the blue forage caps, seem to have been particularly prized by the Confederates. Few captured officers failed to experience a tug-of-war for their headgear.[42]

When the battered battalion of wounded and shellshocked filed out of the Crater between a double row of Confederates, Union artillery opened momentarily. At least one Federal private had his arm torn off by his own ordnance. And even after that danger had been surmounted they were not safe: one officer of colored troops reported a Negro soldier was shot by a guard halfway back to the Gee house.[43]

The Confederates put the Crater, with its swarms of bloodthirsty flies, to immediate use. They dug a little shelf inside the rear palisade, from which they could shoot at the Yankees. Firing between the lines continued unabated after the position had been recaptured.

General Burnside was staggered by his division commanders' reports. Potter in particular brought bad news: at 2:30 he reported his division all but destroyed. More than half of his regiments were thought to be captured almost to a man, and those that were left were badly depleted. He did not exaggerate greatly, for most of his regiments had been cut in half and he was justified in his fear that he would be unable to hold the length of trenches formerly assigned to him. Ledlie and Ferrero made no immediate reports, but each of their divisions had suffered brutal punishment. Fragments of Willcox's division remained effective for duty — mostly those who had been routed from Humphrey's morning assault and had since been reformed. Willcox moved into the trenches left empty by Ord's withdrawal and saved Burnside the mortification of having to ask that his entire corps be relieved.[44]

Mummified in the official correspondence between Burnside and his subordinates is the evidence of frustration, anguish, and outrage. Burnside shared all of these emotions. He must have remembered his efforts to get Meade to continue the struggle with bitter irony when, that evening, Meade announced the return of the rest of the Confederate army from the James. Meade wanted him to "strengthen the line of works where any obstacles have to-day been removed" and warned him to marshal his reserves against a possible counterattack.[45]

The Confederates, who had been so near the end of their tether they were disinclined even to feign an attack, did not try Burnside's strength. While the IX Corps commander feverishly tried to reorganize what was left of his corps, Generals Meade and Grant retired to their respective head-quarters. So ignorant were they of the predicament in which they had left Burnside that Grant wired him, before the Crater was recaptured, to learn how many of his men the Confederates had taken in their presumed victory. Then, after what ordinarily would have been dinner, Meade telegramed Burnside to ask if he still held the Crater and whether he could get his wounded off safely. General Burnside figured that either Meade knew what the situation was and was taunting him, or he cared too little about the IX Corps to bother to learn what the rest of the army could plainly see. Burnside flung Meade's message away and told the officer who had delivered it that he would answer no such insulting communication. Peeved at the lack of a response, Meade forwarded two more queries that night, but the enraged Burnside threw them both away. When the com-mander of the Army of the Potomac finally went to bed, near midnight, he still did not know whether the IX Corps held the Crater.[46]

General Potter complained that few of the wounded had been brought off; Confederates commented on the unusually small ratio of wounded taken from the Crater. The two observations speak to the extent of the butchery that took place inside that crucible. Yet, in little pockets and shellholes in the clay, many of those wounded remained. As the sun set over that dreadful day, they began to keen with the pain of their wounds and to call for water.[47]

CHAPTER VI

"Let's all go home!"

The sun that rose on the last day of July uncovered a scene of apocalyptic horror. The red and yellow clay of Virginia's underbelly lay riven and exposed — blasted into fragments by the mine, scored by shot and shell, and wildly furrowed by the frantic diggings of desperate men. Two hundred bodies littered the gantlet between the reestablished lines, most of them clothed in blue uniforms beneath a heavy film of dust. The air still hung unbearably close as the sun resumed its cruel broiling of the dead and wounded, some of whom yet survived. They had no water, nor was there anyone left who dared carry it to them.

General Meade supplied Burnside with a letter addressed to Robert E. Lee but told the IX Corps commander to try to bury the dead and bring in the wounded with only a local truce on his own front, without delivering the letter; only if the informal arrangement was not acceptable was he authorized to submit the written request. A formal appeal to recover the dead was usually considered an admission of defeat; perhaps Meade was reluctant to make that acknowledgement, though the matter was hardly in doubt. The stranded Union casualties suffered greatly for Meade's hesitance.[1]

Burnside sent a staff member across the ravaged landscape to make the initial inquiry, but the local Confederate commanders were unwilling to accede to a truce without higher authority. The Union officer then returned with the required letter, which a courier took to Lee's headquarters. The only humanitarian gesture accorded the Yankees that day was permission to distribute water and whiskey to the wounded. With a canteen or so apiece, the sunburned handful of men who had survived thus far were left to endure another long day without shade. Many were doubtless unable to raise the filled canteens to their mouths. The dead had already begun to stink fearfully.[2]

Lest he trespass on the domain of General Beauregard, in whose department the Crater lay, Lee forwarded Meade's letter to him. By the time the message reached Beauregard, it was too late in the afternoon to begin a truce long enough to bury all the dead. Rather than extend it through the night or break it into two periods, Beauregard put it off until five A.M., August 1.

The burial parties finally moved forward in the same glimmer of dawn that had lighted the charge of Ledlie's division. Twenty-four cumulative hours under a merciless summer sun had baked all the dead a uniform black, so that Negro and white could be distinguished only by the hair, and their bloating flesh strained at the seams and buttons of their clothing. Often their pants or shirts had burst open; in some cases so had the skin itself. Many of the bodies were shot to pieces, and maggots covered the myriad wounds. Flies swarmed over the few wounded who still breathed. So fragile were the corpses that no attempt was made to retrieve them to their respective sides. Instead, Confederate and Union soldiers worked beside each other to dig long trenches, and they flopped the dead into them indiscriminately, touching them only with their shovels whenever possible.[3]

Union officers counted 220 Federals thrown into the mass graves, while only a score of wounded were recovered. One field officer saw some bewildered members of the Christian Commission struggling with a handcart full of "stimulants and delicacies, including ice," which they hoped to distribute to the maimed; these young clerics found little market for their benevolence. Most of the few remaining wounded were Negroes: their disproportionate number among the survivors may have resulted from a natural tolerance for heat, or from their understandable disinclination to crawl into the Confederate lines and surrender. So numerous and scattered were the casualties that the four-hour truce had to be extended to six hours before all the fetid remains could be gotten underground. By eleven o'clock the job was done. The meeting between the lines had been courteous — even pleasant, according to a New Hampshire captain. Amid the smell of death the enemies had traded coffee and tobacco with the callous indifference of the veteran, and one Confederate had leapt to the parapet and shouted "Let's all go home!" But once the last stiffened arm was finally tamped beneath the soil, the belligerents took to their trenches and the war began again with, if anything, even greater rancor than before. Despite the cordiality of the truce, after the Crater the Confederates seemed to harbor a heightened animosity for the army that had them under siege. A matron at Chimborazo Hospital in Richmond, who had previously remarked upon the respect wounded Confederates bore for their opponents, saw such considerations come to an end with the casualties from the Crater. Men of Mahone's division arrived at her hospital cursing and snarling at the Yankees, proudly brandishing muskets they would not relinquish — muskets with the bloody hair of their brained adversaries imbedded in the locks.[4]

Colonel Henry Thomas, of the U.S. Colored Troops, fell afoul of the enemy pickets while trying to make his way back to Union lines after the truce. He was detained for nearly a full day before the Confederates released him. While his case was being reviewed at Bushrod Johnson's headquarters he overheard the Confederates talking about the slaughter of the blacks, before and after the surrender. He was told, with obvious exaggeration, that only three dozen of them were taken alive. He saw some of them around Johnson's headquarters; rather than being confined as prisoners of war they were working on fatigue duty, under guard.[5]

The degree to which the Negro prisoners were mistreated after the battle is somewhat overdrawn, but the men captured at the Crater did seem to suffer more than the average Union prisoner. As always, part of their neglect is attributable to the meager supplies available to the Confederacy and to the extreme shorthandedness of the two divisions around the Crater the evening of July 30; but there was an undeniable element of animosity toward the Negro soldiers and those who were perceived as their agitators. No food was distributed to the prisoners Saturay night, and worse yet, no water; nor were they provided with shelter or blankets. The night after the battle all the prisoners, black and white, were crowded into a stone-littered field to sleep, going crazy with thirst. Officers and men were robbed of their possessions by their guards. That was unusual so near the front, but there are indications these guards consisted of reserves, or militia.

When the column of filthy unfortunates was marched into Petersburg on Sunday morning, it came through the city in a formation designed both to amuse the citizens and humiliate the prisoners. At the head of the column were the senior officers, four abreast, followed by four Negroes. Four more Union officers followed, then four more blacks, and so on, until first the supply of officers was exhausted and then the supply of colored troops. Residents jeered the dejected mass, one woman calling out, "Birds of a feather will flock together." The bitterness with which survivors of the march recalled the event suggests it was every bit as mortifying as the Confederates intended. As might be expected, some of the Union officers magnified the insult, imagining the legless General Bartlett placed in front of the column, bareback on a spavined old nag. Their march ended on an island in the Appomattox, where they spent another night under the open sky. Some raw bacon was issued, and at last water was available in endless quantity.

The following day cattle cars came for the officers. While they were on their way to Columbia, South Carolina, a second set of trains started down the tracks of the Southside Railroad for Danville, carrying the enlisted men: Andersonville was already too full for this large a catch.[6]

Even after their capture, the black troops did not suffer indignities and cruelty solely at the hands of Confederates. One Virginia surgeon in charge of the Petersburg hospital assigned five Union medical officers to assist him with the Federal wounded. He gave them the freedom of the camp and a detail of enlisted prisoners to act as nurses, but when these Northern doctors — prisoners from a different battle — had finished with the white wounded, they chose to relax. According to the Virginian, Dr.

John Claiborne, the owner of a nearby estate called him to his property. Claiborne said he found the grounds littered with a hundred and fifty groaning, wounded Negroes. They had lain there since the previous afternoon, almost all robbed naked and totally unattended. The doctor made straight for the Union prisoner-surgeons, whom he found "lounging in front of their quarters, doing nothing." One Confederate officer was already cursing them for their breach of faith, and Claiborne joined in. They steadfastly refused to do anything more until Claiborne ostentatiously called for a provost guard to take them away to prison. Only then did these surgeons agree to treat the Negroes.[7]

While all the burying had been going on around the Crater, Confederate authorities had been particularly anxious to bring the truce to an end. They, themselves, were preparing to explode a mine about six hundred yards nearer the Appomattox. The indefatigable Captain Douglas had arranged a magazine before Gracie's Salient, just beyond Burnside's right, on the front of the XVIII Corps. As soon as the truce was over he touched off his four safety fuses, but forty-five minutes later nothing had happened. A Confederate named Black, a man of the same mold as Henry Reese, ventured into the tunnel and found three of the fuses burned out; the fourth was sputtering hopelessly. It was the best fuse the Confederacy could supply, but it wasn't good enough. Douglas postponed the detonation and had his men dig a little farther, thinking perhaps that he had fallen short of the enemy line. In the next few days his sappers packed eight big barrels of powder into two new chambers. At six-thirty on the evening of August 5 he tried it again. There was no assault planned to follow the explosion, but that was just as well: the mine blew an unimpressive spout of dirt into the air some forty yards in front of Ord's extreme left, doing no damage whatsoever to his trenches. There was a frustrated flurry of artillery fire, but the only upshot of the entire episode was that another Union fort earned its name when Colonel Griffin Stedman was killed by a stray piece of canister.[8]

For a few weeks after the Crater fight there was a perfect paranoia about mining operations. Captain Douglas was only one of several Confederate engineer officers engaged in the search for and construction of new tunnels. Lieutenant Colonel William Blackford was in charge of the engineers in the area of the Crater itself, where he kept busy long after the battle was over, digging for the gallery the Pennsylvanians had run. He also drilled a number of new holes in the hope of uncovering more Union mines, sometimes creating a panic in his own camp when other Confederates heard the picks and shovels his men were swinging. Blackford's operations were hampered by a gruesome development he had not considered. The malodorous gases from the dead bodies buried in the Crater had permeated every underground fissure in the vicinity; because of the explosion these fissures radiated in every direction. The combined stench of black powder and decomposition stopped his miners at every turn, and Blackford himself was almost overcome by the effluvia when he crawled into a tunnel to investigate the complaint. Eventually, by the use of some winnowing fans and lengths of homemade ducting, he was able to ventilate his countermine enough to continue probing for the original shaft Pleasants had driven. After weeks of groping in subterranean arcs around the corpse-packed Crater, he found it.[9]

The human loss in the Crater was not so great as in many of the other battles of 1864, but it went far beyond the 220 dead men buried under the flag of truce. There were the hundreds of bodies that had been rolled into the bottom of the Crater by the victorious Confederates, to be covered with loose earth while the defensive lines were reconstructed on this ghostly foundation. Many of Elliott's men had been spontaneously entombed there, as well. A review of the casualties shows that Union forces lost 504 killed, 1,881 wounded, and another 1,413 captured or missing. Somewhat fewer than 400 Confederates died, many in the initial explosion; more than 700 were wounded, and another 40 fell into Union hands or were simply never found. One calculation marks the total Confederate loss at 1,612, fewer than half the Union casualties. Of the 3,798 men lost in the Army of the Potomac, all but about three hundred came from Burnside's IX Corps. More than a third of all the Union casualties were from Ferrero's division. The colored troops accounted for more than forty-one percent of the known killed.

Those relatives of soldiers who knew what had become of their menfolk were extremely lucky. Because of the large numbers of prisoners and the difficulty in identifying the dead, no one could be certain if a missing man were still alive. The wife of Private Jeremiah Batchelder of the 11th New Hampshire was notified by the sergeant left in command of his company that her husband was presumed to be a prisoner; two weeks after the battle she wrote the sergeant to learn how to get in touch with Jeremiah. The sergeant replied, "... if he is a prisoner he will write to you[.] if he is dead we shall not know anything more of him[.]" No letter ever came, and Mrs. Batchelder never saw her husband again.[10]

The disaster was, however, of sufficient proportions that General Meade insisted upon a court of inquiry, principally to clear himself of any culpability. He appointed a board from within his own army, but when it was made clear to him that higher authority was necessary for such a court he asked Grant to use his influence to persuade President Lincoln to legitimize Meade's choices. Lincoln did, and when the court opened its hearings on August 6 it still consisted of the four men Meade had named: Generals Winfield Hancock and Nelson Miles of the II Corps, Romeyn B. Ayres of the V Corps, and Colonel Edward Schriver of Meade's own staff.[11]

Burnside made haste to complain about the appointments to the court. He sensed, perhaps, that he was about to be crucified, and he wished to have the investigation conducted by officers more objective than those who had taken part in the battle. As he stressed to the Secretary of War, three of those on the court had commanded troops that failed to support his corps, which Burnside felt contributed to the disaster. The fourth member was none other than Meade's own inspector general, who was not likely to find much fault with his chief. Considering that Hancock had expressed prejudice against Burnside in past months and Ayres already had decided that the failure was due to Burnside's improper deployment of troops, Burnside had good reason to suspect he would not get a fair hearing. Unbelievably, President Lincoln assured him that he would.[12]

Meade gave his testimony first. He submitted a blizzard of documents and statements that tended to incriminate General Burnside, some of which seemed to extend beyond the scope of the investigation. Meade gave the court an account of Burnside's argument with him at IX Corps headquarters, for which — as well for his "ungentlemanly" dispatch — Meade had preferred charges against him. He repeated several times that Burnside had made no report to him until the day after the battle; when Burnside objected that none of this had anything to do with fixing the blame for the failure of the assault, the court coolly overruled him. Not only did the examining officers find the extraneous material pertinent, they also cited the technical fact that Burnside ought to have objected at the moment the evidence was submitted, rather than waiting until the end of the first day's testimony.[13]

The court met for a few hours each day of the second week in August. On the tenth General Burnside asked Meade a few questions before taking the stand himself. He convinced Meade to modify his statements about Burnside's failure to report, and made the point that it was Meade himself who ordered a withdrawal at 9:00 A.M., when Warren's front was virtually clear of Confederate infantry. After this exchange Burnside was sworn in, and he began to recount his difficulties in digging the mine almost entirely without the assistance of Meade's staff. He went into great detail about his reasons for choosing the Negro troops to lead the assault and explained why he had finally cast lots when that decision was vetoed. He also complained of the failure to send in Warren's corps when it would have been useful. When he continued his testimony on August 11 and 12 he was questioned about the preparations he had made in his parapets to accommodate the assault. He admitted that he had required little to be done, both because of the dangers involved and because the obstructions were already riddled beyond effectiveness. Burnside estimated it had taken only five minutes from the time of the explosion to get the first division moving, a fact later corroborated by General Willcox, who characterized the infantry obstructions as "no obstacle whatever."

Had Stephen Weld not been a prisoner, the court might have had testimony from a man hostile to Burnside who could have told of Ledlie's men moving toward the Crater by 4:49 A.M. The manner in which the court questioned Burnside and following witnesses indicated that the judges were leaning toward this failure to remove the abatis and break down the trenches as the principal cause of the fragmented movement of the first division and, by extension, of the entire failure. General Ledlie, who had conveniently requested leave of absence, was never examined. No one was ever able to ask him whether his men moved by the flank simply because he failed to instruct his brigadiers to do otherwise, and the brigadiers in question were both in a Confederate prison. Nor did anyone ask Burnside if he failed to level his parapets because he feared for the success of the operation. Burnside offered nothing of the kind: had he wished to use that defence, he might have cited Meade's worried order of 5:00 P.M., July 30, directing him to strengthen his works where he might have torn them down. After a final barrage of leading questions by Meade's inspector general, Burnside left the stand. The next day he departed the army on twenty days' furlough, never to return.[14]

Toward the end of Burnside's leave of absence, the court reconvened. Forty-two more officers were examined, from General Grant down to a pair of regimental surgeons. Even General Ayres stepped down from his impartial seat on the court to offer his preconceived notions about the failure of the assault. General Grant, possibly sensing the drift of the court, wrote Burnside that he might as well remain at home in Providence a while longer, because his return to the Army of the Potomac just then would be injudicious.[15]

The court's predictable findings were delivered on September 9. Burnside was held principally accountable. He was blamed for not leveling his parapets; for allowing the troops to advance by the flank; for failure to obey Meade's orders to advance quickly, or take Ledlie's men out of the way; and, inexplicably, for not properly fortifying the crest that was never gained. Ledlie and Ferrero were found somewhat responsible for a combination of cowardice and negligence, Colonel Bliss was censured for remaining behind while most of his brigade advanced, and Orlando Willcox was chastised for a general want of effort. The findings did not name Meade specifically, but in deference perhaps to objectivity the court observed that, in his absence, a single officer on the spot ought to have been authorized to command all the troops on the field. The remark was made very gently: there was no reference to Burnside's prophetic July 3 appeal to "say when and how the other two corps shall come in to my support," and the court stopped far short of offering Meade the same criticism it had aimed at every other commander who failed to come near the fighting.[16]

110

The decision fixed the light in which the actors in the tragedy would be viewed. General Burnside was never again assigned to duty. Ledlie was relieved of command and allowed to vanish from the army in a more honorable manner than he deserved, while Willcox and Ferrero continued in undistinguished division command. Colonel Bliss, though a graduate of West Point and colonel of his regiment during most of the war, was never tendered the almost routine brevet as brigadier general.

However, that was not the end of the matter. As was its wont during Christmas recesses, the Joint Congressional Committee on the Conduct of the War investigated the disaster. The committee was as friendly to Burnside as the court had been hostile to him, and it had no vested interest in finding him responsible. It spent almost a month gathering the necessary testimony and reaching its conclusions. The congressmen interviewed Burnside and some others at Washington, including Colonel Pleasants, who had not been on hand before; then they travelled to City Point and Petersburg to hear Grant, Meade, and everyone else who was still on duty with the army.

Two months before the end of the war, the committee published its independent results. Their main suspect was Meade, whom they blamed for forcing Burnside to change his plan of attack and find a substitute for his trained, fresh division of Negroes. They criticized supporting troops — including the V Corps, in which Romeyn Ayres commanded a division, and Hancock's II Corps, wherein was Miles's division — for failing to give sufficient assistance to Burnside. Meade came under further scrutiny for withdrawing all support from Burnside's flanks before he could extricate the IX Corps. The congressmen discounted the pretext of the unprepared parapets: if there had not been sufficient room for men to leave the trenches, they reasoned, how was such a large force so quickly pushed forward that the front became overcrowded? The only fault the committee found with General Burnside was the manner in which he had finally chosen the leading division, which they judged less than commendable. Despite that criticism, they suggested that the choice of Ledlie's division was not, in itself, indicative of poor judgment. The original choice of the colored division, these solons believed, was the best; the battle was lost when Meade denied Burnside that choice.[17]

The committee's review of the affair did Burnside little good. Within ten weeks of the report's publication the new President accepted his resignation, and the war was over. The opinion of most of the Army of the Potomac's officers fossilized against him, and that soon translated into a majority of public opinion. The Joint Committee's reports were retired to the uppermost shelves of a few obscure collections in public and private libraries, while the judgment of the court of inquiry and the Army of the Potomac went into the history books.

The Crater never ceased to be a significant landmark for those who had fought there, but it quickly diminished in strategic importance. Soon it was just another sector of the Confederate lines, albeit still the closest to the Yankee works. In mid-August Grant's offensive operations gravitated back up to Deep Bottom, then down to the Weldon Railroad. From there the open-field fighting was carried on to the west, in the vicinity of the Boydton Plank Road. Never again would enemies grapple in the Crater, and only when Lee's equally-disastrous assault swallowed Fort Stedman would the tedium of the siege at Elliott's Salient be interrupted. There would be a brush on the picket line outside the Crater in April, but when Union soldiers finally marched into the resurrected Confederate fort over Henry Pleasants's mine there would be no one to confront them: no Stephen Elliott; no William Mahone. Northern cameramen would clamber over the rough bombproofs, blissfully unaware they trod the graves of several hundred dead men, and Yankee soldiers would pose for them, unimpeded by the familiar sting of the sharpshooters.[18]

William Griffith resumed tenancy on his farm again after the armies abandoned it. His house, in the angle of the Jerusalem Plank Road and the Baxter Road, had burned in the earliest days of the siege, and he could only afford to build a rude cabin for himself and his sons. The pastures he had maintained were a barren waste; his cultivated fields were trenched and burrowed beyond use. He and his neighbors immediately began the years-long process of razing the miles of forts and intervening earthworks, but while Fort Morton was disappearing on the other side of Poor Creek, Mr. Griffith took note of the steady stream of visitors who passed his door to see the nearby Crater. Old and tired, he pondered the possibility of supplementing his livelihood from the attraction the war had placed in his hands. He fenced off the site of the explosion, put up a booth where tourists could pay the expected two bits, and added a relic shop that he supplied from the endless trove of broken and twisted fragments in the sides of the pit. He laid out paths, and paved the main walkway to the Crater in flagstones. Within three years of the battle he was profiting enough to build the Crater Saloon, for the use of the guests. Sometimes veterans of the battle refused to pay his admission. Mr. Griffith waived it for them, at least those who were ex-Confederates.[19]

Griffith could not commence his enterprise immediately after the war, though. A year after Appomattox, Lieutenant Colonel James Moore of the U.S. Army was charged with the task of reinterring the hundreds of Union dead from the Petersburg siege. First he found the site for a cemetery, on a farm near the Vaughn Road, southeast of the city. Then, with a hundred men and ten wagons, he began a systematic sweep of every square foot of ground adjacent to the Union lines and every battlefield. His hundred men would line up at arm's length and stroll for a distance of five hundred yards, searching closely for signs of the disturbed earth that might disclose a grave. Stakes and blazes marked the ground they already covered. When the reburial detail neared the Crater it was confronted with the thickest mass of graves on the whole Petersburg front. Suffering miserably from the sight and smell of the decayed bodies, those involuntary sextons began hauling bodies away by the score. On the second anniversary of the battle they were busy at that site, and on that day alone three hundred bodies were exhumed from either the Crater or the trench graves outside it. Before Colonel Moore's men moved on, they found 669 bodies. A contemporary account notes that the dead who were found in common graves were remarkably well preserved. Still, not a man in the Crater could be identified, and it would have been incredibly good luck if none of General Elliott's buried South Carolinians was inadvertently reinterred as a Union soldier.[20]

All the dead were carted down the Vaughn Road and separated into individual graves in the new Poplar Grove National Cemetery. There they lie today, six thousand and more of them on the now-tranquil scene of another of William Mahone's victories. Somewhere beneath the four thousand stones marked "Unknown" are the bones of John Bross, from Illinois; Cornelius Kalaher, of Boston; Jeremiah Batchelder, of Hampton, New Hampshire; Wesley Stanley, of New York; and the gallant Christopher Pennell.[21]

Throughout the summer of 1866 the burial corps continued its work, and the federal government offered five dollars for every set of bones that was turned over with a skull intact. Many civilians reportedly went into the business of selling such remains, some of which were of a dubious Union character and questionable origin. Residents complained that the unearthing of so many decomposing bodies was responsible for a particularly virulent form of dysentery that swept Petersburg and killed a number of people.[22] Yet the burial corps — and Mr. Griffith, whose plow unearthed a mass grave of Negroes and whose sons might have been busy collecting five-dollar rewards — did not find all the victims of the Crater. More than six decades later, when the Griffith family had sold the land, it was remolded into a golf course. In 1931, in the course of building traps and smoothing the greens, workmen uncovered another twenty-nine skeletons. Identified as those of Union soldiers, they were collected in flag-draped coffins and removed to Poplar Grove. Townspeople looked on as these veterans rejoined their comrades, and a doughboy played "Taps."[23]

The next year, the federal government established the Petersburg National Military Park, and in 1936 the Crater was incorporated in the park. Except for a small archaeological dig in 1978, the terrain around the Crater has remained essentially undisturbed since that time. Despite the efforts of the unenviable burial corps, all the incentives of financial reward, and the opportunities for chance findings over a dozen decades, the probability exists that somewhere in the Virginia clay still lie the remains of men who struggled to capture or defend Elliott's Salient that sweltering 30th of July, 1864.[24]

CHAPTER VII

Conclusions

As might be expected from two assemblies as biased as the court of inquiry and the Committee on the Conduct of the War, neither really struck the mark in its assignment of blame. The weakness of the court's principal indictment — that the parapets were not leveled and the troops were thus misaligned — has already been demonstrated. Someone suggested it might have been desirable to provide the Crater position with immediate field artillery support, for which the Union trenches were not prepared, but as it turned out the maze of entrenchments behind the Confederate works would have prohibited such artillery from deploying.

The court's added criticism, that Burnside failed to withdraw Ledlie's division when it could not be advanced, ignores that the front was too narrow for an orderly withdrawal. Ledlie's troops would have had to pull back through Potter's and Willcox's men, and would have caused nearly the same disruption as the repulse of Ferrero's brigades. The court's finding in regard to General Meade, on the other hand, seems deliberately diluted. The conclusion that another officer ought to have had command of all the engaged troops "while the commanding general was not present in person to witness the operations" is simply another way of saying that Meade should have been there himself. This limp reproof borders on hypocrisy, following as it does the condemnation of three other officers for their failure to go near enough to the battle to exercise effective command over their troops.[1]

If there were a single culprit to be chosen, one might readily point to James H. Ledlie, who has been called "the Union's worst general."[2] Ledlie's apparent failure to relay the correct battle orders to his brigadiers was an essential element of the disaster. Had Bartlett and Marshall known what was expected of them, and had Ledlie's want of courage not prevented him from going out to reinforce those expectations, the first division could probably have been dissuaded from the self-protective impulse that led to defeat. It seems unlikely that Burnside erred in transmitting his own orders to Ledlie, for he did so in the presence of Willcox and Potter, both of whom understood him perfectly.

There have been many attempts to place the responsibility squarely on Burnside for choosing Ledlie to lead the assault. All such attempts were necessarily made after Ledlie's incompetence and cowardice became matters of public knowledge: prior to the Crater, they were not. Ledlie had come highly recommended by General John Foster, one of

Burnside's most trusted friends. His first action with the IX Corps had been south of the North Anna River, where he wasted his isolated brigade against a fortified Confederate battery, but that fiasco went unseen even by Ledlie's division commander. Burnside, who had been on the other side of the river, knew the story only through Ledlie's own report, in which he characterized his bloody repulse as heroic defence. His drunken neglect of duty at Petersburg on June 17 was hidden from his superiors by his personal staff officers, some of whom were already developing an outright contempt for him. (Burnside blamed that day's failure on the heavy artillerymen, whose absence from the battle may actually have been Ledlie's fault.) Charles Mills, a Massachusetts officer serving as Ledlie's aide, wrote after the North Anna debacle that he still thought Ledlie had considerable ability. "He is brave to rashness in a fight," Mills added, with unintended irony. Just after the Crater, though he blamed the defeat on Ferrero's men, that same officer said of Ledlie "I never met a man so thoroughly blackguard, . . . or one who had less sense of his duty."[3] Ledlie's greatest capacity seemed to be the ability to conceal his mistakes. Burnside had some confidence in him, for he regularly supported efforts to have his commission confirmed. And even if rumors of Ledlie's incompetence drifted up to headquarters, Burnside would have been the last to pay them heed: it had been just such a campaign of rumors that had destroyed his effectiveness as commander of the Army of the Potomac. But General Grant, who admitted he knew of the choice of Ledlie before the battle, said he considered him the "worst" division commander in the IX Corps. If that were so, Grant was even more culpable than Burnside for allowing him to lead the assault. Grant's statement, however, was made almost five months after the battle, and it is not likely he thought so poorly of Ledlie before the Crater as after.[4] He was either deluding himself or exercising his usual generosity in accepting responsibility — or both.

If the choice of Ledlie resulted in disaster, the search for ultimate blame degenerates into a philosophical analysis of causality. The corps commander chose him by trusting to luck. Ambrose Burnside had always been a gambler — at cards, in business, and on the battlefield — and except for the Battle of Fredericksburg his luck had been very good during this war. So Burnside can be held to account for his gambler's instinct. That same logic carries on to Meade, whose interference with Burnside's original plan made necessary the choice that put Ledlie's division in front: had Meade only allowed his subordinate to carry out his initial scheme, all might have been well.

That is probably true. Untried as they were, Ferrero's own men were extremely eager and they knew exactly what they were supposed to do. Had the colored troops been loosed in the confusion of the moments after the explosion, the Confederates would have been in a poor position to mount even as stiff a resistance as those same Negro troops later overcame. Even General Grant admitted they could probably have done it. And when General Warren was asked by the court of inquiry what might have been done to improve the chances of success, he said the leading element ought to have diverged to the left and right, to sweep the Confederate lines and protect the flanks — precisely the tactical plan Burnside had originally submitted to Meade.[5]

This line of reasoning leads to the conclusion that General Meade deserves the greatest censure; the responsibility does not continue to Grant because Meade seems never to have presented Burnside's entire plan to him. The congressional committeemen came to that same essential determination, though no one has questioned whether Grant knew Burnside's full plan until now.

Yet the process should go further. Why, for instance, did Meade interfere? He may truly have feared the competence of a green division, or the political consequences of sacrificing black troops. Looking at the correspondence of early July, however, one gets the impression that Meade felt a compelling need to assert his authority as army commander; he felt it with Ambrose Burnside more than with anyone else. Burnside had previously been his superior, and he still outranked him in the usual manner of determining seniority. Especially after Burnside's message of July 3, Meade might have been expected to guard his prerogative with some jealousy. It is not unreasonble to suppose he was looking for a chance to exercise that prerogative in some noticeable but seemingly insignificant manner, as a frustrated editor might shuffle some punctuation in an aggravatingly perfect manuscript. Just as the rearrangement of critical punctuation marks can render an excellent essay gibberish, changes in the vital elements of a battle order can transform certain victory into rout. It was Burnside's singular misfortune that Meade chose to tamper with such vital elements.

There was, aside from Meade's apprehension that Burnside was trying to wangle control of the army from him, his ossified opinion that the younger man was not a proper commander. He had come to that belief in the winter of 1862 and 1863, when the ever-humble Burnside — beset by prodding superiors and unsupportive subordinates — was frequently heard despairing of his ability to lead the Army of the Potomac. Though at first Meade felt Burnside's worst problem was his own admission of self-doubt, Meade had since joined the majority of eastern army officers in the conclusion that Burnside was wholly incompetent to command anything at all.[6] Whenever there was a mixup between Burnside and another corps commander, Meade tended to assume that Burnside was at fault, and he had been incredibly short with him all summer.[7] The same undercurrent of contempt permeated most of the various staffs throughout the rest of the army, and was extended to the IX Corps in general. As Walt Whitman's brother expressed it, "our Corps never had a fair chance since we came in this Army."[8]

That pervasive attitude contributed both to the train of thought that led Meade to discount Burnside's arrangements and to the undue readiness of the other corps and division commanders to withdraw from what was perceived as Burnside's fight. When things looked grim, but Burnside was still advocating a continuation of the struggle, the other commanders would have had to harbor a particular respect for his opinion in order to be persuaded. They had long since abandoned any such respect, if indeed they ever bore it, and he had a reputation for head-butting when his offensives floundered; an excellent opportunity was thereby squandered at midmorning on July 30.

One thing is certain. Whoever or whatever precipitated the failure of the assault, it was Meade's direct order — abetted by the aforementioned lack of confidence in Burnside — that turned mere repulse into calamity. After the general order to withdraw, the men in the Crater found it difficult to defend themselves because every Confederate for a quarter-mile in either direction was permitted to turn his attention on them, keeping their heads down or blocking their retreat with that fearful crossfire. The worst carnage was in the Crater, which remained a relatively safe location until Meade called off the other three corps; thereafter the IX Corps was on its own, and the mortars were able to close in for their almost leisurely slaughter of men who could neither fight back nor run.

For all of that, the extent of the disaster could have been drastically reduced at a much earlier moment. Well before six o'clock, Henry Pleasants had come to General Potter with a badly blistered hand. Pleasants, acting as Potter's volunteer aide that day, had been on the other side of the Crater trying to move Ledlie's division forward. The men would not budge from the rifle pits they were digging, no matter how brutally the volatile Pleasants slapped them with his saber. His only reward for his trouble was the blisters.[9] Though Burnside missed the early note from Loring on this subject, such reports eventually filtered back to him. This had been the obstacle he had feared more than anything. Had Burnside — or Meade, for that matter — called off the assault at that first hitch, the Union casualties could have been counted in the dozens. It would probably have been unreasonable to expect either of them to fritter away so fair a chance, but especially so for Burnside, who neither had, nor wished to usurp, authority to cancel the operation. But more compelling than this was the fact that, in the eyes of the army and the public, this was his mine. He had done it all himself, and if there was a failure anywhere between the fuse and the end of the fight, he knew he would be held accountable. In fact it was smugly supposed by many that he would not succeed. Thus, the general disdain for Burnside and his corps serves to explain both why he was reluctant to give up the contest and why his fellow commanders were willing to let him get out of his scrape by himself. As in other battles of this and every war, the principal villains were jealously and prejudice at the highest levels.

INTRODUCTION TO THE APPENDICES

Appendix A lists Union and Confederate forces involved in the battle of the Crater on July 30, 1864. Of the Union infantry units, only those who were involved in the actual assault on the exploded fort are listed. Union artillery units listed only include those who fired on the Confederate positions opposing the assaulting infantry units (See *O.R. Atlas* Plate LXIV, No. 3). All other Union units on the Petersburg line, although they may have made demonstrations or fired on Confederate positions to the right and left of Elliott's Salient, are not included. Likewise, Confederate forces not involved in the fighting against the assaulting IX and X Corps forces are not included.

Appendix B, Union and Confederate casualties, is derived from the *Official Records* and the research of Mr. Bryce Suderow in his article in the June-July, 1985 issue of *The Kepi* magazine. Using the standard sources, Mr. Suderow has expanded his research by consulting local Southern newspapers printed right after the battle. The authors of this book have updated these figures when new information became available, such as the latest Virginia Regimental Histories Series volumes in print. These final figures, we believe, constitute the most up-to-date casualty figures available. It must be noted that killed totals will almost always be higher due to the mortally wounded soldiers who died after the figures were reported, plus the fact that some units only reported total casualties.

Appendix D, like Appendix A, lists Union and Confederate units involved in the fighting at Deep Bottom on July 27, 28, and 29. For Confederate casualties at Deep Bottom, we again rely on the work of Mr. Suderow. This time we use his manuscript, "The First Battle of Deep Bottom, Virginia, July 26 to 29, 1864," for the most updated listing of Confederate losses. We would like to offer our sincere thanks Mr. Suderow for allowing us to quote extensively from his findings.

Abbreviations used in the appendices are: (K) killed in action; (MW) mortally wounded in action; (W) wounded; (P) taken prisoner or missing.

APPENDIX A

ORGANIZATION OF FEDERAL FORCES AT THE BATTLE OF THE CRATER PETERSBURG, VIRGINIA — JULY 30, 1864[1]

UNITED STATES ARMY
LIEUTENANT GENERAL ULYSSES S. GRANT
Commander-In-Chief

Adjutant General & Chief of Staff — Brigadier General John A. Rawlins
Assist. Adjutant General — Lieutenant Colonel Theodore S. Bowers
Assist. Adjutant General — Captain Ely S. Parker
Assist. Inspector General — Lieutenant Colonel William L. Duff
Assist. Quartermaster — Captain Henry W. Janes
Aide de Camp — Colonel Orville E. Babcock
Aide de Camp — Colonel Cyrus B. Comstock
Aide de Camp — Lieutenant Colonel Frederick T. Dent
Aide de Camp to General Rawlins — Lieutenant William M. Dunn
Aide de Camp — Major Peter T. Hudson
Aide de Camp — Colonel Horace Porter
Chief Commissary — Lieutenant Colonel Michael R. Morgan
Chief Quartermaster — Brigadier General Rufus Ingalls
Military Secretary — Lieutenant Colonel Adam Badeau
Military Secretary — Lieutenant Colonel William R. Rowley

ARMY OF THE POTOMAC
MAJOR GENERAL GEORGE GORDON MEADE
Commanding

Chief of Artillery — Brigadier General Henry J. Hunt
Chief Engineer — Major James C. Duane
Chief of Staff — Andrew A. Humphreys
Volunteer Engineer Brigade — Brigadier General Henry W. Benham
Battalion U. S. Engineers — Captain George H. Mendell
Provost Guard — Brigadier General Marsena R. Patrick
Signal Corps — Captain Benjamin F. Fisher

NINTH ARMY CORPS
MAJOR GENERAL AMBROSE E. BURNSIDE
Commanding

Aide de Camp — Lieutenant Colonel James L. Van Buren
Assist. Inspector General — Lieutenant Colonel Charles G. Loring
Chief of Staff — Brigadier General Julius White
Escort — 3rd New Jersey Cavalry (detachment) — Lieutenant John S. Hough

Provost Guard — 8th United States — Captain Milton Cogswell

FIRST DIVISION — Brigadier General James H. Ledlie
  First Brigade — Brigadier General William Francis Bartlett (P)
      Lieutenant Colonel Joseph H. Barnes
    21st Massachusetts — Captain William H. Clark (MW)
    29th Massachusetts — Lieutenant Colonel Joseph H. Barnes
      Captain Willard D. Tripp
    56th Massachusetts — Captain Charles D. Lamb
    57th Massachusetts — Major Albert Prescott (K)
      Captain George H. Howe (K)
      Lieutenant Albert Doty
    59th Massachusetts — Colonel Jacob Parker Gould (MW)
      Lieutenant Colonel John Hodges, Jr. (K)
      Captain Ezra Palmer Gould
    100th Pennsylvania — Major Thomas J. Hamilton (W & P)
      Captain Joseph H. Pentecost
  Second Brigade — Colonel Elisha G. Marshall (P)
      Lieutenant Colonel Gilbert P. Robinson
    3rd Maryland Battalion — Lieutenant Colonel Gilbert P. Robinson
      Captain David J. Weaver
    14th New York Heavy Artillery — Major Charles Chipman
    179th New York — Major John Barton (K)
      Captain Albert A. Terrill
    2nd Pennsylvania Provisional Heavy Artillery (112th Penn. Regt.) —
      Lieutenant Colonel Benjamin Griffin Barney (W)
      Captain James W. Haig

  Acting Engineers
    35th Massachusetts — Captain Clifton Aurelius Blanchard

SECOND DIVISION — Brigadier General Robert B. Potter
  First Brigade — Colonel Zenas R. Bliss
    36th Massachusetts — Captain Thaddeus L. Barker
    58th Massachusetts — Captain Everett S. Horton
    2nd New York Mounted Rifles — Colonel John Fisk
    51st New York — Major John G. Wright (W)
      Captain George Washington Whitman
    45th Pennsylvania — Captain Theodore Gregg
    48th Pennsylvania — Colonel Henry Pleasants
    4th Rhode Island — Major James T. P. Bucklin
  Second Brigade — Brigadier General Simon G. Griffin
    31st Maine — Captain James Dean
    32nd Maine — Captain Joseph B. Hammond
    2nd Maryland — Lieutenant Colonel Henry Howard, Jr. (MW)
      Captain James H. Wilson

122

6th New Hampshire — Captain Samuel G. Goodwin
9th New Hampshire — Captain John B. Cooper
11th New Hampshire — Captain Arthur C. Locke
17th Vermont — Lieutenant Colonel Charles Cummings

Acting Engineers
7th Rhode Island — Captain Percy Daniels

THIRD DIVISION — Brigadier General Orlando B. Willcox
First Brigade — Brigadier General John Hartranft
8th Michigan — Lieutenant Colonel Ralph Ely
27th Michigan (1st & 2nd Cos. Mich. S.S. attached)
Captain Edward S. Leadbeater
109th New York — Captain Edwin Evans
13th Ohio Dismounted Cavalry — Colonel Noah H. Hixon
51st Pennsylvania — Colonel William J. Bolton (W)
Major Lane S. Hart
37th Wisconsin — Colonel Samuel Harriman
38th Wisconsin (5 Cos.) — Lieutenant Colonel Colwert K. Pler

Second Brigade — Colonel William Humphrey
1st Michigan Sharpshooters — Captain Elmer C. Dicey (P)
2nd Michigan — Captain John L. Young (K)
Captain Ebenezer C. Tullock
20th Michigan — Lieutenant Colonel Byron M. Cutcheon
24th New York Cavalry (Dismounted) — Lieutenant Colonel Walter C. Newberry
46th New York — Captain Alphons Serviere
60th Ohio (9th & 10th Cos. Ohio S.S. attached) — Major Martin Avery
50th Pennsylvania — Lieutenant Colonel Edward Overton, Jr.

Acting Engineers
17th Michigan — Colonel Constant Luce

FOURTH DIVISION — Brigadier General Edward Ferrero
First Brigade — Lieutenant Colonel Joshua K. Sigfried
27th U.S.C.T. — Lieutenant Colonel Charles J. Wright (W)
30th U.S.C.T. — Colonel Delevan Bates (K)
— Lieutenant Colonel Hiram A. Oakman
39th U.S.C.T. — Colonel Ozora P. Stearns
43rd U.S.C.T. — Lieutenant Colonel H. Seymour Hall (W)
— Captain Jesse Wilkinson

Second Brigade — Colonel Henry Goddard Thomas
19th U.S.C.T. — Lieutenant Colonel Joseph G. Perkins
23rd U.S.C.T. — Colonel Cleveland J. Campbell
28th U.S.C.T. — Colonel Charles S. Russell

29th U.S.C.T. — Lieutenant Colonel John A. Bross (K)
Major T. Jefferson Brown
31st U.S.C.T. — Captain Thomas Wright

Artillery Brigade — Lieutenant Colonel J. Albert Monroe[2]
Maine Light, 2nd Battery (B) — Captain Albert F. Thomas
Maine Light, 3rd Battery (C) — Captain Ezekiel R. Mayo
Maine Light, 7th Battery (G) — Captain Adelbert B. Twitchell
Massachusetts Light, 11th Battery — Captain Edward J. Jones
New York Light, 19th Battery — Captain Edward W. Rogers
New York Light, 34th Battery — Captain Jacob Roemer
Pennsylvania Light, Battery D — Captain George W. Durell
Vermont Light, 3rd Battery — Captain Romeo H. Start
Mortar Battery (2nd Penn. Prov. H. A.) — Captain Benjamin F. Smiley

FIFTH CORPS ARTILLERY — Colonel Charles S. Wainwright
1st New York Light, Battery B — Lieutenant Robert E. Rogers
1st New York Light, Battery E — Lieutenant James B. Hazelton
1st New York Light, Battery H — Captain Charles E. Mink
5th United States, Battery D — Lieutenant William E. Van Reed

SIXTH CORPS ARTILLERY — Captain William Hexamer
Maine Light, 4th Battery (D) — Lieutenant Charles W. White
New York Light, 3rd Battery — Captain William A. Harn

ARMY OF THE JAMES
MAJOR GENERAL BENJAMIN BUTLER
Commanding

SIEGE ARTILLERY — Colonel Henry L. Abbot
1st Connecticut Heavy Artillery — Colonel Henry L. Abbot
Company A — Captain Edward A. Gillett
Company B — Captain Albert F. Booker
Company M — Captain Franklin A. Pratt

EIGHTEENTH ARMY CORPS
MAJOR GENERAL EDWARD O. C. ORD
Commanding
Chief Engineer — Captain Francis U. Farquhar

TENTH ARMY CORPS
(Attached to the Eighteenth Army Corps)

SECOND DIVISION — Brigadier General John W. Turner
First Brigade — Colonel N. Martin Curtis
3rd New York — Captain George W. Warren
112th New York — Lieutenant Colonel John F. Smith

124

117th New York — Lieutenant Colonel Rufus Daggett
142nd New York — Lieutenant Colonel Albert M. Barney

Second Brigade — Lieutenant Colonel William B. Coan
47th New York — Captain Charles A. Moore
48th New York — Major Samuel M. Swartwout (K)
Captain William H. Dunbar
76th Pennsylvania — Major William S. Diller
97th Pennsylvania — Captain Isaiah Price

Third Brigade — Colonel Louis Bell
13th Indiana (3 Cos.) — Lieutenant Samuel M. Zent
9th Maine — Captain Robert J. Gray
4th New Hampshire — Captain Frank W. Parker
115th New York — Lieutenant Colonel Nathan J. Johnson
169th New York — Major James A. Colvin

* * * * * * * *

ORGANIZATION OF CONFEDERATES AT THE
BATTLE OF THE CRATER
PETERSBURG — JULY 30, 1864

ARMY OF NORTHERN VIRGINIA[3]
GENERAL ROBERT E. LEE
Commanding

Aide de Camp & Assist. Military Secretary — Major Charles Marshall
Aide de Camp & Assist. Adjutant General — Colonel Walter H. Taylor
Aide de Camp & Assist. Inspector General — Major Charles S. Venable
Chief of Artillery — Brigadier General William N. Pendleton
Chief Commissary — Lieutenant Colonel Robert G. Cole
Chief Engineer — Colonel Walter Husted Stevens
Chief of Ordnance — Lieutenant Colonel Briscoe G. Baldwin
Chief Quartermaster — Lieutenant Colonel James L. Corley
Judge Advocate General — Major Henry E. Young
Medical Director — Surgeon Lafayette Guild
Military Sect. & Act. Assist. Chief of Artillery — Colonel Armistead L. Long

THIRD CORPS
MAJOR GENERAL AMBROSE P. HILL
Commanding

RICHARD H. ANDERSON'S DIVISION — Brigadier General William
Mahone
Mahone's (VA.) Brigade — Colonel David Weisiger (W)
Colonel George Thomas Rogers

6th Virginia — Colonel George Thomas Rogers
  Lieutenant Colonel Henry Watson Williamson (W)
12th Virginia — Captain Richard W. Jones
16th Virginia — Lieutenant Colonel Richard Owen Whitehead
41st Virginia — Major William H. Etheridge
61st Virginia — Lieutenant Colonel William H. Stewart

Wilcox (Ala.) Brigade — Colonel John C. C. Sanders
8th Alabama — Captain M. W. Mordecai
9th Alabama — Colonel J. Horace King
10th Alabama — Captain W. L. Brewster
11th Alabama — Lieutenant Colonel George Edward Tayloe
14th Alabama — Captain Elias Folk (K)

Wright's (GA.) Brigade — Lieutenant Colonel Matthew R. Hall
3rd Georgia — Lieutenant Colonel Claiborne Snead
22nd Georgia — Colonel George H. Jones
48th Georgia — Lieutenant Colonel Reuben W. Carswell
64th Georgia — Colonel John W. Evans (K)
  Colonel Walter H. Weems

ARTILLERY
ARMY OF NORTHERN VIRGINIA
BRIGADIER GENERAL WILLIAM N. PENDLETON
Chief of Artillery

FIRST CORPS — Lieutenant Colonel Frank Huger
Haskell's Battalion — Major John C. Haskell
  Branch (N.C.) Battery — Captain Henry G. Flanner
  Nelson (Va.) Battery — Captain James N. Lamkin

13th Battalion Virginia Light Artillery — Major Wade Hampton Gibbs (W)
Company A, Otey Battery — Captain David Norvell Walker
Company B, Ringgold Battery — Captain Crispin Dickenson
Company C, Davidson's Battery — Lieutenant John H. Chamberlayne
Battery of mortars manned by men from Otey and Ringgold Batteries—
  Lieutenant Jack Langhorne

THIRD CORPS — Colonel Reuben Lindsay Walker
Pegram's Battalion — Lieutenant Colonel William J. Pegram
  Crenshaw's (Va.) Battery — Captain Thomas Ellett
  Letcher (Va.) Light Artillery — Captain Thomas A. Brander

DEPARTMENT OF NORTH CAROLINA AND SOUTHERN VIRGINIA[4]
LIEUTENANT GENERAL PIERRE G. T. BEAUREGARD
Commanding

JOHNSON'S DIVISION — Major General Bushrod Rust Johnson
Ransom's (N.C.) Brigade — Colonel Lee M. McAfee
24th North Carolina — Colonel William John Clarke
25th North Carolina — Major William Simmons Grady (MW)
35th North Carolina — Colonel James Theodore Johnson
49th North Carolina — Lieutenant Colonel John A. Flemming (K)
Lieutenant Colonel James Taylor Davis
56th North Carolina — Captain Lawson Harrill
Elliott's (S.C.) Brigade — Brigadier General Stephen Elliott (W)
Colonel Fitz William McMaster
17th South Carolina — Colonel Fitz William McMaster
Major John R. Culp
18th South Carolina — Captain R. H. Glenn
22nd South Carolina — Colonel David G. Fleming (K)
Captain James Nelson Shedd
23rd South Carolina — Captain E. R. White (W)
26th South Carolina — Colonel Alexander D. Smith

Wise's (Va.) Brigade — Colonel J. Thomas Goode
26th Virginia — Captain Napoleon B. Street
34th Virginia — Major John R. Bagby
46th Virginia — Captain George Norris
59th Virginia — Captain Henry Wood (W)

HOKE'S DIVISION — Major General Robert F. Hoke
Clingman's (N.C.) Brigade — Brigadier General Thomas L. Clingman
61st North Carolina — Colonel James Dillard Radcliffe

Colquitt's (Ga.) Brigade (temporarily assigned to Johnson's Division) —
Brigadier General Alfred H. Colquitt
6th Georgia — Colonel John T. Lofton
19th Georgia — Colonel James H. Neal
23rd Georgia — Colonel James H. Huggins
27th Georgia — Major Hezekiah Bussey
28th Georgia — Captain John A. Johnson

ARTILLERY
DEPARTMENT OF SOUTHERN VIRGINIA AND NORTH CAROLINA
COLONEL HILARY POLARD JONES
Commanding

Branch's Battalion — Major James C. Coit
Halifax (Va.) Battery — Captain Samuel T. Wright
Petersburg (Va.) Battery — Captain Richard G. Pegram

APPENDIX B
CASUALTIES AT THE BATTLE OF THE CRATER
UNION FORCES[1]

	K&MW	Wounded	Missing	Total
NINTH CORPS				
1st Division · Staff	0	0	2	2
1st Brigade	28	105	148	281
2nd Brigade	27	106	197	330
Acting Engineers	10	28	3	41
Total 1st Division	65	239	350	654
2nd Division · Staff	0	0	0	0
1st Brigade	37	151	159	347
2nd Brigade	55	199	227	481
Acting Engineers	0	4	0	4
Total 2nd Division	92	354	386	832
3rd Division · Staff	1	0	0	1
1st Brigade	87	243	111	441
2nd Brigade	18	110	88	216
Acting Engineers	0	1	0	1
Total 3rd Division	106	354	199	659
4th Division · Staff	0	0	0	0
1st Brigade	54	333	168	555
2nd Brigade	155	364	253	772
Total 4th Division	209	697	421	1,327
Artillery Brigade	1	2	0	3
TOTAL NINTH CORPS	473	1,646	1,356	3,475

Total strength of the Ninth Corps on July 20, 1864 . . . . 15,272[2]

	K&MW	Wounded	Missing	Total
TENTH CORPS				
2nd Division · Staff	0	1	0	1
1st Brigade	3	29	0	32
2nd Brigade	14	103	19	136
3rd Brigade	14	102	38	154
TOTAL TENTH CORPS	31	235	57	323

Strength Tenth Corps, 2nd Division on July 20, 1864 . . . . . approx. 1,500[2]

	K&MW	Wounded	Missing	Total
TOTAL UNION ARMY	504	1,881	1,413	3,798

Strength Union Army at the Crater . . . . .approx. 16,772

NOTE: There were no reported casualties for the Union artillery involved.

128

CONFEDERATE FORCES
ARMY OF NORTHERN VIRGINIA[4]

	K & MW	Wounded	Missing	Total
A. P. HILL'S CORPS (III)				
Mahone's Division · Staff	0	1	0	1
Saunders's Ala. Brigade	n/a	n/a	n/a	89
Wright's Ga. Brigade	70	139	22	231
Weisiger's Va. Brigade	94	159	14	267
Total Mahone's Division	164 +	299 +	36 +	588

Strength Mahone's Division involved at the Crater . . . . . . approx. 2,250[5]

ARMY OF SOUTHERN VIRGINIA AND NORTH CAROLINA[6]

	K & MW	Wounded	Missing	Total
Johnson's Division				
Ransom's N.C. Brigade	17	60	8	85
Wise's Va. Brigade	25	86	0	111
Elliott's S.C. Brigade	125	222	351	698
Total Johnson's Division	167	368	359	894
Hoke's Division				
Clingman's N.C. Brigade (61st N.C.)	6	33	0	39
Colquitt's Ga. Brigade	4	27	0	31
Total Hoke's Division	10	60	0	70
Total A.S.V. & N.C.	177	428	359	964

Strength A.S.U. & N C. Division involved at the Crater . . . . approx. 6,600[7]

	K & MW	Wounded	Missing	Total
Confederate Artillery				
R. Pegram's Battery	22	0	8	30
Other Batteries	n/a	n/a	n/a	30
Total artillery	22 +	0 +	8 +	60[8]

Strength of Confederate artillery involved at the Crater . . . . . . approx. 580[9]

	K & MW	Wounded	Missing	Total
Total Confederate Casualties	361 +	727 +	403 +	1,612

Total Confederate strength involved at the Crater . . . . . . approx. 9,430[10]

* * * * * * * *

CONFEDERATE CASUALTIES IN THE EXPLOSION OF THE MINE[11]

	Killed	Wounded	Total
18th South Carolina Infantry	39	38	77
22nd South Carolina Infantry	n/a	n/a	170
Richard Pegram's Battery	22	0	22
Total	61 +	38 +	278

APPENDIX C

RECIPIENTS OF THE U.S. MEDAL OF HONOR
AND
CONFEDERATE ROLL OF HONOR
AT THE
BATTLE OF THE CRATER
****

CONFEDERATE ROLL OF HONOR[1]

ARMY OF NORTHERN VIRGINIA
MAHONE'S DIVISION

Saunders's Alabama Brigade
Sergeant John E. Deaton, Co. E, 8th Alabama Infantry
Captured the 2nd Michigan Infantry colors.
Private John M. Critcher, Co. K, 9th Alabama Infantry
Captured the 20th Michigan Infantry colors.
Private James N. Keeton, Co. G, 11th Alabama Infantry
Captured guidon, Stars and Stripes, regiment unknown.

Weisiger's Brigade
Private Walter B. Wellons, Co. H, 6th Virginia Infantry
Captured the 11th New Hampshire Infantry colors.
Lieut. Colonel Richard Owen Whitehead, F&S, 16th Virginia Infantry
Captured Union Stars and Stripes.
Captain Leroy Richardson Kilby, Co. B, 16th Virginia Infantry
Captured the 100th Pennsylvania Infantry colors.
Lieutenant Joseph B. Goodwin, Co. F, 16th Virginia Infantry
Captured Union Stars and Stripes.
Corporal Solomon V. Butler, Co. D, 16th Virginia Infantry
Captured the 28th U.S.C.T. colors.
Private David Barnes, Co. G, 16th Virginia Infantry
Captured Union Stars and Stripes.
Private Addison J. Sadler, Co. F, 16th Virginia Infantry
Captured the 58th Massachusetts Infantry state colors.
Private W. F. Lane, Co. G, 16th Virginia Infantry
Captured Union Stars and Stripes.
Private Lemuel Tucker, Co. B, 41st Virginia Infantry
Captured a portion of a Union flag and staff.
Private John W. Miles, Co. H, 41st Virginia Infantry
Captured Union regimental colors, regiment unknown.
Lieutenant St. Julien Wilson, Co. C, 61st Virginia Infantry
Captured the 57th Massachusetts Infantry colors.
Lieutenant Julius J. Billsoly, Co. D, 61st Virginia Infantry
Captured Union Stars and Stripes.

Reason not given for the awards to the following:
    Corporal B. F. Martin, Co. E, 61st Virginia Infantry
    Corporal T. R. Collins, Co. unkn., 61st Virginia Infantry
    Private William H. Cooper, Co. C, 61st Virginia Infantry
    Private R. S. Jones, Co. D, 61st Virginia Infantry
    Private A. Jackson, Co. F, 61st Virginia Infantry
    Private D. C. Cannou, Co. G, 61st Virginia Infantry
    Private J. T. Rushing, Co. I, 61st Virginia Infantry
    Private C. J. Falk, Co. K, 61st Virginia Infantry

Wright's Georgia Brigade
    Corporal Furney I. Herndon, Co. F, 3rd Georgia Infantry
    Captured the 58th Massachusetts Infantry colors.

MEMBERS OF MAHONE'S DIVISION CREDITED WITH THE CAPTURE OF UNION COLORS BUT NOT LISTED ON ROLL OF HONOR[2]

Weisiger's Brigade
    Sergeant Peter F. Howell, Co. G, 61st Virginia Infantry
    Captured Union regimental colors, regiment unknown.
    Corporal William H. Harrison, Co. A, 61st Virginia Infantry
    Captured the 31st Maine Infantry colors.
    Private John Edgar Foreman, Co. E, 61st Virginia Infantry
    Captured portion of staff and fringe, regiment unknown.

UNITED STATES MEDAL OF HONOR[3]

NINTH ARMY CORPS

First Division
    Captain Charles H. Houghton, Co. L, 14th New York Heavy Artillery
    Conspicuous gallantry.
    Sergeant James Hill, Co. C, 14th New York Heavy Artillery
    Capture of Confederate flag.
    Color Sergeant Conrad Homan, Co. A, 29th Massachusetts Infantry
    Fought way through enemy lines with regimental colors after all of color guard was killed or wounded.

Second Division
    Corporal Frank Hogan, Co. A, 45th Pennsylvania Infantry
    Captured flag of the 6th Virginia Infantry.
    Sergeant Major Abraham Cohn, 6th New Hampshire Infantry
    Bravely advanced on Confederate line under severe fire.
    Corporal Charles H. Knight, Co. I, 9th New Hampshire Infantry
    Entered Crater and although wounded took several Confederate prisoners back to Federal lines.

Sergeant Charles J. Simons, Co. A, 9th New Hampshire Infantry
One of first to enter crater and captured many prisoners. He was then captured, but escaped.

Sergeant Leander A. Wilkins, Co. H, 9th New Hampshire Infantry
Recaptured colors of the 21st Massachusetts Infantry in hand-to-hand fighting.

Lieutenant Harlan J. Swift, Co. H, 2nd New York Mounted Rifles
Captured four Confederates trying to reach their second line of entrenchments. Returned them to his regiment.

Sergeant William H. Mathews, Co. E, 2nd Maryland Infantry (Entered under name of Henry Sivel).
Came upon several Confederates of the 17th South Carolina Infantry. Killed one and took three prisoners.

Sergeant Benjamin F. McAlwee, Co. D, 3rd Maryland Infantry Battalion
Picked up a shell with a burning fuse, throwing it over the parapet into a ditch where it exploded.

Sergeant George Schnieder, Co. A, 3rd Maryland Infantry Battalion
After the color sergeant was shot down, he seized the colors and planted them on the enemy's works during a charge.

Private James Welsh, Co. E, 4th Rhode Island Infantry
Took charge of regimental colors when the color sergeant had been wounded and the color corporal was killed, saving the colors from capture.

Third Division
Sergeant Charles H. De Puy, Co. H, 1st Michigan Sharpshooters
Aided General Bartlett in working the guns of the exploded fort.

Corporal Sidney Haight, Co. E, 1st Michigan Sharpshooters
Stayed on line after his regiment retreated continuing fire on the enemy.

Private Charles M. Thatcher, Co. B, 1st Michigan Sharpshooters
Did not retreat and continued firing until captured.

Private Robert F. Dodd, Co. E, 27th Michigan Infantry
Assisted in carrying wounded from in front of the crater while under heavy fire.

Colonel Isaac S. Catlin, F & S, 109th New York Infantry
Wounded while trying to rally troops, he returned to action and again was wounded which cost him his leg.

Private Nathaniel Gwynne, Co. H, 13th Ohio Cavalry (Dismounted)
Only 15 years old, not yet mustered into service, he participated in a charge and lost his arm to a shell blast.

Fourth Division
Colonel Delavan Bates, F & S, 30th U.S. Colored Troops
Gallantry in action, fell shot in the face while in front of his regiment.

Lieutenant Andrew Davidson, Co. H, 30th U.S. Colored Troops
After his colonel, major and one-third of the regimental officers fell, he rallied the regiment and saved it from destruction.

Sergeant Decatur Dorsey, Co. B, 39th U.S. Colored Troops
Planted the colors on the Confederate works in advance of his regiment. Carrying the colors, he rallied the men when they were driven back to the Union works.

Captain Albert D. Wright, Co. G, 43rd U.S. Colored Troops
Advance beyond enemy lines and captured the colors and color guard and then was severely wounded.

EIGHTEENTH CORPS

First Division
Sergeant Walter Jamieson, Co. B, 139th New York Infantry
Although his regiment was not involved in the battle, he went out between the lines and carried a wounded officer back to the Union lines.

APPENDIX D

ORGANIZATION OF FEDERAL FORCES AT DEEP BOTTOM, VIRGINIA[1]
(Darbytown, Strawberry Plains, and New Market Road)

ARMY OF THE POTOMAC
MAJOR GENERAL GEORGE GORDON MEADE
Commanding

SECOND ARMY CORPS
MAJOR GENERAL WINFIELD SCOTT HANCOCK
Commanding

FIRST DIVISION — Brigadier General Francis C. Barlow
First Brigade — Brigadier General Nelson A. Miles
    28th Massachusetts — Major James Fleming
    26th Michigan — Captain Asa G. Dailey
    5th New Hampshire — Major James E. Larkin
    2nd New York Heavy Artillery — Major William A. McKay
    61st New York — Major George W. Scott
    81st Pennsylvania — Captain Lawrence Mercer
    140th Pennsylvania — Captain William A. F. Stockton
    183rd Pennsylvania — Major George T. Egbert

Consolidated Brigade — Colonel Levin Crandell
    7th New York (4 cos.) — Captain Jacob Scheu
    39th New York — Captain David A. Allen
    52nd New York — Captain Henry P. Ritzius
    57th New York — Captain George W. Jones
    63rd New York (6 cos.) — Captain Michael H. Kenneally
    69th New York (6 cos.) — Lieutenant James J. Smith
    88th New York (4 cos.) — Captain John Smith
    111th New York — Captain Lewis W. Husk
    125th New York — Captain Nelson Penfield
    126th New York — Lieutenant Henry M. Lee

Fourth Brigade — Lieutenant Colonel K. Oscar Broady
    7th New York Heavy Artillery — Major Edward A. Springsteed
    64th New York — Captain William Glenny
    66th New York — Lieutenant Nathaniel P. Lane
    53rd Pennsylvania — Captain Philip H. Schreyer
    116th Pennsylvania — Captain Garrett Nowlen
    145th Pennsylvania — Captain James H. Hamlin
    148th Pennsylvania — Captain James F. Weaver

Brigade Artillery Attached[2]
Massachusetts Light, 10th Battery — Captain J. Henry Sleeper
1st Rhode Island Light, Battery B — Captain T. Frederick Brown

SECOND DIVISION — Major General John Gibbon
First Brigade — Lieutenant Colonel Francis E. Pierce
19th Maine — Captain Joseph W. Spaulding
15th Massachusetts (2 cos.) — Captain Henry T. Dudley
20th Massachusetts (7 cos. & a detachment of 19th Mass.) —
Captain Henry L. Patten
1st Company (Andrew) Massachusetts S.S. — Captain Isaac N.
Mudgett
7th Michigan — Lieutenant Colonel Samuel N. Smith
1st Minnesota (2 cos.) — Captain James C. Farwell
59th New York — Lieutenant Colonel Horace P. Rugg
152nd New York — Major Timothy O'Brien
184th Pennsylvania (7 cos.) — Major Charles Kleckner
36th Wisconsin — Lieutenant Colonel Clement E. Warner

Second Brigade — Colonel Mathew Murphy
8th New York Heavy Artillery — Major Erastus M. Spaulding
155th New York — Major John Byrne
164th New York — Major John Beattie
170th New York — Colonel James P. McIvor
182nd New York (69th N.Y. National Guard Arty.) — Captain John
Coonam

Third Brigade — Colonel Thomas A. Smyth
14th Connecticut — Captain John C. Broatch
1st Delaware — Major William F. Smith
2nd Delaware (3 cos.) — Lieutenant Philip Johnson
12th New Jersey — Lieutenant Colonel Richard S. Thompson
10th New York (6 cos.) — Lieutenant Colonel George F. Hopper
108th New York — Captain William H. Andrews
4th Ohio (4 cos.) — Lieutenant Frank J. Spalter
69th Pennsylvania — Lieutenant Colonel William Davis
106th Pennsylvania (3 cos.) — Lieutenant Colonel John Irvin
7th West Virginia (4 cos.) — Captain Isaac B. Fisher

Brigade Artillery Attached
1st Pennsylvania Light, Battery F — Captain R. Bruce Ricketts
5th United States, Batteries C & I — Lieutenant James Gillis

THIRD DIVISION — Brigadier General Gershom Mott
First Brigade — Brigadier General P. Regis De Trobriand
20th Indiana — Lieutenant Colonel George W. Meikel
1st Maine Heavy Artillery — Colonel Daniel Chaplin

17th Maine — Lieutenant Colonel Charles B. Merrill
40th New York (6 cos.) — Captain Madison M. Cannon
73rd New York (5 cos. 74th New York attached) — Lieutenant Colonel
   Michael W. Burnes
86th New York — Major Michael B. Stafford
124th New York — Lieutenant Colonel Charles H. Weygant
99th Pennsylvania — Lieutenant Colonel Edwin R. Biles
110th Pennsylvania — Captain William Stewart
2nd U.S. Sharpshooters (8 cos.) — Captain Abraham Wright

Second Brigade — Colonel Daniel Chaplin
               Colonel Henry J. Madill
   1st Massachusetts Heavy Artillery — Major Nathaniel Shatswell
   5th Michigan — Colonel John Pulford
   93rd New York — Lieutenant Colonel Benjamin C. Butler
   57th Pennsylvania (8 cos.) — Lieutenant Colonel William B. Neeper
   63rd Pennsylvania — Lieutenant Colonel John A. Danks
   84th Pennsylvania — Major George Zinn
   105th Pennsylvania — Colonel Calvin A. Craig
   141st Pennsylvania — Lieutenant Colonel Casper W. Tyler
   1st U.S. Sharpshooters — Captain William G. Andrews

Third Brigade — Colonel Robert McAllister
   11th Massachusetts (7 cos.) — Major Abram L. Lockwood
   5th New Jersey — Captain Thomas C. Godfrey
   6th New Jersey — Lieutenant Colonel Stephen R. Gilkyson
   7th New Jersey — Captain Thomas C. Thompson
   8th New Jersey — Major Virgil M. Healy
   11th New Jersey — Lieutenant Colonel John Schoonover
   120th New York (1 co., 72nd New York attached)– Lieutenant Colonel
      John R. Tappen

Brigade Artillery Attached
   New Hampshire Light, 1st Battery — Captain Frederick M. Edgell
   Maine Light, 6th Battery (F) — Captain Edwin B. Dow
   New Jersey Light, 3rd Battery — Captain Christian Woerner

Artillery Brigade — Major John G. Hazard
   1st New Jersey Light, Battery B — Captain A. Judson Clark
   4th New York Heavy, Company D — Captain James H. Wood
   4th New York Heavy, Company L — Lieutenant Frank Seymour
   1st New York Light, Battery G — Captain Nelson Ames
   New York Light, 11th Battery — Captain John E. Burton
   New York Light, 12th Battery — Captain George F. McKnight
   1st Rhode Island Light, Battery A — Lieutenant Walter S. Perrin
   4th United States, Battery K — Lieutenant John W. Roder

ARMY OF THE JAMES[3]
MAJOR GENERAL BENJAMIN FRANKLIN BUTLER
Commanding

TENTH ARMY CORPS
MAJOR GENERAL DAVID B. BIRNEY
Commanding

FIRST DIVISION
  Third Brigade — Brigadier General Robert S. Foster
  10th Connecticut — Colonel John L. Otis
  11th Maine — Colonel Harris M. Plaisted
  1st Maryland Cavalry (dismounted) — Colonel Andrew W. Evans
  24th Massachusetts — Colonel Francis A. Osborn
  100th New York — Colonel George B. Dandy
  Connecticut Light Artillery, 1st Battery — Lieutenant George P. Bliss

NINETEENTH ARMY CORPS[4]
(Temporarily under command of the Tenth Army Corps)

SECOND DIVISION
  First Brigade — Brigadier General Henry W. Birge
  9th Connecticut — Colonel Thomas W. Cahill
  12th Maine — Colonel William R. Kimball
  14th Maine — Colonel Thomas W. Porter
  26th Massachusetts — Colonel Alpha B. Farr
  14th New Hampshire — Colonel Robert Wilson
  75th New York — Colonel Robert B. Merritt

CAVALRY CORPS[5]
MAJOR GENERAL PHILIP H. SHERIDAN
Commanding

FIRST DIVISION — Brigadier General Alfred T. A. Torbert
  First Brigade — Brigadier General George A. Custer
  1st Michigan — Lieutenant Colonel Peter Stagg
  5th Michigan — Colonel Russell A. Alger
  6th Michigan — Colonel James H. Kidd
  7th Michigan — Major Melvin Brewer
  3rd U.S. Artillery, Battery C — Lieutenant Colonel Dunbar R. Ransom

  Second Brigade — Colonel Thomas C. Devin
  4th New York — Colonel Louis P. DiCesnola
  6th New York — Major William E. Beardsley
  9th New York — Lieutenant Colonel George S. Nichols
  17th Pennsylvania — Lieutenant Colonel James Q. Anderson
  2nd U.S. Artillery, Batteries B & L — Lieutenant Edward Heaton

Reserve Brigade — Brigadier General Wesley Merritt
   19th New York (1st Dragoons) — Colonel Alfred Gibbs
   6th Pennsylvania — Major James Starr
   1st Rhode Island (8 cos.) — Major Preston M. Farrington
   1st United States — Captain Nelson B. Sweitzer
   2nd United States — Captain David S. Gordon
   5th United States — Lieutenant Jeremiah C. Denney
   2nd U.S. Artillery, Battery D — Lieutenant Edward B. Williston

SECOND DIVISION — Brigadier General David McM. Gregg
  First Brigade — Brigadier General Henry E. Davies, Jr.
   1st Massachusetts — Lieutenant Colonel Samuel E. Chamberlain
   1st New Jersey — Lieutenant Colonel John W. Kester
   10th New York — Colonel William Irvine
   6th Ohio — Colonel William Stedman
   1st Pennsylvania — Lieutenant Colonel David Gardner
   2nd U.S. Artillery, Battery A — Lieutenant W. Neil Dennison

  Second Brigade — Colonel J. Irvin Gregg
   1st Maine — Major Sidney W. Thaxter
   2nd Pennsylvania — Lieutenant Colonel Joseph P. Brinton
   4th Pennsylvania — Major William M. Biddle
   8th Pennsylvania — Lieutenant Colonel Samuel Wilson
   13th Pennsylvania — Major George F. McCabe
   16th Pennsylvania — Lieutenant Colonel John K. Robinson

KAUTZ'S DIVISION (Army of the James) — Brigadier General August V. Kautz
  First Brigade — Colonel Robert M. West
   3rd New York — Colonel George W. Lewis
   5th Pennsylvania — Lieutenant Colonel Christopher Kleinz

  Second Brigade — Colonel Samuel P. Spear
   1st District of Columbia — Major J. Stannard Baker
   11th Pennsylvania — Major Franklin A. Stratton

  Artillery
   Wisconsin Light, 4th Battery — Captain George B. Easterly

UNITED STATES NAVY[6]
NORTH ATLANTIC BLOCKADING SQUADRON
ACTING REAR ADMIRAL SAMUEL PHILLIPS LEE
Commanding

James River Division — Captain Melancton Smith
  U.S.S. Agawam — Commander Alexander C. Rhind
  U.S.S. Mendota — Commander Edward T. Nichols

* * * * * * * *

138

CONFEDERATE FORCES[7]

DEPARTMENT OF RICHMOND
LIEUTENANT GENERAL RICHARD S. EWELL
Commanding

Reserves
   1st Regiment Virginia Reserves — Lieutenant Colonel Richard T. W. Duke

Cavalry Brigade — Brigadier General Martin W. Gary
   Hampton Legion — Colonel Thomas M. Logan
   7th South Carolina — Colonel Alexander Cheves Haskell
   24th Virginia — Colonel William Todd Robins

Unattached
   25th Virginia Battalion Infantry — Lieutenant Colonel Wyatt M. Eliott

Artillery Defences — Lieutenant Colonel John C. Pemberton
   First Division (Inner Line) — Lieutenant Colonel John W. Atkinson
   10th Virginia Battalion Heavy Artillery — Major James O. Hensley
   19th Virginia Battalion Heavy Artillery — Major N. R. Cary

Second Division (Inner Line) — Lieutenant Colonel James Howard
   18th Virginia Battalion Heavy Artillery — Major Mark B. Hardin
   20th Virginia Battalion Heavy Artillery — Major James E. Robertson

   Unattached — Louisiana Guard Artillery — Captain Charles A. Green

Light Artillery — Lieutenant Colonel Charles E. Lightfoot
   Carolina (Va.) Artillery — Captain Thomas R. Thornton
   2nd Nelson (Va.) Artillery — Captain J. Henry Rives
   Surry (Va.) Artillery — Captain James D. Hankins

Chaffin's Bluff — Lieutenant Colonel John M. Maury

Stark's Battalion Light Artillery — Major Alexander W. Stark
   Mathews (Va.) Artillery — Captain Andrew D. Armistead
   McComas (Va.) Artillery — Captain David A. French

ARMY OF NORTHERN VIRGINIA[8]
GENERAL ROBERT E. LEE
Commanding

FIRST CORPS
LEUTENANT GENERAL RICHARD H. ANDERSON
Commanding

KERSHAW'S DIVISION — Major General Joseph Brevard Kershaw

Kershaw's Brigade — Colonel John Williford Henagan
  2nd South Carolina — Colonel John D. Kennedy
  3rd South Carolina — Colonel William D. Rutherford
  7th South Carolina — Captain Elijah J. Goggans
  8th South Carolina — Lieutenant Colonel Eli T. Stackhouse
  15th South Carolina — Colonel John B. Davis
  3rd South Carolina Battalion — Lieutenant Colonel William Georg
    Rice

Humphrey's Brigade — Brigadier General Benjamin Grubb Humphrey
  13th Mississippi — Major George L. Donald
  17th Mississippi — Captain Jesse C. Cochran
  18th Mississippi — Colonel Thomas M. Griffin
  21st Mississippi — Colonel Daniel N. Moody

Wofford's Brigade — Brigadier General William T. Wofford
  16th Georgia — Major James S. Gholston
  18th Georgia — Colonel Joseph Armstrong
  24th Georgia — Colonel Christopher Columbus Sanders
  Cobb's Georgia Legion — Lieutenant Colonel Luther J. Glenn
  Phillips' Georgia Legion — Lieutenant Colonel Joseph Hamilton
  3rd Georgia Battalion S.S. — Lieutenant Colonel Nathan
    Hutchins, Jr.

Bryan's Brigade — Colonel James Phillip Simms
  10th Georgia — Colonel Wilis C. Holt
  50th Georgia — Colonel Peter McGlashan
  51st Georgia — Colonel Edward Ball
  53rd Georgia — Colonel Wiley F. Hartsfield, Jr.

THIRD CORPS
LIEUTENANT GENERAL AMBROSE POWELL HILL
Commanding

WILCOX'S DIVISION — Brigadier General James Conner[9]
Lane's Brigade — Colonel John Decatur Barry
  7th North Carolina — Captain James G. Harris
  18th North Carolina — Lieutenant Colonel John W. McGill
  28th North Carolina — Major Samuel N. Stowe
  33rd North Carolina — Captain W. J. Callais
  37th North Carolina — Colonel William M. Barbour

McGowan's Brigade — Lieutenant Colonel Isaac Foster Hunt
  1st South Carolina — Lieutenant Colonel Andrew P. Butler
  12th South Carolina — Captain Robert M. Kerr
  13th South Carolina — Major William Lester
  14th South Carolina — Lieutenant Colonel Edward Croft
  Orr's Rifles — Major William M. Haden (K)

HETH'S DIVISION — Major General Henry Heth
Davis' Brigade — Brigadier General Joseph R. Davis
   2nd Mississippi — Colonel John M. Stone
   11th Mississippi — Lieutenant Colonel William B. Lowry
   26th Mississippi — Colonel Arthur E. Reynolds
   42nd Mississippi — Lieutenant Colonel Andrew M. Nelson
   1st Confederate Battalion — Captain J. M. Johnson

Cooke's Brigade — Brigadier General John Rogers Cooke
   15th North Carolina — Lieutenant Colonel William H. Yarborough
   27th North Carolina — Colonel John A. Gilmer, Jr.
   46th North Carolina — Lieutenant Colonel Alexander C. McAllister
   48th North Carolina — Colonel Samuel H. Walkup

McRae's Brigade — Brigadier General William MacRae
   11th North Carolina — Colonel William J. Martin
   26th North Carolina — Colonel John R. Lane
   44th North Carolina — Colonel Thomas C. Singeltary
   47th North Carolina — Colonel George H. Faribault
   52nd North Carolina — Colonel Marcus A. Parks

Archer's Brigade — Brigadier General James J. Archer
   1st Tennessee — Lieutenant Colonel Newton J. George
   7th Tennessee — Lieutenant Colonel Samuel G. Shepard
   14th Tennessee — Colonel William McComb
   13th Alabama — Lieutenant Colonel James Aiken

Walker's Brigade — Brigadier General Birkett Davenport Fry
   22nd Virginia Battalion — Lieutenant Colonel Edward P. Tayloe
   40th Virginia — Lieutenant Colonel Arthur S. Cunningham
   47th Virginia — Colonel Robert M. Mayo
   55th Virginia — Colonel William S. Christian
   2nd Maryland Battalion — Lieutenant Colonel James R. Herbert

CAVALRY CORPS[10]

LEE'S (Fitzhugh) DIVISION — Major General Fitzhugh Lee
Wickham's Brigade — Brigadier General Williams Carter Wickham
   1st Virginia — Major Charles R. Irving
   2nd Virginia — Colonel Thomas T. Munford
   3rd Virginia — Colonel Thomas H. Owen
   4th Virginia — Colonel William H. Payne

Lomax's Brigade — Brigadier General Lunsford Lindsey Lomax
   5th Virginia — Colonel Reuben B. Boston
   6th Virginia — Colonel Julian Harrison
   15th Virginia — Captain John Cooper

LEE'S (W. H. F.) DIVISION — Major General William H. F. Lee
Barringer's Brigade — Brigadier General Rufus Barringer
1st North Carolina — Colonel William H. Cheek
2nd North Carolina — Colonel William P. Roberts
4th North Carolina — Colonel Dennis D. Ferebee
5th North Carolina — Lieutenant Colonel Stephen B. Evans

Chambliss' Brigade — Brigadier General John R. Chambliss, Jr.
9th Virginia — Colonel Richard L. T. Beale
10th Virginia — Colonel J. Lucius Davis
13th Virginia — Colonel Jefferson C. Phillips

ARTILLERY
ARMY OF NORTHERN VIRGINIA
BRIGADIER GENERAL WILLIAM NELSON PENDLETON
Chief of Artillery

SECOND CORPS — Brig. Gen. Armistead Lindsay Long
Brown's Battalion — Lieutenant Colonel Robert A. Hardaway
Powhatan (Va.) Artillery — Captain Willis J. Dance
2nd Company Richmond Howitzers — Captain Lorraine F. Jones
3rd Company Richmond Howitzers — Captain Benjamin H. Smith, Jr.
Rockbridge (Va.) Artillery — Captain Archibald Graham
Salem Flying (Va.) Artillery — Captain Charles B. Griffin

Carter's Battalion — Lieutenant Colonel Thomas H. Carter
Morris (Va.) Artillery — Captain Samuel H. Pendleton
Orange (Va.) Artillery — Captain Charles W. Fry
King William (Va.) Artillery — Captain William P. Carter
Jefferson Davis (Ala.) Artillery — Captain William J. Reese

Cutshaw's Battalion — Major Wilfred Emory Cutshaw
Charlottesville (Va.) Artillery — Captain James McD Carrington
Staunton (Va.) Artillery — Captain Asher W. Garber
Courtney (Va.) Artillery — Captain William A. Tanner

THIRD CORPS ARTILLERY — Colonel Reuben Lindsay Walker

Poague's Battalion — Lieutenant Colonel William T. Poague
Madison (Ms.) Artillery — Captain J. Richards
Albemarle (Va.) Artillery — Captain James W. Wyatt
Brooke (Va.) Artillery — Captain Addison W. Utterback
Charlotte (N.C.) Artillery — Captain Arthur B. Williams

* * * * * * * *

CASUALTIES AT DEEP BOTTOM, JULY 26 TO JULY 29, 1864[11]

UNION

	Killed	Wounded	Missing	Total
SECOND CORPS				
First Division	15	43	17	75
Second Division	0	17	28	45
Third Division	11	49	8	68
Artillery Brigade	0	0	0	0
Total II Army Corps	26	109	53	188

NOTE: Strength of Second Corps — 13,521

	Killed	Wounded	Missing	Total
TENTH CORPS — First Division				
Third Brigade (Foster)	5	51	0	56

NOTE: Strength of Foster's Brigade — 3,590

	Killed	Wounded	Missing	Total
XIX CORPS — Second Division				
First Brigade (Birge)	1	0	0	1

NOTE: Strength of Birge's Brigade — 2,600

	Killed	Wounded	Missing	Total
CAVALRY CORPS				
First Division	10	60	5	75
Second Division	20	118	28	166
Kautz's Division	0	2	0	2
Total Cavalry Corps	30	180	33	243

NOTE: Strength of Sheridan's Cavalry Corps, with Kautz's Division — 8,597

	Killed	Wounded	Missing	Total
Total Union	62	340	86	488

NOTE: Total Union Army Strength — 28,303[12]

CONFEDERATE[13]

	Killed	Wounded	Missing	Total
DEPARTMENT OF RICHMOND				
Cavalry Brigade (Grays)	4	36	3	43
1st Reg't. Va. Reserves		(Not Available)		
25th Va. Battl. Inf.		(Not Available)		
Artillery Defenses		(Not Available)		
Total Dept. of Richmond	4 +	36 +	3 +	43 +
ARMY OF NORTHERN VIRGINIA				
FIRST CORPS — Kershaw's Division				
Kershaw's Brigade	25	122	29	176
Humphrey's Brigade		(20 Total)	19	39
Wofford's Brigade		(Not Available)		
Bryan's Brigade		(Not Available)		
Total First Corps	35 +	132 +	48 +	215 +
THIRD CORPS				
Wilcox's Divison				
Lane's Brigade	11	50	77	138
McGowan's Brigade	21	153	65	239
Heth's Divison				
Davis' Brigade		(Not Available)		
Cooke's Brigade		(Not Available)		
McRae's Brigade		(Not Available)		
Archer's Brigade		(Not Available)		
Walker's Brigade (Fry)		(Not Available)		
Total Third Corps	32 +	203 +	142 +	377 +
CAVALRY CORPS				
Lee's (Fitzhugh) Division		(Not Available)		
Lee's (W. H. F.) Division		(Not Available)		
Total Cavalry Corps		(Not Available)		
ARTILLERY				
Second Corps	0	0	0	0
Third Corps		(Not Available)		
Total Artillery	0	0	0	0
TOTAL CONFEDERATE	71 +	371 +	193 +	635 +

NOTE: Total Confederate strength — 16,984[14]

APPENDIX E

Confederate Artillery at the Battle of the Crater

In a speech entitled "The Boy Gunners of Lee," delivered to the R. E. Lee Confederate Veterans Camp No. 1 in 1916, Jennings C. Wise, author of the classic two-volume *The Long Arm of Lee or The History of the Artillery of the Army of Northern Virginia,* spoke to the veterans about instances where the artillery of the Confederacy "saved Lee from defeat." He included, of course, the battle of the Crater. Few students of the Civil War would not include the Confederate artillery's performance on July 30, 1864 as one of their finest moments of the war. The target of over eighty Union guns and thousands of blueclad troops, they were able to maintain a constant fire on the Crater, the surrounding entrenchments, and the no-man's-land between the lines for over eight hours. Although many of the Confederate gunners were killed or wounded, not one of their batteries was put out of commission. They were able to pour a continuous fire into the confused blue mass until the Crater area was finally recaptured by the Confederates around 1 P.M.

Over the years the actual Confederate batteries present at the battle of the Crater were a mystery to many. Because of the fact that several of the battalions were split between the north and south sides of the Appomattox River, it became just as difficult to determine who was *not* there as who was there. Researching the usual sources, plus digging into actual battery records and papers, we are able to list for the first time, we believe, the batteries that were present, who commanded them, and what they did on July 30 to help win this very impressive Confederate victory.

The Confederate artillery south of the Appomattox River on the Petersburg line on July 30, 1864 was commanded by Lieutenant Colonel Frank Huger. He had taken temporary command from General E. Porter Alexander, the artillery commander of Longstreet's First Corps. Alexander was wounded in the hand in late June and was home on leave when the mine was sprung. General Beauregard's artillery was commanded by Colonel Hilary P. Jones.

The Confederate artillery in the battle was able to form a horseshoe-shaped ring around the Crater. Even though the Union spotters were supposed to have known exactly where each battery was located, save one (Haskell's mortars, along Jerusalem Plank Road), the Confederates were so expertly dug in and protected, the Union artillery was unable to eliminate them.[1]

The following, starting with Richard Pegram's blown-up battery, is a listing of the batteries as they were positioned on July 30, in clockwise order.

Captain Richard Pegram's Company Light Artillery (Va.). Formerly Branch's Field Artillery, also known as Lee's Life Guards and the Petersburg Artillery, this unit was made mostly from men from Petersburg and evolved from the 12th Virginia Infantry. At the time of the battle they were assigned to Major James C. Coit's battalion of Beauregard's Department of Southern Virginia and North Carolina. The target of Henry Pleasants's mine, they were at the apex of Elliott's Salient on July 30, equipped with four 12-pound Napoleons. Captain Richard Gregory Pegram, a cousin of Lieutenant Colonel William Pegram, commanded the battery but was not present at the explosion or the ensuing battle. Relieved after two days in the trenches by Lieutenants Hamlin and Chandler, Pegram was at his headquarters in Petersburg on the morning of the 30th. He hurried to the scene of the explosion but was sent back to his headquarters by Major Coit to find the rest of his battery's personnel. Pegram's two left guns were destroyed by the explosion. The two right guns, unharmed, were captured by Sergeant Wesley Stanley of the 14th New York Heavy Artillery and put into service against the Confederates until the late afternoon.[2]

The **13th Virginia Light Artillery Battalion** had three batteries placed on the line south of Pegram's battery. Park of Colonel Reuben Lindsay Walker's artillery of the Third Corps, Army of Northern Virginia, they were commanded by Major Wade Hampton Gibbs on July 30, who was severely wounded when he took charge of an abandoned gun. Command was then assumed by Captain David Norvell Walker of Otey's battery. Major William Miller Owen of the Washington Light Artillery (La.) took command of the battalion the next day. The following are the three batteries of the 13th Virginia Battalion involved in the fighting on the south side of the Crater.[3]

Company C — Davidson's Battery. Named for Captain George S. Davidson. The battery was commanded by Captain John Hampden Chamberlayne, who was away on sick leave on July 70. The battery was temporarily commanded by Lieutenant James C. Otey and equipped with two 12 pound Napoleons. Their exact position was on the Confederate line 373 yards south of the Crater, south of but touching Baxter Road. Only one gun, the left, was in a position to fire on the Crater area but was very effective. Right after the explosion Lieutenant Otey fled in fear and the gun was taken over by battalion commander Gibbs, along with staff from Alexander's command and Major Preston of Wise's brigade. Also, Chamberlayne, leaving the hospital, returned to his battery and assisted in its operation the rest of the day. After Gibbs's wounding, the battery was commanded by Captain David Walker.[4]

Company A — Otey Battery. Named for Captain George G. Otey, who died on October 21, 1862. They were equipped with two 12-pound

Napoleons and commanded by Captain David Norvell Walker on July 30. They were on the Confederate line south of the Crater, 100 yards south of Davidson's Battery. When Walker went to command Davidson's battery, after the wounding of Gibbs's, the guns were commanded by Lieutenant Jack Langhorne.[5]

Company B — Ringgold's Battery. Formerly Captain Timothy H. Stamps's Battery. Commanded by Captain Crispin Dickerson on July 30, equipped with four 12 pound Napoleons, their position was on the Confederate line 100 yards south of Otey's Battery. Guns were kept loaded with a double load of grape and canister and kept in a position aimed at the Elliott's Salient area. During the battle, Captain Alexander F. Bagby of the 34th Virginia (Wise's brigade) was assigned to the guns and was killed in action. Only two of the four guns were in a position to fire on the Crater area.[6]

Langhorne's Battery. Made up of "10 to 12" men from Otey's Battery and "3 or 4" men from Ringgold's Battery, this temporary battery was commanded by Captain John (Jack) B. Langhorne of Otey's Battery. They were equipped with three mortars (12-pound Coehorns) from the "Mortar Train" in late June or early July, 1864. Their position was about 100 to 150 yards to the rear of Otey's battery near the south side of Baxter Road, beside a bombproof, said to be about 400 yards from the Crater. During the battle Langhorne was sent back to his battery and his place was taken by Sergeant A. Whit Smith of Otey's Battery.[7]

Major John C. Haskell's Battalion was made up of batteries from various Confederate states and was assigned to Longstreet's First Corps, Army of Northern Virginia. The battalion only had Lamkin's and Flanner's batteries on the Petersburg line on July 30. Assigned 16 mortars (probably all 12-pound Coehorns) by Alexander, they lined up along the east side of Jerusalem Plank Road from Baxter Road to near the Blandford cemetery with six mortars. The rest of their mortars were placed further east in the many ravines and bombproofs between the Crater and the Jerusalem Plank Road. They were ordered by General Alexander, before he left the front on leave, to place their mortars, but not to dig in or throw up breastworks so that the enemy would not detect their location.[8]

Captain Henry G. Flanner's Battery. Company F, 13th Battalion North Carolina Artillery. Formerly 1st Company, Company H, 40th Regiment N.C. Troops (3rd Regiment N.C. Artillery.) Commanded by Captain Flanner, assigned to Haskell's Battalion, the battery was posted with six 12-pound Napoleons on the east side of the Jerusalem Plank Road at the intersection with Baxter Road. Flanner boasted after the war that his battery "is entitled to the credit of preventing the Federal army from entering Petersburg." Strong claim, but Flanner's battery was very important to the Confederate defence on July 30 and was a target for many Union guns.[9]

Captain James Nelson Lamkin's Company Va. Light Artillery (Co. B). Known as one of the two Nelson Light Artillery units from Nelson County, they were also known as Captain Woodville Latham's Company. The were sent from South Carolina in early May, 1864 where they left their field pieces. Captain Lamkin, assisted personally by Haskell, commanded the two 12-pound Coehorn mortars that moved to within 50 yards of the Crater on July 30 and poured devastating fire on the mass of Union troops in the Crater.[10]

Lieutenant Colonel William J. Pegram's Battalion, assigned to the Third Corps artillery, Army of Northern Virginia, commanded by Colonel Reuben Lindsay Walker, had two batteries in action on the day of the battle.

Letcher Artillery, Richmond. Known as Captain Greenlee Davidson's Company Va. Light Artillery (Davidson was killed on May 3, 1863 at Chancellorsville). Commanded on July 30 by Captain Thomas Alexander Brander, this battery was part of the Provisional Army of Virginia and assigned to Lieutenant Colonel Pegram's Battalion at the time of the battle. The battery of four 12-pound Napoleons was brought up with Ellet's battery after the explosion and posted on Cemetery Hill approximately 300 to 400 yards northwest of the Crater.

Captain Thomas Ellet's Company Va. Light Artillery. Formerly Captain William Crenshaw's Company Va. Light Artillery, they were also part of Lieutenant Colonel Pegram's Battalion on July 30. Commanded by Captain Ellet, they were equipped with four 12 pound Napoleons and were placed next to Brander's Battery on Cemetery Hill. Both Ellet's and Brander's batteries may have arrived with Mahone's men from a part of the Confederate line well south of the City of Petersburg.[11]

Captain Samuel T. Wright's Company Va. Heavy Artillery. Known as the Halifax Artillery of Halifax County, they served as Company C, 12th Battalion Louisiana Heavy Artillerty (DeGournay's Battalion). When DeGournay's command was sent to the Department of Mississippi, Wright's Battery stayed behind in Virginia. Wright was assigned to Coit's Battalion, Beauregard's department, and was in command at the time of the battle. Posted on a hill 100 or so yards to the rear of McAfee's N.C. brigade and 555 yards northwest of the Crater, they, along with Davidson's battery, were recognized as providing the most effective fire on the Union troops. It was said that Wright's Battery fired 500 to 600 shell and canister that day. The ground was torn up all around them by Union mortars but they were unable to knock out this battery.[12]

BIBLIOGRAPHY

Articles

Adams, Capt. J. C. (30th U.S.C.T.). "Battle of the Crater," *National Tribune,* June 25, 1903.

Anderson, Colonel James (Union officer). "In the Trenches at Petersburg," *Confederate Veteran,* Volume XXXIV, No. 1, (January, 1926), p. 23.

"Annals of the War, Chapters of Unwritten History; The Petersburg Mine," *Philadelphia Weekly Times,* April 24, 1880.

Bacon, James T. "Capt. George B. Lake," (22nd South Carolina Inf.). *Confederate Veteran,* Volume II, No. 5, (May, 1894), pp. 153.

Ballou, Lieut. Daniel R., (12th Rhode Island Inf.). "The Petersburg Mine," *National Tribune,* June 5, 1913.

Barnwell, Robert W. "A View on the Crater Battle," *Confederate Veteran,* Volume XXXIII, No. 5 (May, 1925), pp. 176-178.

Bates, Brig. General Delevan. (30th U.S.C.T.). "A Day with the Colored Troops," *National Tribune,* January 30, 1908.

Bausum, Daniel F. "Personal Reminiscences of Sergeant Daniel F. Bausum, Co. K, 48th Regt., Penna. Vol. Inf., 1861-1865; Read before the Society November 27th, 1912," Pub. of the Schuylkill County Historical Society, Vol. IV, pp. 240-249, Pottsville, Pa., 1914.

Beaty, B. L. (Co. K, 26th South Carolina Inf.). "The Battle of the Crater," *Sketches and Reminiscences* by Joshua Hilary Hudson. Columbia: The State Company, 1903, pp. 46-61.

Beecham, Capt. R. K. (29th U.S.C.T.). "Adventures of an Iron Brigade Man," 2 parts. *National Tribune,* November 20 & 27, 1902.

Beller, Lieut. James W. (Battery E, 2nd Pennsylvania Provisional H. A.). "The Mine Explosion," *National Tribune,* June 20, 1889.

Bernard, George S. (12th Virginia Inf.). "Who Were They," *The Maine Bugle.* Campaign II, Call III, (July 1895), pp. 218-221.

_____ "Great Battle of the Crater: The Work of Mahone and Weisiger at the Fight," *Southern Historical Society Papers,* Volume II, p.p. 204-221.

Bosbyshell, Major Oliver C. (48th Pennsylvania Inf.). "The Petersburg Mine," *The Maine Bugle,* Campaign III, Call III, (July, 1896), pp. 211-223.

Bowley, Lieut. Freeman S. (30th U.S.C.T.) "The Petersburg Mine," *War Paper No. 3, California M.O.L.L.U.S., (November 6, 1889), pp. 1-17.*

_____ "The Crater," *National Tribune,* November 6, 1884.

Branson, Sgt. Daniel F. (45th Pennsylvania Inf.). "The Petersburg Mine," *National Tribune,* September 13, 1911.

Burbank, Captain Horace H. (31st Maine Inf.). "The Battle of 'The Crater,' *War Papers,* Maine M.O.L.L.U.S., Volume I, pp. 283-294.

Case, Ervin T. "Battle of the Mine," *Personal Narratives of the Battles of the Rebellion, Being Papers Read Before the Rhode Island Soldiers and Sailors Historical Society,* Series I, No. 1, (1879), pp. 5-37.

Chambers, Capt. H. A. (49th North Carolina Inf.). "The Bloody Crater," *Confederate Veteran,* Volume XXXI, No. 5, (May, 1923), pp. 174-177.

Coit, Major James C. (Coit's Battl. Artillery) "Letter from Major J. C. Coit, August 2, 1879," *Southern Historical Society Papers,* Volume X, pp. 123-130.

Clark, George (11th Alabama Inf.). "Alabamians in the Crater Battle," *Confederate Veteran,* Volume III, No. 3, (March, 1895), pp. 68-70.

Cross, Thomas H. (Co. A, 16th Virginia Inf.). "Battle of the Crater," *National Tribune,* February 25, 1882.

Crawford, Robert F. "The Civil War Letters of S. Rodman and Linton Smith," (4th Delaware Inf.). *Delaware History,* Volume XXI, No. 2, Fall-Winter, 1984, pp. 86-116.

Culver, Asst. Surgeon J. B. (48th Pennsylvania Inf.). "The Petersburg Mine," *National Tribune,* September 4, 1919.

Cutcheon, General Byron M. "The Twentieth Michigan Regiment in the Assault on Petersburg, July, 1864," *Michigan Pioneer and Historical Society,* Volume XXX, pp. 127-139.

Davies, A. M. (34th Virginia Inf.). "Petersburg - The Battle of the Crater," *Blue and Gray,* Volume III, No. 5, (May, 1894), pp. 249-252.

Day, W. A. (49th North Carolina Inf.). "Battle of the Crater," *Confederate Veteran,* Volume XI, No. 8, (August, 1903), pp. 355-356.

_____ "The Breastworks at Petersburg," *Confederate Veteran,* Volume XXIX, No. 5, (May, 1921), pp. 173-175.

Draper, Joseph (10th Alabama Inf.). "Who Fought in the Battle of the Crater," *Confederate Veteran,* Volume VIII, No. 11, (November, 1900), p. 502.

Etheredge, Major William H. (41st Virginia Inf.). "Another Story of the Crater Battle," *Confederate Veteran* Volume XV, No. 4, (April, 1907), p. 167. (Also see *S.H.S.P.,* Volume XXXVII, p. 203.)

Fagan, W. L. (8th Alabama Inf.). "The Petersburg Crater," *Philadelphia Weekly Times,* January 6, 1883.

Featherston, Captain John C. (9th Alabama Inf.). "Graphic Account of Battle of Crater," *Southern Historical Society Papers,* Volume XXXIII, pp. 358-374.
(Also see *S.H.S.P.,* Volume XXXVI, pp. 161-178 and *Confederate Veteran,* Volume XIV, No. 1, [January, 1906), pp. 23-26.)

_____ "The Battle of the Crater," Address to the 48th Pennsylvania Association, Pottsville, Pa. *Confederate Veteran,* Volume XXXIV, No. 8 (August, 1926), p. 298.

_____ "Incidents of the Battle of the Crater," *Confederate Veteran,* Volume XIV, No. 3 (March, 1906), pp. 107-108.

Flanner, Henry H. "Flanners' North Carolina Battery at the Battle of the Crater," *Southern Historical Society Papers,* Vol. V, pp. 247-248.

Floyd, N. J. (9th Alabama Inf.) "Concerning the Battle of the Crater," *Confederate Veteran,* Volume XVI, No. 4, (April, 1908), p. 159.

George, Major Larry, U.S. Army. "Battle of the Crater: A Combat Engineer Case Study," *Military Review;* Vol. LXIV, No. 2, (February, 1984), pp. 35-47.

Hale, C. Wesly. "1926 Crater Findings Recalled," *Progress-Index,* (Petersburg), n.d.

Hall, Henry S. (43rd U.S.C.T.) "Mine Run to Petersburg," *War Talks in Kansas,* Kansas M.O.L.L.U.S., 1906, pp. 219-249.

Haas, James F. "The Famous 48th," *Schuylkill County in the Civil War,* A Publication of the Historical Society of Schuylkill County, Vol. VII, No. 3, 1961.

Herbert, Col. Hilary A. "History of the Eighth Alabama Volunteer Regiment, C.S.A.," ed. by Maurice S. Fortin. *The Alabama Historical Quarterly,* Volume XXXIX, No. 1, 2, 3, and 4, 1977, pp. 145-201.

Holsinger, Capt. Frank, (19th U.S.C.T.). "The Colored Troops at the Mine," *National Tribune,* October 19, 1905.

Houghton, Major Charles H. (14th New York H. A.) "In the Crater," *Battles and Leaders of the Civil War.* New York: The Century Co., 1884-1888, Volume IV, pp. 561-562.

Kilmer, George L. "The Dash Into the Crater," *Century Magazine,* September, 1887, pp. 775-776.

Kenfield, Capt. Frank (17th Vermont Inf.). "Captured by the Rebels: A Vermonter at Petersburg, 1864," *Vermont History,* Volume XXXVI, No. 4, (Autumn, 1968), pp. 230-235.

Laughton, Captain John E. (12th Virginia Inf.). "The Sharpshooters of Mahone's Brigade," *Southern Historical Society Papers,* Volume XXII, pp. 103-104.

LoPiano, Tom, Jr. "Gallantry in the Crater," (Col. Elisha Marshall) *Arms Gazette,* (July, 1979), pp. 16-48.

McAlpine, Newton. "Sketch of Company I, 61st Virginia Infantry, Mahone's Brigade, C.S.A.," *Southern Historical Society Papers,* Volume XXIV, pp. 98-108.

McCabe, William G. (Pegram's Battl.) "Defence of Petersburg," *Southern Historical Society Papers,* Volume II, pp. 256-306.

McMaster, Colonel F. W. (17th South Carolina Inf.). "The Battle of the Crater, July 30, 1864," *Southern Historical Society Papers,* Volume X, pp. 119-130.

McWhiney, Grady and Jack Jay Jenkins. "The Union's Worst General, (Brig. Gen. James Ledlie)" *Civil War Times Illustrated,* Volume XIV, No. 3 (June, 1975), pp. 30-39.

Mills, Luther Rice (26th Virginia Inf.). "Letters From the Trenches," *Wake Forest Student,* Volume XXXI, (1911/12), pp. 285-310.

Newberry, Walter C. (24th New York Inf.). "The Petersburg Mine," *Military*

Essays and Recollections, Illinois M.O.L.L.U.S., Volume III, pp. 111-124.

Owen, William Miller (Gibb's Battl.). "The Artillery Defenders of Fort Gregg," *Southern Historical Society Papers,* Volume XIX, pp. 65-71.

Paul, Frank (A.A.G., 18th Corps.). "Why it was a Failure," *Philadelphia Weekly Times,* April 24, 1880.

Phillips, B. F. (9th Alabama Inf.). "Wilcox's Alabamians in Virginia," *Confederate Veteran,* Volume XV, No. 11, (November, 1907), p. 490.

Pollard, Henry R. "Edwards Bagby of Virginia," (34th Virginia Inf.) *Confederate Veteran,* Volume XXVII, No. 12, (December, 1919), pp. 453-458.

Porter, Capt. Charles H. (39th Massachusetts Inf.). "The Petersburg Mine," *Papers of the Military Historical Society of Massachusetts,* Volume V, pp. 221-239.

Powell, Major William H. "The Battle of the Petersburg Crater," *Battles and Leaders of the Civil War.* New York: The Century Co., 1884-1888, Volume IV, pp. 545-560.

Proctor, Capt. D. E. (Co. F, 30th U.S.C.T.). "The Massacre in the Crater," *National Tribune,* October 17, 1907.

Pryor, Anne Banister. "A Child's Recollections of War," *Confederate Veteran,* Volume XXXIX, No. 2, (February, 1931), pp. 54-57.

Richards, Capt. R. G. (Co. G, 45th Pennsylvania Inf.). "The Blunder at the Petersburg Mine," *National Tribune,* June 18, 1925.

Robinson, Lieut. W. P. (Ringgold Battery). "Artillery in Battle of the Crater," *Confederate Veteran,* Volume XIX, No. 4, (April, 1911), pp. 164-166.

Rogers, Col. George T. (6th Virginia Inf.). "The Crater Battle, 30th July, 1864," *Confederate Veteran.* Volume III, No. 1, (January, 1895), pp. 12-14.

_____ "Crater Battle; Reply to Mr. Clark," *Confederate Veteran,* Volume III, No. 5, (May, 1895), p. 137.

Roulhac, Thomas S. "The Forty-Ninth N.C. Infantry, C.S.A.," *Southern Historical Society Papers,* Volume XXIII, pp. 58-78.

Rowland, J. C. (Co. A, 112th New York Inf.). "The Petersburg Mine," *National Tribune,* July 18, 1907.

Shearman, Sumner U. "Battle of the Crater and Experiences of Prison Life." *Personal Narratives of the Events of the War of the Rebellion, Being Papers Read Before the Rhode Island Soldiers and Sailors Historical Society.* Fifth Series, No. 8 (1898), pp. 5-38.

Sholes, Albert E. (4th Rhode Island Inf.) "The Crater Fight Vividly Portrayed," *National Tribune,* January 12, 1928.

Soldier, (48th Pennsylvania Inf.). "The Petersburg Mine," *National Tribune,* January 17, 1884.

Spear, Jamin A. (Co. K, 57th Massachusetts Inf.). "Fighting Them Over," *National Tribune,* June 20, 1889.

Stewart, Lieut. Col. William H. (61st Virginia Inf.). "Carnage at 'The Crater' Near Petersburg," *Confederate Veteran,* Volume I, No. 2, (February 1893), pp. 41-42.

_____ "Crater Legion of Mahone's Brigade," *Confederate Veteran,* Volume XI, No. 12, (December, 1903), pp. 557-558.

_____ "The Charge of the Crater," *Southern Historical Society Papers,* Volume XXV, pp. 77-90.

_____ "Field of Blood was the Crater," *Southern Historical Society Papers,* Volume XXXIII, pp. 351-357.

Suderow, Bryce A. "Confederate Casualties at the Crater," *The Kepi,* Volume III, No. 3, (June-July, 1985). pp. 22-33.

Thomas, Major General Henry G. (4th Div., 9th Corps). "Twenty-Two Hours Prisoner of War in Dixie," *War Papers,* Maine M.O.L.L.U.S., Volume I, 1898, pp. 29-48.

_____ "The Colored Troops at Petersburg," *Battles and Leaders of the Civil War.* New York: The Century Co., 1884-1888, Volume IV, pp. 563-567.

Thrash, A. B. (25th North Carolina Inf.). "Vivid Reminiscence of the Crater," *Confederate Veteran,* Volume XIV, No. 11, (November, 1908), pp. 508-509.

Tribou, Charles E. (Co. I, 58th Massachusetts Inf.). "At the Crater," *National Tribune,* June 29, 1911.

Vance, P. M. (11th Alabama Inf.). "Incidents of the Crater Battle," *Confederate Veteran,* Volume XIV, No. 4, (April, 1906), pp. 178-179.

Venable, M. W. (Conf. Engineers). "In the Trenches at Petersburg," *Confederate Veteran,* Volume XXXIV, No. 2, (February, 1926), pp. 59-61.

Way, Lieut. D. S., (A.D.C., 18th Corps.). "The Battle of the Crater," *National Tribune,* June 4, 1903.

Weld, Brig. General Stephen M. (58th Massachusetts Inf.). "The Petersburg Mine," *Papers of the Military Historical Society of Massachusetts,* Volume V, pp. 207-219.

Wentz, A., (Co. A, 14th New York H. A.). "Closing Days of the War," Part 3. *National Tribune,* February 11, 1904.

White, Col. Daniel, (31st Maine Inf.). "Charging the Crater," *National Tribune,* June 21, 1883.

Wilson, Clarence, (2nd Pennsylvania Provisional H. A.). "The Petersburg Mine," *National Tribune,* July 3, 1919.

Wise, Jennings C. "The Boy Gunners of Lee," *Southern Historical Society Papers,* Volume XLII, pp. 152-173.

W. R. S. (?). "The Sharpshooters of Mahone's Old Brigade at the Crater," *Southern Historical Society Papers,* Volume XXVIII, pp. 307-308.

General Histories, Biographies, Published Diaries, and Letters

Abbot, Bvt. Brig. General Henry L. *Siege Artillery in the Campaigns Against Richmond.* New York: D. Van Nostrand, Publisher, 1868.

Agassiz, George R., ed. *Meade's Headquarters, 1863-1865, Letters of Colonel Theodore Lyman.* Boston: The Atlantic Monthly Press, 1922.

Alexander, E. Porter. *Military Memoirs of a Confederate.* Dayton, Ohio: Morningside Bookshop, 1977.

Benedict, G. G. *Vermont in the Civil War.* Volume II. Burlington, Vt.: The Free Press Association, 1888.

Bernard, George S. *War Talks of Confederate Veterans.* Dayton, Ohio: Morningside Bookshop, 1981.

Beyer, W. F. & O. F. Keydel, eds. *Deeds of Valor From the Records in the Archives of the United States Government. How American Heroes Won the Medal of Honor.* 2 volumes. Detroit: The Perrien-Keydel Company, 1907.

Blackford, W. W. *War Years with Jeb Stuart.* New York: Charles Scribner's Sons, 1945.

Blake, Nelson M. *William Mahone of Virginia, Soldier and Political Insurgent.* Richmond: Garrett and Massie, 1935.

Catton, Bruce. *The Army of the Potomac: A Stillness at Appomattox.* New York: Doubleday & Company, Inc., 1953.

Chase, Lieut. James Judson. (32nd Maine Inf.) *The Charge at Day-Break: Scenes and Incidents at the Battle of the Mine Explosion, Near Petersburg, Va., July 30, 1864.* Lewiston: Printed at the Journal Office, 1875.

Claiborne, John Herbert, M.D. *Seventy-Five Years in Old Virginia.* New York: The Neale Publishing Co., 1904.

Cleaves, Freeman. *Meade at Gettysburg.* Norman, Ok.: University of Oklahoma Press, 1960.

Cullen, Joseph P. "The Siege of Petersburg" *Civil War Times Illustrated,* Vol. IX (Aug. 1970).

Cummings, Charles M. *Yankee Quaker Confederate General: The Curious Career of Bushrod Rust Johnson.* Rutherford, N.J.: Fairleigh Dickinson University Press, 1971.

Davis, William C. *Death in the Trenches: Grant at Petersburg.* Alexandria: Time-Life Books, 1986.

De Trobriand, Philippe Regis. *Four Years with the Army of the Potomac.* Boston: Ticknor and Company, 1889.

Dunlop, W. S. *Lee's Sharpshooters: The Forefront of Battle.* Dayton, Ohio: Morningside Bookshop, 1982.

Dyer, Frederick H. *A Compendium of the Rebellion.* Des Moines, Iowa: Dyer Publishing, 1908.

Evans, Clement A., ed. *Confederate Military History.* 19 volumes. Expanded Biographical Volumes. Wilmington, N.C.: Broadfoot Publishing Co., 1987-88.

Frassanito, William A. *Grant and Lee: The Virginia Campaigns, 1864-1865.* New York: Charles Scribner's Sons, 1983.

Freeman, Douglas Southall. *Lee's Lieutenants: A Study in Command.* 3 vols. New York: Charles Scribner's Sons, 1942-44.

_____ *R. E. Lee, A Biography.* 4 Volumes. New York: Charles Scribner's Sons, 1935.

Govan, Gilbert E. and James W. Livingood. *The Haskell Memoirs, John Cheves Haskell.* New York: G. P. Putnam's Sons, 1960.

Grant, Ulysses S. *Personal Memoirs of U.S. Grant.* 2 vols. New York: Charles L. Webster & Co., 1885.

Hagood, Johnson. *Memoirs of the War of Secession From the Original Manuscripts of Johnson Hagood.* Columbia: The State Company, 1910.

Harrison, W. B. *Petersburg, Virginia, the Cockade City of the Union.* Petersburg: Virginia Printing and Manufacturing Co., 1909.

Hoar, Jay S. *The South's Last Boys in Gray.* Bowling Green, Oh.: Bowling Green State University Popular Press, 1986.

Howe, Thomas J. *The Petersburg Campaign, Wasted Valor: June 15-18, 1864.* The Virginia Civil War Battles and Leaders Series. Lynchburg: H. E. Howard, Inc., 1988.

Humphreys, Andrew A. *The Virginia Campaigns of '64 and '65.* New York: Charles Scribner's Sons, 1899.

Krick, Robert K. *Lee's Colonels: A Biographical Register of the Field Officers of the Army of Northern Virginia.* 2nd Edition Revised. Dayton, Oh.: Press of Morningside Bookshop, 1984.

Landman, Charles. *The Red Book of Michigan.* Detroit: E. B. Smith & Company, 1871.

Landrum, J. B. O. *The History of Spartanburg County.* Spartanburg, S.C.: n.p., 1954.

Lee, Robert E. *The Wartime Papers of Robert E. Lee.* New York: Bramhall House, 1961.

Longacre, Edward G., ed. *From Antietam to Fort Fisher.* Rutherford, N.J.: Fairleigh Dickinson University Press, 1985.

_____ *The Man Behind the Guns: A Biography of General Henry J. Hunt, Commander of Artillery, Army of the Potomac.* New York: A. S. Barnes and Company, 1977.

Loving, Jerome M. *Civil War Letters of George Washington Whitman.* Durham: Duke University Press, 1975.

Mahone, General William. *The Battle of the Crater.* Petersburg: The Franklin Press Co., n.d.

McInnes, Hugh. *Civil War Letters.* Parsons, W. V.: McClain Printing Company, 1981.

Meade, George. *The Life and Letters of George Gordon Meade, Major General, United States Army.* 2 vols. New York: Charles Scribner's Sons, 1913.

Montague, Ludwell Lee. *Gloucester County in the Civil War.* Gloucester, Va.: The DeHardit Press, 1965.

Nevins, Allan, ed. *A Diary of Battle: The Personal Journals of Colonel Charles S. Wainwright 1861-1865.* New York: Harcourt, Brace & World, Inc., 1962.

Palfrey, Francis W. *Memoir of William Francis Bartlett.* Boston: Houghton, Osgood and Company, 1878.

Pearce, T. H., ed. *Diary of Captain Henry A. Chambers,* Wendell: Broadfoot's Bookmark, 1983 (49th North Carolina Inf.).

Pember, Phoebe Yates, *A Southern Woman's Story.* New York: G. W. Carleton & Co., 1879.

Pleasants, Henry, Jr., *The Tragedy of the Crater.* Boston: The Christopher Publishing House, 1938.

Pleasants, Henry, Jr. and George H. Straley. *Inferno at Petersburg.* Philadelphia: Chilton Company, 1961.

Poore, Ben Perley. *The Life and Public Services of Ambrose E. Burnside, Soldier-Citizen-Statesman.* Providence: J. A. & R. A. Reid, Publishers, 1882.

Porter, Horace. *Campaigning with Grant.* New York: The Century Co., 1897.

Post, Lydia Minturn, ed. *Soldiers' Letters from Camp, Battle-field and Prison.* New York: Bunce & Huntington, Publishers, 1865.

Robertson, James I., Jr., ed. *The Civil War Letters of General Robert McAllister.* New Brunswick, N.J.: Rutgers University Press, 1965.

_____ *General A. P. Hill: The Story of a Confederate Warrior.* New York: Random House, 1987.

Roman, Alfred. *The Military Operations of General Beauregard in the War Between the States 1861-1865.* 2 vols. New York: Harper and Brothers, 1883-1884.

Rosenburg, Charles E. *The Cholera Years: The United States in 1832, 1849, and 1866.* Chicago: The University of Chicago Press, 1962.

Sauers, Richard A. *Advance the Colors: Pennsylvania Civil War Battle Flags.* Harrisburg: Capitol Preservation Committee, 1987.

Sheridan, Philip H. *Personal Memoirs of P. H. Sheridan.* New York: Charles L. Webster & Company, 1888.

Silliker, Ruth L., ed. *The Rebel Yell & Yankee Hurrah: The Civil War Journal of a Maine Volunteer.* Camden, Me.: Down East Books, 1985.

Simon, John Y., ed. *The Papers of Ulysses S. Grant.* 14 volumes. Carbondale, Ill.: Southern Illinois University Press, 1984.

Sommers, Richard J. *Richmond Redeemed: The Siege of Petersburg.* Garden City, N.Y.: Doubleday & Company, Inc., 1981.

Sparks, David S., ed. *Inside Lincoln's Army: The Diary of Marsena Rudolph Patrick, Provost Marshal General, Army of the Potomac.* New York: Thomas Yoseloff, 1964.

Stevenson, Silas, M.D. *Account of the Battle of the Mine or Battle of the Crater in Front of Petersburg, Va. July 30th, 1864.* New Castle, Pa.: John A. Leathers, Printer, 1914.

Stewart, William H. *A Pair of Blankets.* New York: Broadway Publishing Co., 1911.

Stribling, Robert M. *Gettysburg Campaign and Campaigns of 1864 and 1865 in Virginia.* Petersburg: The Franklin Press Co., 1905.

The Cockade City of the Union, Petersburg, Virginia. n.p., 1906.

Wallace, Francis B. *Memorial of the Patriotism of Schuylkill County in the American Slaveholder's Rebellion.* Pottsville: Benjamin Nannan, 1865.

Wallace, Lee A., Jr. *A Guide to Virginia Military Organizations 1861-1865.* Revised 2nd Edition. Lynchburg: H. E. Howard, Inc., 1986.

Warner, Ezra J. *Generals in Blue: Lives of the Union Commanders.* Baton Rouge: Louisiana State University Press, 1964.

_____ *Generals in Gray: Lives of the Confederate Commanders.* Baton Rouge: Louisiana State University Press, 1959.

Williams, George W. *A History of the Negro Troops in the War of the Rebellion.* New York: Harper & Brothers, Franklin Square, 1888.

Wise, George. *Campaigns and Battles of the Army of Northern Virginia.* New York: The Neale Publishing Company, 1916.

Wise, Jennings Cropper. *The Long Arm of Lee.* 2 vols. Lynchburg: J. P. Bell Company, Inc., 1912.

Wise, John S. *The End of an Era.* Boston: Houghton, Mifflin and Company, 1902.

Williams, T. Harry *P.G.T. Beauregard: Napoleon in Gray.* Baton Rouge: Louisiana State University Press, 1954.

Woodbury, Augustus. *Major General Ambrose E. Burnside and the Ninth Army Corps.* Providence: Sidney S. Rider and Brother, 1867.

Woodward, C. Vann, ed. *Mary Chestnut's Civil War.* New Haven, Ct.: Yale University Press, 1981.

Yeary, Miss Mamie, comp. *Reminiscences of the Boys in Gray 1861-1865.* Dayton: Morningside Books, 1986.

Manuscripts

Annapolis, Md. — United States Naval Academy.
Snyder, Midshipman J. C. "The Petersburg Mine, An Essay Submitted to the Head of the Department of English, History, and Government," 1950.

Ann Arbor, Mi. — Clements Library, University of Michigan:
Parker, Lieut. Hilon A. Letters. (10th New York H. A.).

Ann Arbor, Mi. — Bentley Historical Library, University of Michigan:
  Baird, Lieutenant William Memoirs (23rd U.S.C.T.)
Brunswick, Me. — Letters of Private Jeremiah Batchelder (Co. I, 11th New Hampshire Inf.). Private collection of Warren B. Randall.
Carlisle Barracks, Pa. — United States Military History Institute:
  Bliss, Zenas R. Memoirs, pp. 121-147 (1st Brig., 2nd Div., 9th Corps).
  Buterbaugh, Elias L. Letter (Union Signal Corps). Lewis Leigh Collection.
  Hawkes, Lieutenant Colonel George P. Diary (21st Massachusetts Inf.)
  Jones, Peleg Gardner (7th Rhode Island Acting Engineers) "Letters and Record of Events of," *Civil War Times Illustrated* Collection.
  Mills, Charles (56th Massachusetts Inf.). "Through Blood and Fire," G. A. Coco Collection.
  Scroggs, Lieut. Joseph J. Diary (5th U.S.C.T.) *Civil War Times Illustrated* Collection.
  Tuttle Brothers Letters (81st New York Inf.).
Chapel Hill, N.C. — Univer. of North Carolina, Southern Historical Collection:
  Alexander, Edward P., Papers, M-7, Volume 49 (1st Corps Art., A. of N.V.)
  Bernard, George S. Papers (1891-1904), No. 3930 (12th Va. Inf.)
Charlottesville, Va. — University of Virginia Library:
  Adkins, Elizabeth F. Civil War Papers, 1865 and n.d.
  Christiancy, Henry Clay. Diary, 1862-1864 (1st Michigan Inf.)
  Daniel, John Warwick. Papers, No. 158, Box No. 23 (1905)
  Douglas, Capt. Hugh Thomas, C.S.A. "The Petersburg Crater," (Engineers)
  _____ "Confederate Counter-mining in Front of Petersburg"
  Chevy Chase, Md. Diary of Elbert Corbin (Battery B, 1st New York Light Artillery "Rogers' Battery"). Private collection of Thomas E. Corbin.
Cinnaminson, N.J. — Michael Cavanaugh Collection:
  Cleveland, Private Fisher. A. Letter (35th Massachusetts Inf. Acting Engineers), August 8, 1864.
Columbia, S.C. — South Carolina Department of Archives and History:
  Alexander, Lieutenant A. N. Letters (Co. F, 22nd South Carolina Inf.). "Twenty-Second South Carolina Infantry"
Columbia, S.C. — University of South Carolina, The South Caroliniana Library:
  Elliott, Stephen Jr. Letters
  McMaster, Fitz William. Letters (17th South Carolina Inf.).
  Moseley, J. McG. Letters (South Carolina unit)

Columbiana, Ala. — County Museum and Archives:
Fleming, A. T. Letter, August 3, 1864. (10th Alabama Inf.)
Concord, N.H. — New Hampshire Historical Society.
Bell, Louis H. Letters, Box 3, Folder 7, Bell Family Papers (4th New Hampshire).
Jones, J. N. Diary (6th New Hampshire Inf.)
9th New Hampshire Collection.
Lexington, Va. — Virginia Military Institute:
Mahone, William. File.
Montpelier, Vt. — Vermont Historical Society Library
Cummings, Charles. Papers, MS-A28 (17th Vermont Inf.)
Mount Laurel, N.J. — Diary of Sgt. Samuel Beddall (48th Pa. Inf.). Private collection of Frank Beddall.
Petersburg, Va. — Petersburg National Battlefield:
Park Research Library:
Archaeological Report, Crater, 1978.
Bearss, Edwin C, "Documentation for Troop Movement Maps for the Battle of the Crater, July 30, 1864," February, 1966. Includes 5 overlay maps, 30" x 18" (Map Collection File)
Calkins, Christopher M. "The History of Poplar Grove National Cemetery.
Russell, William. Diary (Co. H, 26th Virginia Infantry.)
Wallace, Lee A., Jr. "A History of Petersburg National Military Park Virginia," 1983.
Manuscript Collection:
Johnson, Bushrod. Report, August 20, 1864 — Cat. No. 281.
Morgan, George. Letters (48th Pennsylvania Inf.) Cat. No. 642.
Research Files, Battle of the Crater No. 8:
Bishop, Captain Carter R. "History of the Battle of the Crater"
Bishop, Carter R. Letter to Miss Laura Lee Richardson, February 13, 1932.
Campbell, Charles. Diary, May 13 to July 22, 1864. Transcribed by Chris Calkins.
Cutchin, Color Cpl. J. Frank "Reminiscences of the Charge of the Crater" (Co. A, 16th Virginia Infantry), n.d.
Goode, J. Thomas. Letter to George S. Bernard
Guy, George W. "A List of Men Blown up at the Crater Battle," 1937
Harrison, Thomas, Park Historian. "Route of Mahone's Troops to the Crater Battlefield," Nov., 1961.
Jackson, C. R. "Report on Artillery Operations in the Battle of the Crater," 1934.
Rich, Alonzo G. Letter to his father, July 31, 1864. (Co. G, 36th Massachusetts Inf.)
Taylor, Raleigh C. "The Battle of the Crater, Hammering Fails for the Last Time," 1938.

Philadelphia, Pa. — Civil War Library and Museum.
  Bolton, William H. Journal (51st Pennsylvania Inf.).
  Hamilton, Major Isaac. Papers (110th Pennsylvania Inf.).
  Morrison, Lieut. John W. "The Mine Explosion, Petersburg, Va., July
    30th, 1864" (Co. E, 100th Pennsylvania Inf.).
  Papers of the 100th Pennsylvania Infantry ("Roundheads").
Philadelphia, Pa. — Historical Society of Pennsylvania
  Humphreys, Andrew A. Papers.
  Meade, George G. Papers.
Raleigh, N.C. — North Carolina Department of Cultural Resources:
  Mabry, Robert C. Letters, August 1864 (6th Virginia Inf.).
Richmond, Va. — Virginia State Library:
  Dobie, David F. Letters (118th New York Inf.).
Richmond, Va. — Virginia Historical Society:
  Pergram-Johnson-McIntosh Papers: William Pegram's letters to his
    wife, Virginia.
Santa Barbara, Ca. — University of California at, Library.
  Cook, Edward L. Manuscript (100th New York Inf.)
University Park, Pa. — Pennsylvania State University, Pattee Library
  Gyla McDowell Papers: Hamilton R. Dunlap diary and letters. (100th
    Pennsylvania Inf.)
Washington, D.C. — Bryce A. Suderow, "The First Battle of Deep Bottom,
    Virginia July 26-29, 1864," Private manuscript, 1986.
Washington, D.C. — Library of Congress
  Comstock, Cyrus B. Diary (U.S. Grant's Headquarters Staff).
  Hunt, Henry J. Papers (Chief of Artillery, Army of Potomac).
  Larned, Daniel Reed, Papers. (Burnside's Asst. Adjutant General).
  Wilcox, Cadmus. Papers (A. P. Hill's 3rd Corps).
Washington, D.C. — National Archives.
  Compiled Service Records, 18th, 21st South Carolina Inf., 6th Vir-
    ginia Inf., 15th Virginia Cavalry, R. G. 109, M 270.

Maps

U.S. War Department. *Atlas to Accompany the Official Records of the
Union and Confederate Armies, 1861-1865.* Washington: Government Printing Office, 1891-1895.

Newspapers

Boston Globe, The
Evening Post, The (New York)
Harper's Weekly
National Tribune, The (Washington, D.C.)
New York Herald, The
New York Times, The

New York Tribune
Philadelphia Inquirier, The
Pottsville Journal, The
Pottsville Republican, The
Progress-Index, The (Petersburg)
Richmond Examiner, The
Richmond Times Dispatch, The
Richmond Whig

Official Documents

Confederate States of America. *Confederate Roll of Honor.* Adjutant and Inspector General's Office, Richmond, August 10, 1864.

State of Massachusetts. *A Record of the Dedication of the Statue of Major General William Francis Bartlett.* Boston: Wright and Potter Printing Company State Printers, 1905.

U.S. Congress. *Report of the Committee on the Conduct of the War on the Attack on Petersburg on the 30th Day of July, 1864.* Washington: U.S. Government Printing Office, 1865.

_____ *Medal of Honor Recipients 1863-1978.* Washington: U.S. Government Printing Office, 1979.

U.S. War Department, comp. *War of the Rebellion: A Compilation of the Official Records of the Union and Confederate Armies.* 128 vols. Washington: Government Printing Office, 1880-1901.

Unit Histories

Albert, Allen D., ed. *History of the Forty Fifth Pennsylvania Veteran Volunteer Infantry 1861-1865.* Williamsport, Pa.: Grit Publishing Company, 1912.

Allen, George H. *Forty-six Months with the Fourth R. I. Volunteers in the War of 1861 to 1865.* Providence: J. A. & R. A. Reid, Printers, 1887.

Anderson, Captain John. *The Fifty-Seventh Regiment Massachusetts Volunteers in the War of the Rebellion.* Boston: E. B. Stillings & Co., Printers, 1896.

Billings, John D. *The History of the Tenth Massachusetts Battery of Light Artillery in the War of the Rebellion.* Boston: Hall & Whiting, Publishers, 1881.

Bosbyshell, Oliver C. *The 48th in the War, Being a Narrative of the Campaigns of the 48th Regiment, Pennsylvania Veteran Volunteers, during the War of the Rebellion.* Philadelphia: Avil Printing Co., 1895.

Caldwell, J. F. J. *The History of a Brigade of South Carolinians, Known First as "Gregg's," and Subsequently as "McGowan's Brigade."* Philadelphia: King & Baird, Printers, 1866.

Cavanaugh, Michael A. *6th Virginia Infantry.* Lynchburg: H. E. Howard, Inc., 1988.

Clark, James H. *The Iron Hearted Regiment: Being an Account of the Battles, Marches and Gallant Deeds Performed by the 115th Regiment N.Y. Volunteers.* Albany: J. Munsell, 1865.

Clark, Walter, comp. *A History of the Several Regiments and Battalions from North Carolina in the Great War, 1861-65.* 5 vols. Raleigh: E. M. Uzzell, 1901.

Cogswell, Leander W. *A History of the Eleventh New Hampshire Regiment Volunteers Infantry.* Concord: Republican Press Association, 1891.

Copp, Colonel Elbridge J. *Remniscences of the War of the Rebellion 1861-1865.* Nashua, N.H.: The Telegraph Publishing Company, 1911. (3rd New Hampshire Inf.)

Cufell, Charles A. *History of Durell's Battery in the Civil War (Independent Battery D, Pennsylvania Volunteer Artillery)* Philadelphia: Craig, Finley & Co., 1903.

Cushman, Frederick E. *History of the 58th Regt. Massachusetts Volunteers from the 15th Day of September, 1863 to the Close of the Rebellion.* Washington, D.C.: Gibson Brothers, Printers, 1865.

Cutchins, John A. *A Famous Command: The Richmond Light Infantry Blues.* Richmond: Garrett & Massie, 1934 (46th Va. Inf.)

Dickert, D. Augustus. *History of Kershaw's Brigade.* Newberry, S.C.: Elbert H. Aull, Company, 1899.

Eden, Major R. C. *The Sword and Gun: A History of the 37th Wisconsin Volunteer Infantry from its First Organization to its Final Muster Out.* Madison: Atwood & Rublee, Printers, 1865.

Elliott, Charles Pinckney. *Elliott's Brigade: How It Held the Crater and Saved Petersburg.* Savannah: Review Printing Company, n.d.

Embick, Milton A., ed. *Military History of the Third Division, Ninth Corps, Army of the Potomac.* Harrisburg: C. E. Aughinbaugh, 1913.

Gould, Joseph. *The Story of the Forty-Eighth: A Record of the Campaigns of the Forty-Eighth Regiment Pennsylvania Volunteer Infantry during the Four Eventful Years of Its Service in the War for the Preservation of the Union.* Philadelphia: Alfred M. Slocum Company, 1908.

Hanks, O. T., *History of Captain B. F. Benton's Company, Hood's Texas Brigade, 1861-1865.* Austin: W. M. Morrison Books, 1984. (1st Texas Inf.)

History of the Thirty-Fifth Massachusetts Volunteers 1862-1865. Boston: Mills, Knight & Co. Printers, 1884.

History of the Thirty-Sixth Regiment Massachusetts Volunteers 1862-1865. Boston: Press of Rockwell and Churchill, 1884.

Hopkins, William P. *The Seventh Regiment Rhode Island Volunteers in the Civil War 1862-1865.* Boston: The Providence Press, 1903.

Houston, Henry C. *The Thirty-Second Maine Regiment of Infantry Volunteers: An Historical Sketch.* Portland: Southworth Brothers, 1903.

Jackman, Capt. Lyman. *History of the Sixth New Hampshire Regiment in the War for the Union.* Concord: Republican Press Association, 1891.

Jackson, Harry F. & Thomas F. O'Donnell. *Back Home in Oneida: Herman Clarke and His Letters.* New York: Syracuse University Press, 1965. (117th New York Inf.)

Jordan, Weymouth T., Jr., ed., and Louis H. Manarin. *North Carolina Troops: A Roster.* 11 Volumes. Raleigh: 1975-1987.

Lord, Edward O. *History of the Ninth New Hampshire Volunteers in the War of the Rebellion.* Concord: Republican Press Association, 1895.

Marvel, William. *Race of the Soil, The Ninth New Hampshire Regiment in the Civil War.* Wilmington, N.C.: Broadfoot Publishing Co., 1988.

Maxfield, Albert and Robert Brady, Jr. *Roster and Statistical Record of Company D, Eleventh Regiment Maine Infantry Volunteers, with a Sketch of its Services in the War of the Rebellion.* New York: n.p., 1890.

Osborne, William H. *The History of the Twenty-ninth Regiment of Massachusetts Volunteer Infantry, in the Late War of the Rebellion.* Boston: Albert G. Wright, Printer, 1877.

Palmer, Abraham J. *The History of the Forty-Eighth New York State Volunteers.* New York: Charles T. Dillingham, 1885.

Pegram Battalion Association. *Annual Reunion of Pegram Battalion Association in the Hall of House of Delegates, Richmond, Va., May 21st, 1886, when the Battle-Flag of the Battalion was Presented by Capt. W. Gordon McCabe, Adjutant.* Richmond: Wm. Ellis Jones, Book and Job Printer, 1886.

Parker, Thomas H. *History of the 51st Regiment of P. V. and V. V. from Its Organization at Camp Curtin, Harrisburg, Pa. in 1861, to Its Being Mustered Out of the United States Service at Alexandria, Va. July 27th, 1865.* Philadelphia: King & Baird Printers, 1869.

Pierce, Lieutenant S. W. *Battlefields and Camp Fires of the Thirty-Eighth: An Authentic Narrative and Record of the Organization of the Thirty-Eighth Regiment of Wis. Vol. Inf'y and the Part Taken by It in the Late War.* Milwaukee: Daily Wisconsin Printing House, 1866.

Price, Isaiah. *History of the Ninety Seventh Regiment Pennsylvani Infantry During the War of the Rebellion, 1861-65, with the Biographical Sketches of Its Field and Staff Officers and a Complete Record of Each Officer and Enlisted Man.* Philadelphia: B.&P. Printers, 1875.

Roe, Alfred S. *The Thirty-Ninth Regiment Massachusetts Volunteers 1862-1865.* Worcester: Published by Regimental Veteran Association, 1914.

Shaver, Lewellyn A. *A History of the Sixtieth Alabama Regiment, Gracie's Alabama Brigade.* Montgomery: Barrett & Brown, 1867.

The Story of One Regiment; The Eleventh Maine Infantry Volunteers in the War of the Rebellion. New York: Regimental Association, 1896.

Twitchell, Quartermaster Sergeant A. S. *History of the Seventh Maine Light Artillery in the Great Rebellion.* Boston: E. B. Stillings & Co., 1892.

Walcott, Charles F. *History of the Twenty-First Regiment Massachusetts Volunteers in the War for the Preservation of the Union 1861-1865, with Statistics of the War and Rebel Prisons.* Boston: Houghton Mifflin and Company, 1882.

Walker, Francis A. *History of the Second Army Corps of the Army of the Potomac.* New York: Charles Scribner's Sons, 1886.

Ward, George W. *History of the Second Pennsylvania Veteran Heavy Artillery (112th Regiment Pennsylvania Volunteers) from 1861 to 1866, Including the Provisional Second Penn'a. Heavy Artillery.* Philadelphia: George W. Ward Printer, 1904.

Weld, Stephen M. *War Diary and Letters of Stephen Minot Weld 1861-1865.* Boston: Massachusetts Historical Society, 1979.

ENDNOTES
Chapter I

1. William C. Davis, *Death in the Trenches: Grant at Petersburg* (Alexandria, Va.: 1986), 9; Richard Wayne Lukes, *Campaign for Petersburg* (Washington: 1970), 3-4. The "Cockade City" earned its nickname during the War of 1812, because so many of its citizens wore the patriotic red, white and blue rosettes known as cockades.
2. Lukes, *Campaign for Petersburg,* 10-17.
3. *Ibid.,* 16; *War of the Rebellion: Official Records of the Union and Confederate Armies,* 128 vols. (Washington: 1880-1901), Series I, Vol. XL, Part 1, 251-265. Hereafter cited as *O.R.,* with Series I understood unless otherwise noted.
4. *O.R.* XL, i, 522; George R. Agassiz, ed., *Meade's Headquarters, 1863-1865: Letters of Colonel Theodore Lyman* (Boston: 1922), 164-168. For the accusation that Ledlie was drunk and avoiding duty, see the George P. Hawkes diary, U.S. Army Military History Institute, entry of June 17, 1864, and Gregory A. Coco, ed., *Through Blood and Fire: The Civil War Letters of Major Charles J. Mills, 1862-1865* (n.p.: 1982) 114-115.
5. *O.R.,* XL, i, 572-573, and ii, 179-181.
6. *Ibid.,* ii, 220.
7. Henry Pleasants, Jr. and George H. Straley, *Inferno at Petersburg* (Philadelphia: 1961), 12-18; Joseph Gould, *The Story of the Forty-Eighth* (Philadelphia: 1908), 25, 208.
8. *O.R.,* XL, ii, 396.
9. *Report of the Committee on the Conduct of the War on the Attack on Petersburg* (Washington: 1865), 10, 156. Hereafter referred to as *J.C.C.W. Report.*
10. Agassiz, *Meade's Headquarters,* 128; D. R. Larned to "My Dear Sister," June 5 and 20, 1864, Daniel Reed Larned Papers, Library of Congress; *J.C.C.W. Report,* 156.
11. *O.R.* XIX, ii, 314; *J.C.C.W. Report,* 126-127, 156. One of James Duane's last acts as McClellan's engineer was to order the pontoon train from the upper Potomac to Washington. He sent that order by regular mail, rather than telegraph or special messenger, which added a fatal six days to the delivery time. See *O.R.* XXI, 148.
12. *J.C.C.W. Report,* 126-127.
13. Henry C. Heisler to "Dear Sister," July 20, 1864, Henry C. Heisler Papers, Library of Congress; Appeal Application dated August 21, 1891, Henry Reese Pension File, no. 293594, National Archives; *Schuylkill County in the Civil War* (n.p.: Historical Society of Schuylkill County, 1961), 61; Samuel Beddall diary, collection of Frank Beddall, entry of July 3, 1864.
14. Oliver C. Bosbyshell, *The 48th in the War* (Philadelphia: 1895), 166; *J.C.C.W. Report,* 126-127.
15. *Ibid.,* 127.
16. Samuel Beddall diary, June 26-July 5, 1864; Gould, *The Story of the Forty-Eighth,* 419, 426, 448.
17. *The National Tribune,* January 17, 1884; Charles Campbell diary, Petersburg National Battlefield Park, entry of June 30 and July 2, 1864.
18. *Ibid.,* July 3-10, 1864; Anne Banister Pryor, "A Child's Recollection of War," *Confederate Veteran,* XXXIX, 54-55; *O.R.* XL, i, 782-786.
19. *O.R.* XL, 2, 484.
20. *Ibid.,* 1, 557; *The National Tribune,* January 17, 1884 and September 4, 1919.
21. Gould, *The Story of the Forty-Eighth,* 273; Bosbyshell, *The 48th in the War,* 164.

22. *O.R.* XL, i, 558. A theodolite is a more primitive version of the modern transit.
23. *Ibid.,* 557-558; *New York Herald,* August 1, 1864.
24. *The National Tribune,* September 4, 1919.
25. Samuel Beddall diary, July 14-16, 1864.
26. *Ibid.,* July 7 and 11, 1864.
27. *O.R.* XL, ii, 557 and iii, 300-301.
28. E. P. Alexander, *Military Memoirs of a Confederate* (New York: 1907), 563-564.
29. Hugh T. Douglas, "The Petersburg Crater," University of Virginia Library.
30. *O.R.* XL, iii, 301, 354; Bosbyshell, *The 48th in the War,* 168; *J.C.C.W. Report,* 127. Pleasants reported the exact length of the gallery was 510 and 8/10 feet. The left lateral gallery ran 37 feet and the right, 38 feet.
31. *Ibid.; O.R.* XL, i, 557.
32. *J.C.C.W. Report,* 128; *O.R.* XL, ii, 528.
33. *J.C.C.W. Report,* 129.

Chapter II

1. *J.C.C.W. Report,* 140; *Personal Memoirs of U.S. Grant,* 2 vols. (New York: 1885), vol. I, 551-552, vol. II, 307-308.
2. *O.R.,* XL, ii, 608.
3. *Ibid.* For evidence of Meade's well-known temper, see Agassiz, *Meade's Headquarters,* 128, and *Personal Memoirs of U.S. Grant,* vol. 2, 538-539.
4. George Meade, *The Life and Letters of George Gordon Meade,* 2 vols. (New York: 1913), vol. 1, 339, 341, 351; Freeman Cleaves, *Meade of Gettysburg* (Norman, Ok.: 1960), 235.
5. *O.R.,* XL, ii, 629-630.
6. *Ibid.*
7. Thomas H. Parker, *History of the 51st Regiment of Pennsylvania Volunteers* (Philadelphia: 1869), 232-233.
8. *O.R.* XL, iii, 304-320; Agassiz, *Meade's Headquarters,* 102; Frederick H. Dyer, *A Compendium of the War of the Rebellion* (Des Moines: 1908), 1726-1731.
9. Agassiz, *Meade's Headquarters,* 148; *J.C.C.W. Report,* 17.
10. *O.R.* XL, iii, 304, 321-322.
11. Henry Goddard Thomas, "The Colored Troops at Petersburg," *Battles and Leaders of the Civil War,* vol. IV, 563.
12. *Ibid.,* 563-564.
13. *O.R.* XL, iii, 474-476.
14. *Ibid.,* 465, 478, 498.
15. *J.C.C.W. Report,* 16-17.
16. *O.R.* XL, iii, 568.
17. *J.C.C.W. Report,* 17.
18. *Ibid.,* 17, 42, 98, 125.

Chapter III

1. Ulysses S. Grant, *Personal Memoirs of U.S. Grant* (New York: 1886), II, 308-10; John Y. Simon, ed., *The Papers of Ulysses S. Grant* (Carbondale, Ill.: 1984), Vol. XI, 266-78. Hereafter, all references will be to Volume XI unless otherwise noted.
2. *O.R.* XL, i, 308-309; Regis De Trobriand, *Four Years with the Army of the Potomac* (Boston: 1889), 604-5; unpublished memoir, Major Isaac Hamilton Papers, Civil War Library and Museum, Philadelphia, Pa., 181.
3. *Ibid.,* 182.
4. P. H. Sheridan, *Personal Memoirs of P. H. Sheridan* (New York: 1888), Vol. I, 446; *O.R.* XL, i, 308-309, 692-693 and iii, 796.

5. *Ibid.,* i, 309; A. A. Humphreys, *The Virginia Campaign of '64 and '65* (New York: 1883), 248.
6. *Atlas to Accompany the Official Records of the Union and Confederate Armies* (Washington: 1891-95), Plate XVII, No. 1.
7. *O.R.* XL, i, 308-309; *Official Records of the Union and Confederate Navies in the War of the Rebellion* (Washington: 1900), Series I, Vol. 10, 318-319, hereafter referred as *O.R. Navy;* D. Augustus Dickert, *History of Kershaw's Brigade with Complete Roll of Companies, Biographical Sketches, Incidents, Anecdotes, etc.* (Newberry, S.C.: 1899), 390. Dickert used the term "300 pounder" in his text, but the shells were reported to be from 100-pounder rifled pivot guns, used because of the extreme distance to the target. See *O.R. Navy,* 10, 319.
8. *O.R.* XL, i, 309-310; *Richmond Examiner,* July 29, 1864; John D. Billings, *The History of the Tenth Massachusetts Battery of Light Artillery in the War of the Rebellion* (Boston: 1881), 232.
9. *O.R.* XL, 1, 310.
10. *O.R.* XL, i, 310-311; Simon, *Grant Papers,* 324.
11. Francis A. Walker, *History of the Second Army Corps in the Army of the Potomac* (New York: 1887), 564; Simon, *Grant Papers,* 325.
12. Simon, *Grant Papers,* 326; *O.R.* XL, iii, 809, 812.
13. Simon, *Grant Papers,* 326; *O.R.* XL, iii, 536.
14. J. F. J. Caldwell, *The History of a Brigade of South Carolinians Known First as "Gregg's," and Subsequently as "McGowan's Brigade."* (Philadelphia: 1866) 169-170.
15. *Ibid.*
16. John Gibbon, Personal Recollections of the Civil War (Dayton, O.: 1978), 248-249.
17. *O.R.,* XL, i, 310-311; Caldwell, *History of a Brigade,* 170. Actually, Kershaw's, Lane's, and McGowan's brigades together lost only 57 in killed during all three days of fighting at Deep Bottom. See listing of Confederate casualties at Deep Bottom in Appendix D.
18. Walker, *Second Corps,* 566; Simon, *Grant Papers,* 334-335; Gibbon, *Recollections,* 250-251.
19. *The Story of One Regiment, The Eleventh Maine Infantry Volunteers in the War of the Rebellion* (New York: 1896), 229.
20. *O.R.* XL, i, 311; Simon, *Grant Papers,* 335.

Chapter IV

1. *J.C.C.W. Report,* 128; *O.R.* XI, iii, 656.
2. *J.C.C.W. Report,* 108, 153, 163.
3. *Ibid.,* 129; *O.R.,* XL, iii, 657.
4. Gould, *The Story of the Forty-Eight,* 224; Declaration for Original Invalid Pension dated May 1, 1879, Jacob Douty Pension File no. 203919, National Archives. A now-vandalized plaque on Lt. Douty's grave in Mt. Moriah Cemetery, Philadelphia, recorded that Douty and Reese tore away some of the tamping to find the fuse. This seems unlikely, both because the forty-eight feet of remaining fuse would have extended beyond the tamping and because two men would have had neither time nor room enough to dismantle — let alone repack — sandbags that had taken the entire regiment twenty hours to stack in place.
5. *J.C.C.W. Report,* 163; *O.R.* XL, iii, 657.

6. F. W. McMaster, "The Battle of the Crater, July 30, 1864," *Southern Historical Society Papers.* (hereafter cited as *SHSP*), X, 120, 124-126; George S. Bernard, *War Talks of Confederate Veterans* (Dayton, Ohio: 1981), 208-209.
7. Agassiz, *Meade's Headquarters,* 198; William H. Osborne, *The History of the Twenty-ninth Regiment of Massachustets Volunteer Infantry* (Boston: 1878), 312-313; Sumner U. Shearman, *Battle of the Crater and Experiences of Prison Life* (Providence: 1898), 10; Horace H. Burbank, "The Battle of the Crater," *War Papers,* Maine MOLLUS, I, 286; Stephen M. Weld, "The Petersburg Mine," *Papers of the Military Historical Society of Massachusetts,* V, 208. The height to which debris was thrown is more often described as eighty to one hundred feet.
8. A. B. Thrash, "Vivid Reminiscences of the Crater," *Confederate Veteran* (hereafter cited as *CV*), XIV, 509; Gordon McCabe, "Defence of Petersburg," *SHSP,* II, 283; J. B. O. Landrum, *The History of Spartanburg County* (Spartanburg, S.C.: 1954), 415-417; James T. Bacon, "Capt. George B. Lake," *CV* II, 153.
9. S. Lipscomb to John W. Daniel, November 30, 1905, John Warwick Daniel Papers, University of Virginia Library; *O.R.* XL, iii, 820.
10. McCabe, "Defence of Petersburg," 284.
11. *O.R.* XL,, 280, McMaster, "The Battle of the Crater," 126; *J.C.C.W. Report,* 171, 206, 222; Weld, "The Petersburg Mine," 208; Osborne, *History of the Twenty-ninth,* 313.
12. Charles H. Porter, "The Petersburg Mine," *Papers of the Military Historical Society of Massachusets,* V, 230; George W. Ward, *History of the Provisional Second Penn'a Heavy Artillery* (Philadelphia: 1904), 196, 203; Weld, "The Petersburg Mine," 209. Captain Douglas, the Confederate engineer, measured the Crater with a tape on the afternoon of July 30, and found it 125 feet long, varying from 20 to 25 feet deep, and "about 50 feet wide." *O.R.* XL, iii, 820; Douglas, "The Petersburg Crater," (Mss).
13. McMaster, "The Battle of the Crater," 124-126.
14. W. P. Robinson, "Artillery in the Battle of the Crater," *CV* XIX, 166.
15. Stephen Elliott to Charlotte Elliott, July 14, 1864, Elliott Family Papers, South Caroliniana Library; John C. Haskell, *The Haskell Memoirs* (New York: 1960), 74.
16. McMaster, "The Battle of the Crater," 121.
17. Mary Boykin Chesnut, *A Diary From Dixie* (Boston: 1949), 434.
18. McMaster, "The Battle of the Crater," 121; *O.R.* XL, i, 790; Thrash, "Vivid Reminiscences of the Crater," 509. The term "cavalier trench," so freely used in reference to the line behind the Crater, implies the work was shallower than the main trenches, similar to the ditches used as cavalry (*chevalier, or cavalier*) impediments during the Napoleonic Wars.
19. *O.R.* XL, i, 547, 567.
20. Ervin T. Case, *Battle of the Mine* (Providence: 1879), 27; Edward O. Lord, ed., *History of the Ninth New Hampshire Volunteers in the War of the Rebellion* (Concord: 1895), 491, 511; John E. Mason to William S. Parsons, August 4, 1864, Edward S. Parsons, Pension File no. 388615, National Archives.
21. W. A. Day, "Battle of the Crater," *CV* XI, 355, and "The Breastworks at Petersburg," *CV* XXIX, 174; T. H. Pearce, ed., *Diary of Captain Henry A. Chambers* (Wendell, N.C.: 1983), 210.
22. *O.R.* XL, i, 789; Daniel White, "Charging the Crater," *The National Tribune,* June 21, 1883; *J.C.C.W. Report,* 203, 206.
23. *O.R.* XL, i, 574, 581; *J.C.C.W. Report,* 202.
24. *O.R.* XL, i, 791.

25. *Ibid.*, 547,567; John Anderson, *The Fifty-seventh Regiment of Massachusetts Volunteers in the War of the Rebellion* (Boston: 1896), 179.
26. *J.C.C.W. Report,* 143-144; *O.R.* XL, iii, 658.
27. *Ibid.,* i, 547-549, 553-554; F. E. C[ushman], *History of the 58th Regt. Massachusetts Vols.* (Washington: 1865), 15.
28. Henry G. Flanner, "Flanner's North Carolina Battery at the Battle of the Crater," SHSP V, 247-248; Alfred Roman, *The Military Operations of General Beauregard in the War Between the States, 1861-1865,* 2 vols. (New York: 1883-1884), 263-264.
29. *J.C.C.W. Report,* 164.
30. *O.R.* XL, iii, 659.
31. *J.C.C.W. Report,* 164.
32. *O.R.* XL, i, 547-567; Allen D. Albert, ed., *History of the Forty-Fifth Regiment Pennsylvania Veteran Volunteer Infantry, 1861-1865* (Williamsport, Pa.: 1912), 153; *Civil War Letters of Hugh McInnes* (Parsons, W.Va.: 1981), 12; George H. Allen, *Forty-six Months With the Fourth R.I. Volunteers in the War of 1861 to 1865* (Providence: 1867), 288; Henry C. Houston, *The Thirty-second Maine Regiment of Infantry Volunteers* (Portland, Me.: 1903), 366.
33. *O.R.* XL, i, 553, 791, and iii, 666; Jerome M. Loving, ed., *Civil War Letters of George Washington Whitman* (Durham, N.C.: 1975), 127-128.
34. *O.R.* XL, iii, 660.
35. John S. Wise, *End of an Era* (Boston: 1900), 367; J. Thomas Goode to George A. Bernard, February 7, 1911, Research Files, Petersburg National Battlefield.
36. *O.R.* XL, i, 586; Byron M. Cutcheon, "The Twentieth Michigan Regiment in the Assault on Petersburg, July, 1864," *Collections and Researches Made by the Michigan Pioneer and Historical Society,* XXX, 135.
37. *O.R.* XL, i, 575, 795; Charles H. Houghton, "In the Crater," *Battles and Leaders of the Civil War* IV, 562.
38. Thomas, "The Colored Troops at Petersburg," 564; *J.C.C.W. Report,* 206, 221-222.
39. Delevan Bates, "A Day With the Colored Troops," *The National Tribune,* January 30, 1908; *O.R.* XXXII, 519-540.
40. *Ibid.,* XL, i, 699-704.
41. Roman, *Beauregard,* II, 263-264; Wise, *End of an Era,* 361.
42. Nelson Morehouse Blake, *William Mahone of Virginia, Soldier and Political Insurgent* (Richmond: 1935), 55; Bernard, *War Talks,* 151; William H. Stewart, "The Charge of the Crater," *SHSP,* XXV, 79.
43. Bernard, *War Talks,* 151; William H. Etheridge, "Another Story of the Crater Battle," *SHSP,* XXXVII, 204.
44. Bernard, *War Talks,* 213-214; McCabe, "Defence of Petersburg," 290.
45. *O.R.* XL, iii, 652-653, 656.
46. Bernard, *War Talks,* 151-152.
47. *O.R.* XL, i, 791.
48. Bates, "A Day With the Colored Troops;" *J.C.C.W. Report,* 228.
49. Freeman S. Bowley, "The Crater," *The National Tribune,* November 6, 1884; Lord, *Ninth New Hampshire,* 494; Bates, "A Day With the Colored Troops."
50. Thomas, "The Colored Troops at Petersburg," 564-565; *O.R.* XL, i, 598.
51. Bowley, "The Crater;" *O.R.* XL, i, 596-598; Bernard, *War Talks,* 183; Bates, "A Day With the Colored Troops." While survivors on both sides claimed their opponents came into battle shouting "No quarter," almost every Confederate account remarks upon the Negro troops and their officers rallying to the cry of "Remember Fort Pillow; no quarter." Some very reputable Confederates reported hearing it themselves. See, for instance, T. H. Pearce, ed.,

Diary of Henry Chambers, 210. It would have been logical for the Union officers to try to inspire their untried troops with some cry such as that, simultaneously instilling both righteous anger and fear of capture. Junior officers and the men might have been expected to encourage each other by repeating it, especially in an age when such shouting was popular. At least one Northern source corroborates that Colonel Sigfried made such a remark while exhorting his men: *Publications of the Historical Society of Schuylkill County, 1903-1953,* I, 290. Before the day was over, these men would have reason to regret having uttered such a cheer.

Chapter V

1. *O.R.* XL, iii, 661.
2. *Ibid.,* i, 598-599; R. K. Beecham, "Adventures of an Iron Brigade Man," *The National Tribune,* November 20, 1902. Captain Beecham, of the 29th U.S.C.T., claimed that Colonel Thomas was nowhere to be found on the front line.
3. *O.R.* XL, i, 567, 596-598.
4. McCabe, "Defence of Petersburg," 290; William H. Stewart, *A Pair of Blankets* (New York: 1911), 154-155.
5. William H. Stewart, "Carnage at 'The Crater' Near Petersburg," *CV* I, 41; Bernard, *War Talks,* 154, 217, 219; William H. Stewart, "The Charge of the Crater," *SHSP* XXV, 81.
6. Bernard, *War Talks,* 214, 217-218.
7. *Ibid.,* 180, 200; *O.R.,* XL, i, 791.
8. Beecham, "Iron Brigade Man;" Bernard, *War Talks,* 185-192. Carter R. Bishop to Laura Lee Richardson, February 13, 1932, Research Files, Petersburg National Battlefield.
9. D. E. Proctor, "The Massacre in the Crater," *The National Tribune,* October 17, 1907; Bowley, "The Crater;" Stewart, "Carnage at 'The Crater,' " 41; Wise, *End of an Era,* 365.
10. Lord, *Ninth New Hampshire,* 498-499; *O.R.* XL, i, 567, 754.
11. Weld, "The Petersburg Mine," 210-211; *War Diary and Letters of Stephen Minot Weld,* 1861-1865 (Boston, 1979), 353-354.
12. Louis Bell to George Bell, August 12, 1864, Bell Family Papers, New Hampshire Historical Society; Weld, "The Petersburg Mine," 211; Edward C. Longacre, ed., *From Antietam to Fort Fisher, The Civil War Letters of Edward King Weightman, 1862-1865* (Rutherford, N.J.: 1985), 204.
13. *O.R.* XL, iii, 661-662; *J.C.C.W. Report,* 174.
14. George T. Rogers, "The Crater Battle, 30th July, 1864," *CV* III, 12; same, "Crater Battle — Reply to Mr. Clark," *CV* III, 137; Michael A. Cavanaugh, *6th Virginia Infantry,* (Lynchburg: 1988), 54; R. C. Mabry to "My Dear Wife," August 1, 1864, North Carolina Department of Cultural Resources; Etheridge, "Another Story of the Crater Battle," 205; George Clark, "Alabamians in the Crater Battle," *CV* III, 68; Bernard, *War Talks,* 187, 225; W. R. S., "The Sharpshooters of Mahone's Old Brigade at the Crater," *SHSP* XXVIII, 308.
15. Haskell, *The Haskell Memoirs,* 76; McCabe, "Defence of Petersburg," 292.
16. McCutcheon, "The Twentieth Michigan," 135-136.
17. *O.R.* XL, iii, 636, 653-654, 662.
18. *Ibid.,* 646, 654, 662, 685; Simon, *Grant Papers,* 346.
19. *J.C.C.W. Report,* 175; Agassiz, *Meade's Headquarters,* 200-201.
20. Francis Winthrop Palfrey, *Memoir of William Francis Bartlett* (Boston: 1878), 119.
21. Bernard, *War Talks,* 215-216; *O.R.,* XL, i, 567, 579.

22. Bernard, *War Talks,* 216; Charles M. Cummings, *Yankee Quaker, Confederate General, The Curious Career of Bushrod Rust Johnson* (Rutherford, N.J.: 1971), 22-34.
23. *O.R.* XL, i, 575, 579; Bowley, "The Crater."
24. Bernard, *War Talks,* 216.
25. Lyman Jackman, *History of the Sixth New Hampshire Regiment in the War of the Union* (Concord: 1891), 317-318.
26. Lord, *Ninth New Hampshire,* 505-507.
27. Bowley, "The Crater."
28. *Ibid.;* Lord, *Ninth New Hampshire,* 501; J. J. Chase, *The Charge at Day-break* (Lewiston, Me.: 1875), 21-24.
29. *Ibid.,* 21; Lord, *Ninth New Hampshire,* 704-705.
30. William H. Powell, "The Battle of the Petersburg Crater," *Battles and Leaders of the Civil War* IV, 558.
31. Jackson, *Sixth New Hampshire,* 316-317.
32. *O.R.* XL, i, 575 and iii, 663. Only General Potter made an attempt to reach his division in the Crater, and he was called back from the disputed ground by Burnside's order for a council of division commanders. See *J.C.C.W. Report,* 193.
33. John C. Featherston, "Graphic Account of Battle of the Crater," *SHSP* XXXIII, 361.
34. George Clark, "Alabamians in the Crater Battle," 68; John C. Featherston, "Incidents of the Battle of the Crater," *CV* XIV, 108.
35. Featherston, "Graphic Account," 361-362; Bowley, "The Crater;" George L. Kilmer, "The Dash Into the Crater," *Century Magazine,* September, 1887, 775-776; George W. Emery to Ludo B. Little, August 11, 1864, 9th New Hampshire Collection, New Hampshire Historical Society.
36. Palfrey, *Bartlett,* 119-122; Bowley, "The Crater;" John H. Claiborne, *Seventy-five Years in Old Virginia* (New York: 1904), 228.
37. *J.C.C.W. Report,* 205.
38. Featherston, "Graphic Account," 364; Freeman S. Bowley, "The Petersburg Mine," *War Paper No. 3,* California MOLLUS, 14; same: "The Crater."
39. Clark, "Alabamians in the Crater Battle," 69; John C. Featherston, "The Battle of the 'Crater' As I Saw It," *CV* XIV, 25; P.M. Vance, "Incidents of the Crater Battle," *CV* XIV, 178.
40. *J.C.C.W. Report,* 205; Albert E. Sholes, "The Crater Fight Vividly Portrayed," *The National Tribune,* January 12, 1928; Lord, *Ninth New Hampshire,* 502-503.
41. Bowley, "The Crater."
42. Clark, "Alabamians in the Crater," 69; Shearman, *Battle of the Crater,* 15; B. F. Phillips, "Wilcox's Alabamians in the Crater," *CV* XV, 490. For the Confederates' fondness for hats see, for instance, Bowley, "The Crater" and Weld, "The Petersburg Mine," 211.
43. Featherston, "Graphic Account," 364; Bowley, "The Crater."
44. *O.R.* XL, i, 575-576 and iii, 666-667.
45. *J.C.C.W. Report,* 259.
46. *Ibid.,* 24-25; *O.R.* XL, iii, 664.
47. *Ibid.,* 665; Featherston, "Graphic Account," 365.

Chapter VI

1. Henry G. Thomas, "Twenty-two Hours a Prisoner of War in Dixie," *War Papers,* Maine MOLLUS, I, 29; *O.R.* XL, iii, 691, 704.
2. Diary of Captain Josiah N. Jones, Miscellaneous Civil War Manuscripts, New Hampshire Historical Society, entry of July 31, 1864.

3. *O.R.* XL, iii, 821; Thomas, "Twenty-two Hours," 29-30; H. P. Dunlap to Robert Dunlap, August 1, 1864, Gyla McDowell Papers, Pattee Library, Pennsylvania State University.
4. *O.R.* XLII, ii, 10; Jones Diary, August 1, 1864; Thomas, "Twenty-two Hours," 30. Phoebe Yates Pember, *A Southern Woman's Story* (New York: 1879), 105-106.
5. *O.R.* XLII, ii, 31-32. A Confederate surgeon counted 150 Negro prisoners in wounded alone, and the parade of prisoners through Petersburg put the lie to the notion that only 36 Negroes were taken alive. See Claiborne, *Seventy-five Years in Old Virginia,* 208, and Palfrey, *Bartlett,* 119.
6. *Ibid.;* Bowley, "The Crater," Beecham, "Iron Brigade Man," *The National Tribune,* November 27, 1902. While the last two officers agreed Bartlett was forced to ride a swaybacked nag, Bartlett himself said he was given an ambulance; neither did he make mention of the infamous parade, though he said "We wouldn't treat cattle as we are being treated." See also Frank Kenfield, "Captured By Rebels: A Vermonter at Petersburg, 1864," *Vermont History,* Autumn, 1968, 233-235.
7. Claiborne, *Seventy-five Years in Old Virginia,* 208-209.
8. *O.R.* XLII, ii, 63-64, 1162-1163.
9. W. W. Blackford, *War Years with Jeb Stuart* (New York: 1945), 266-271.
10. *O.R.* XL, i, 246-249; Bryce Suderow, "Confederate Casualties at the Crater," *The Kepi,* III, no. 3, 22-23 (See Appendix B); Samuel H. Dearborn to Mrs. Jeremiah Batchelder, July 31 and August 13, 1864, Collection of Warren B. Randall; Leander W. Cogswell, *A History of the Eleventh New Hampshire Regiment Volunteer Infantry* (Concord: 1891), unnumbered page, roster of Company H.
11. *O.R.* XL, i, 171.
12. *J.C.C.W. Report,* 26, 180; Agassiz, *Meade's Headquarters,* 94.
13. *J.C.C.W. Report,* 139-151.
14. *Ibid.,* 151-176, 197; *O.R.* XLII, ii, 44, 155; Weld, "The Petersburg Mine," 208.
15. *J.C.C.W. Report,* 177-230; *O.R.* XLII, ii, 641.
16. *J.C.C.W. Report,* 230-232.
17. *Ibid.,* 1-10.
18. *O.R.* XLVI, i, 1039-1040; William Frassanito, *Grant and Lee, The Virginia Campaigns* (New York: 1983), 421.
19. *The Progress-Index,* Petersburg, Virginia, June 20, 1932.
20. *Ibid.;* Christopher M. Calkins, "The History of Poplar Grove National Cemetery," (Mss), Petersburg National Battlefield.
21. *Ibid.; History of the Thirty-Fifth Massachusetts,* roster, 36; Cogswell, *Eleventh New Hampshire, roster; O.R.* XL, i, 579.
22. Calkins, "History of Poplar Grove Cemetery." The Petersburg lady who blamed the sickness on the reburial effort may have been describing Asiatic cholera, which produces similar simptoms. An epidemic of cholera struck the East Coast for the last time that same summer of 1866. See Charles E. Rosenburg, *The Cholera Years, the United States in 1832, 1849, and 1866* (Chicago: 1962), 175-212.
23. *The Progress-Index,* June 20, 1932.
24. Lee A. Wallace, "A History of Petersburg National Military Park, Virginia," (Mss), Petersburg National Battlefield, 47, 55; Archaeological Report, Petersburg National Battlefield.

Chapter VII

1. *J.C.C.W. Report,* 231-232. Meade's provost marshall general, Marsena Patrick, seemed to find the commanding general's absence from the front worth noting. On the morning of the battle Patrick posted himself directly behind Burnside's troops, "Supposing, of course, that Meade would go to the Front at the time." When Meade did not show, Patrick went looking for him. The day followed the disaster, after listening to frustrated V Corps officers who felt they should have been sent in, Patrick observed "If the matter be investigated nothing but Grant's presence will save Meade." See David S. Sparks, ed., *Inside Lincoln's Army, The Diary of Marsena Rudolph Patrick, Provost Marshal General, Army of the Potomac* (New York: 1964), 405-407.
2. Grady McWhiney and Jack Jay Jenkins, "The Union's Worst General," *Civil War Times Illustrated,* June, 1975, 30-39.
3. *O.R.* XVIII, 59, and XXXVI, i, 918; George P. Hawkes diary, June 17, 1864; Coco, *Through Blood and Fire,* 101-102, 145.
4. *J.C.C.W. Report,* 124.
5. *Ibid.,* 125, 181.
6. *The Life and Letters of George Gordon Meade,* 1,351.
7. See, for instance, Agassiz, *Meade's Headquarters,* 128, and D. R. Larned to "My Dear Sister," June 5 and 20, 1864, Daniel Reed Larned Papers.
8. Loving, *Whitman,* 131.
9. *J.C.C.W. Report,* 194.

Appendix A

1. *O.R.* XL, iii, 728-741.
2. *O.R. Atlas,* Plate LXIV, No. 3.
3. *O.R.* XLII, ii, 1214-1221.
4. *Ibid.,* 1224-1228.

Appendix B

1. *O.R.* XL, i, 246-250.
2. *Ibid.* 177.
3. *Ibid.* 178.
4. Suderow "Confederate Casualties at the Crater," 22-33.
5. Suderow, pp. 26-27, cites 2,900-3,000 for Mahone's Division, presumably including all five brigades. Stewart, "The Charge of the Crater," 29, cites 800 for Weisiger's brigade and Featherston, "Graphic Account," 362, counts 628 for Saunders.
6. Suderow, "Confederate Casualties at the Crater," 22-33.
7. *Ibid.*
8. *Ibid.*
9. Ibid.
10. Suderow finds 10,064, but the total of infantry and artillery is 9,430.
11. *O.R.* XL, i, 788.

Appendix C

1. Adjutant and Inspector General's Office, Richmond, August 10, 1864. "Confederate Roll of Honor," General Order No. 64; *O.R.* XL, i, 530, 810-813.
2. *Ibid,* 754,
3. Committee on Veteran Affairs *Medal of Honor Recipients 1863-1978.* (Washington: 1979), Part II, "Civil War," pp. 17-268.

Appendix D

1. *O.R.* XL, iii, 729-741.
2. *O.R.* XL, i, 425-426.
3. *O.R.* XL, iii, 737-741.
4. *O.R.* XL, i, 267.
5. *O.R.* XL, iii, 735-736, 741.
6. *O.R. Navy,* Vol. 10, 318-319.
7. *O.R.* XL, iii, 822-823.
8. *O.R.* XLII, ii, 1214-1221.
9. Simon, *Grant Papers,* 233. Brigadier General James Conner was in command of Lane's and McGowan's brigades at Deep Bottom. Division commander General Cadmus Wilcox remained with Scales's and Thomas's brigade on the Confederate lines between Walthall Junction and the Appomatox River.
10. *O.R.* XLII, ii, 1219-1222.
11. *O.R.* XL, i, 241-246.
12. Suderow, "The First Battle of Deep Bottom," Appendix I, 77-78.
13. *Ibid.,* Appendix IV, 83-86.
14. *Ibid.,* Appendix III, 81-82.

Appendix E

1. Jennings C. Wise, "The Boy Gunners of Lee," *S.H.S.P.,* Volume XLII, 163-164; Jennings C. Wise, *The Long Arm of Lee or The History of the Artillery of the Army of Northern Virginia,* (Lynchburg: 1915), Vol. II, 861-862; *O.R.* XL, i, 759.
2. Lee Wallace, *A Guide to Virginia Military Organizations 1861-1865* (Lynchburg: 1986), 29; *O.R.* XL, i, 579; Bernard, *War Talks,* 207-209.
3. Wallace, *Virginia Military Organizations,* 6; Lieutenant W. P. Robinson, "Artillery in the Battle of the Crater," *C.V.,* Volume XIX, (April, 1911) 165-166; William Miller Owen, "The Artillery Defenders of Fort Gregg," *S.H.S.P.,* Volume XIX, 66.
4. Wallace, *Virginia Military Organizations,* 6; Robinson, "Artillery," 165-166; Wise, *Long Arm of Lee,* 866-867.
5. Wallace, *Virginia Military Organizations,* 6; Robinson, "Artillery," 165-166; Bernard, *War Talks,* 313.
6. Wallace, *Virginia Military Organizations,* 6; Robinson, "Artillery," 165-166.
7. Bernard, *War Talks,* 203, 206-207, 313.
8. Wise, *Long Arm of Lee,* 859.
9. Weymouth T. Jordan, Jr. and Louis H. Manarin, *North Carolina Troops 1861-1865 A Roster,* (Raleigh: 1966), Volume I Artillery, 594; Walter Clark, *Histories of the Several Regiments and Battalions from North Carolina in the Great War 1861-'65.* (Raleigh: 1901), Vol. V, 617-618.
10. Wallace, *Virginia Military Organizations,* 25; *O.R.* XL, i, 759.
11. Wallace, *Virginia Military Organizations,* 19, 175; McCabe, "Defence of Petersburg," 289.
12. Wallace, *Virginia Military Organizations,* 36; Bernard, *War Talks,* 195; E. Porter Alexander, *Military Memoirs of a Confederate.* (Dayton, Oh.; 1977), 570-571.

INDEX

179

CORRECTIONS TO THE NARRATIVE OF THE
BATTLE OF THE CRATER

Page 9 — 4th paragraph. 1st line, change Dinwiddie County to Prince George County.

Page 42 — 1st line, change leaving to leave.

Page 43 — 2nd paragraph, 5th line, change Gibbs to Gibbes. 8th line, change Gibbs to Gibbes.

page 46 — 2nd pargraph, 9th line, comma after tually.

page 85 — 2nd pargraph, 3rd line, change Jersualem to Jerusalem.

page 123 — 30th U.S.C.T., change (K) to (W).

page 126 — Wilcox Brigade, change Sanders to Saunders. 13th Battalion Virginia Light Artillery, change Gibbs to Gibbes

page 129 — Change A.S.U. to A.S.V.

page 146 — 2nd pargraph, 2nd line, change Park to Part. 4th line, change Gibbs to Gibbes. 3rd paragraph, 3rd line, change ^{7}0 to 30^7. Line 9, change Gibbs to Gibbes. Line 12, change Gibbs to Gibbes's.

page 147 — 1st paragraph, 4th line, change Gibbs's to Gibbes's.

page 149 — 13th entry, change p.p. to pp. 18th entry, change "The Battle of 'The Crater,' to "The Battle of 'The Crater,' ".

page 150 — last entry, change "Flanners' to Flanner's.

page 158 — change:

_____ "Confederate Counter-mining in Front of Petersburg"

Chevy Chase, Md. Diary of Elbert Corbin (Battery B, 1st New York

to:

_____ "Confederate Counter-mining in Front of Petersburg"

Chevy Chase, Md. — Diary of Elbert Corbin (Battery B, 1st New York

page 159 — even out entries Jackson, Rich and Taylor at bottom of page with Bishop, Bishop, Campbell, Cutchin, Goode, Guy, and Harrison entries.

page 163 — entry 12, change Pennsylvani to Pennsylvania.

page 177 — 3rd line, change Gibbs to Gibbes.

CORRECTIONS FOR FOOTNOTES SHOULD READ AS FOLLOWS:

Page 165

Armies, 128 vols. (Washington: 1880-1901), Series I, Vol. XL, Part i, 251-265.

19. _O.R.,_ XL, ii, 484.
20. _Ibid.,_ I, 557; _The National Tribune,_ January 17, 1884 and September 4, 1919.

MISSING ENDNOTES FOR CHAPTER 2, PAGE 166

19. _Ibid.,_ 17-18, 161.
20. _Ibid.,_ 90, 98.
21. _Ibid.,_ 124.
22. OR, XL, iii, 612-613; _JCCW Report,_ 98-99.
23. OR, XIX, i, 531; XL, ii, 609; iii, 99, 364, 610, 612; LI, 1169. General Ledlie had already failed Senate confirmation once, and his reappointment had been on

of expiration that summer. See Coco, *Through Blood &*

24. OR, XL, i, 706, iii, 596; *JCCW Report*, 99.
25. OR, XL, iii, 480, 612, 656; *JCCW Report*, 170.
26. Agassiz, *Meade's Headquarters*, 197; *JCCW Report*, 152-153.
27. OR XL, iii, 596; *JCCW Report*, 170; Stephen M. Weld, "The Petersburg Mine," *Papers of the Military Historical Society of Massachusetts*, Vol. V, 208.
28. OR, XL, i, 259-260.
29. Agassiz, *Meade's Headquarters*, 195.
30. *JCCW Report*, 120; Thomas, "The Colored Troops at Petersburg," 563-564.
31. George P. Hawkes diary, June 17, 1864; Coco, *Through Blood and Fire*, 128, 130, 133.
32. OR, XL, i, 535; *History of the Thirty-Fifth Massachusetts Volunteers, 1862-1865* (Boston: Mills, Knight, & Co., 1884), 276.
33. *JCCW Report*, 160, 222.

Page 167
9. *O.R.*, XL, i, 310.

Page 168, Number 12
measured the Crater with a tape on the afternoon of Aug. 1, and found it 125

Page 171
31. Jackman, *Sixth New Hampshire*, 316-317.

Page 173
1. *J.C.C.W. Report*, 231-232. Meade's provost marshal general, Marsena

The day following the disaster, after listening to frustrated V Corps officers

6. *The Life and Letters of George Gordon Meade*, I, 351.

INDEX CORRECTION